HENRY OSMERS

On Eagle's Beak

A History of the Montauk Point Lighthouse

Outskirts Press, Inc.
Denver, Colorado

On Eagle's Beak
A History of the Montauk Point Lighthouse

Outskirts Press, Inc.
http://www.outskirtspress.com

ISBN: 978-1-4327-1346-1

PRINTED IN THE UNITED STATES OF AMERICA

For Terri,

who endured my seemingly endless trips to
libraries and other places, from Brooklyn to Montauk,
and numerous hours spent on the family computer…

and who, over the past few years, has come to understand
the sense of renewal and fulfillment I experience working
at the lighthouse
as part of the wonder, beauty, and magic that is Montauk…

And for

Marilyn, Angie, Joseph and Mike,
who, with Terri & I in the summer of 1970,
made Montauk Point a place of lifelong
memories and enduring friendships.

CONTENTS

LIST OF ILLUSTRATIONS

HENRY OSMERS

ON EAGLE'S BEAK

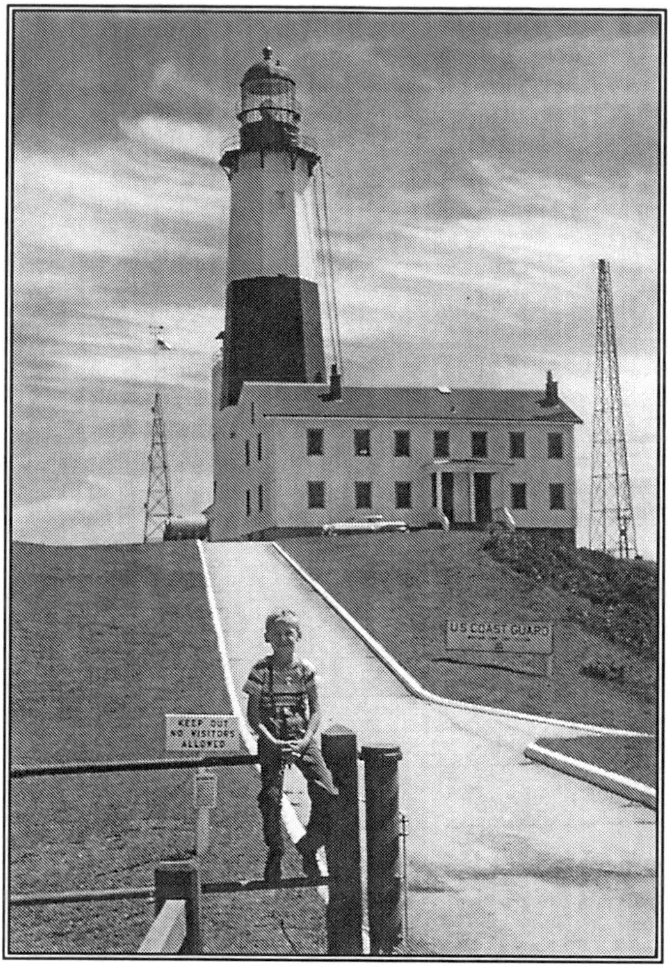

The author at Montauk Point Lighthouse in 1957. (Author Photo)

PREFACE

Like most people, childhood has become a distant and clouded part of my memory, but some experiences remain with me. One of the earliest and most vibrant is a trip with my parents to the tip of Long Island in August of 1957, a hundred-plus mile journey from my home in Elmont, New York. I remember nothing of the ride, but I do recall my first look at the majestic Montauk Point Lighthouse. The most dominant structure on the point, it left me awestruck! But what made this visit truly special was my father handing me his camera and allowing me to take my first-ever photograph, a snapshot of my parents in front of the lighthouse.

As a teenager, the remoteness of Montauk intrigued me. It seemed an adventurous destination, and once I had my driver's license I made a couple of trips to the Point. The most unforgettable visit was on Sunday, July 12, 1970 when a small group of my friends—Terri (now my wife), Marilyn, Angie, Joseph, and Mike—piled into Joseph's old Ford Falcon and made our way to Montauk. We were college students back then, working together in a department store with Sunday as our day off. We had a great time together at Montauk, walking along the beach and climbing on the rocks below the lighthouse. Little did we realize this was the beginning of an annual event, the "Friends Picnic," that continues to this day.

When the lighthouse opened to the public in 1987, I was among its first-year visitors. My wife, Terri, and daughters, Karyn and Jennifer, went along too. Though the girls were too young to grasp the historic significance of the site, they enjoyed running up and down the hills around the lighthouse. Terri and I pored over the exhibits with equal enthusiasm. We were fascinated with the place, but for many years afterwards work, family, and other interests meant that Montauk Lighthouse took a back seat in our lives.

By the spring of 2001, when I learned that the lighthouse museum was looking for tour guides, life was much less busy. I joined the museum as a weekend tour guide. Now in my sixth year as a staff member, I am happily settled in a fun and rewarding part time job. Sometimes, when I'm on duty alone at the top of the tower, I gaze out over the gentle slopes of Montauk toward the State Park where I picnicked with my parents so long ago and played on the beach with my future wife and college friends. These are joyful memories that make me grateful for family and friends, but also for my longtime interest in the Montauk Point Lighthouse.

Serving at the museum is an exhilarating and gratifying opportunity. I drive 60-miles from my home in the town of Shirley to reach the lighthouse, but the trip is worth the time and expense. Meeting people from around the world, witnessing the occasional marriage proposal or wedding ceremony on the property, even answering questions like, "Where's the elevator to the top of the tower?" all add to the unique experience of working at the lighthouse.

There aren't many people who don't love a lighthouse, especially this one. The smiles on the faces of young and old alike as they enter the Montauk Point Lighthouse Museum attest to that. Even if the exhibits are not the most exciting for youngsters, the tower climb certainly is special, with its dizzying height and panoramic view of the sea. And the opulent 3½-order Fresnel lens on display in the museum grabs everyone's attention, young and old. If people leave the museum having learned something about this wonderful and worthy historic site from my presentations, then I have done my job.

Recently, I decided to share the story of Montauk Point Lighthouse in a greater way. That desire is now finding purpose in the publication of this book. I hope the information in the chapters ahead will further extend the public's knowledge and interest in Montauk Point Lighthouse and, by doing so, help ensure its future protection and care. Most of all, I hope that my passion for and commitment to New York's and Long Island's oldest lighthouse shines in these pages as clearly and brightly as the light "on Eagle's Beak."

ACKNOWLEDGEMENTS

This work could not have been accomplished without the assistance of several individuals. First, my gratitude goes to Margaret/Peg Winski for graciously offering and doing an excellent job of reading the first draft. Also, thanks go to her daughter Margaret/Marge Winski for reading the second draft. Their support, advice, and excitement for this project were encouraging and energizing. I am grateful for the assistance of Bob Muller of the Long Island Lighthouse Society for the loan of his Montauk material. His passion for our local lighthouses is infectious, and I am thankful for the time spent with him. Very special thanks go to lighthouse author and researcher Candace Clifford for doing the legwork in Washington, D.C. for material from the National Archives and the Coast Guard Historian's Office.

A number of Long Island librarians helped me "flip over the rocks" to find information that was out of the ordinary, especially at the East Hampton Free Library where I was guided by the delightful and most capable Marci Vail of the Morton Pennypacker Collection. Her advice, encouragement and obvious knowledge of her material were reassuring. She is a credit to her profession. Robin Strong at the

Montauk Library brought a fresh enthusiasm and genuine interest to my work. We spent some pleasant hours pouring over old photos and sharing our love of the lighthouse and the village of Montauk.

Also, thanks to these other fine librarians who provided guidance: Gary Lutz, Patchogue-Medford Library; Susan Caggiano, Southold Free Library; Bob Knoski, Sayville Library; Jennifer Chivvis, Babylon Public Library; June Koffi, Brooklyn Central Library; Julie Greene, East Hampton Free Library, Peggy Ambrosio, Montauk Library. Other libraries that shared material from their Long Island collections: Rogers Memorial Library in Southampton, Brookhaven Free Library, Jamaica Library, Riverhead Free Library, Suffolk County Historical Society Library in Riverhead, Smithtown Library. The Half Hollow Hills Community Library provided material from editions of the *Long Islander*. And, of course, I am thankful to my hometown library where the research began—the Mastics-Moriches-Shirley Community Library in Shirley.

Thanks to Wallace Broege, director of the Suffolk County Historical Society and to librarian Dave Kerkhof for their assistance in providing some of the photographs included in this work. Their sincerity and genuine willingness to assist in this project was refreshing. April at King Visual Technology in Hyattsville, Maryland was very helpful in finding several photos from the National Archives.

Thanks to Montauk Point Lighthouse Museum director Ann Shengold and site manager Tricia Wood for their direction and encouragement in retrieving information from their records. My gratitude goes to former lighthouse tour guide and good friend Henry Aubry for presenting me with much of his own material. The successful organization of information and photographs for the erosion chapter would not have been possible without the gracious assistance of

Greg Donohue. An honorary mention goes to another good friend at the lighthouse, long time tour guide Audrey Loebl. Her inspiration, vitality, and humor taught me much about lighthouse operations and instilled a greater affection for this historic place.

Looking back at the research I conducted pertaining to the formation of the Lighthouse Museum and the subsequent efforts to maintain it over the years, it was clearly evident that Dick White was a hands-on person who always had the best interests of the museum at heart. I've had the privilege of knowing him since the summer of 2001 and am inspired by his passion, enthusiasm, and appreciation for Long Island's most famous landmark. He is a down-to-earth man who rolls up his sleeves to get any job done, such as helping to load barrels with bottled water, juices, and ice in preparation for the annual triathlon (the finish line was at the lighthouse). Moments like these revealed his character and passion for the lighthouse. I appreciate his interest in the success of my project.

Closer to home, I offer thanks to my brother-in-law Anthony Picarello for his skills in scanning and organizing many of the photos used in this book. And, of course, I owe the greatest thanks to Terri, my wife, who endured it all.

(Author's Note—In most cases, quoted material in the following chapters is printed verbatim from the original documents. The use of [sic] appears only where a word or phrase is so unwieldy as to be unrecognizable. Misspellings in a few quoted passages were corrected to avoid repeated use of [sic], and these instances are indicated in the text.)

A splendid sunrise silhouettes Montauk Point Lighthouse in October 1986. (Author Photo)

PROLOGUE

I stand as on some mighty eagle's beak
Eastward the sea absorbing, viewing (nothing but sea and sky)
The tossing waves, the foam, the ships in the distance,
The wild unrest, the snowy, curling caps-
That inbound urge and urge of waves,
Seeking the shores forever.

Walt Whitman
"From Montauk Point," 1888

At the eastern end of Long Island lies nearly 10,000 acres of wonder, mystery and splendor—the Montauk Peninsula. It has seen the meteoric rise and fall of grandiose developers and a continual human invasion that quadruples its numbers in season. Yet, its remote character and overall rugged natural appearance remain intact. The beauty of the seemingly endless rolling hills, the hidden ponds, and the magnificent and colorful bluffs inspire wonder and awe.

Montauk is unique to the rest of Long Island. Far beyond the tidy Hamptons picket fences and fine old colonial homes, strung like a necklace of charming towns along the Montauk Highway, the intersection with Cranberry Hole Road appears at the east end of Amagansett. This is the final outpost of Long Island civilization. Beyond this point lie 17-miles of other-world landscape, a place of bucolic beauty and charm, yet with a definite feel of isolation.

The Montauk Peninsula of long ago was a rugged and isolated environment, home to the resourceful Montaukett Indians, who hunted and farmed the land and fished its abundant waters. After Europeans arrived, pastoral scenes of grazing livestock, cowboys, and cattle drives were common. There were the inevitable tragic shipwrecks too, as more and more vessels plied eastern Long Island waters to fish, hunt whales, and transport settlers seeking opportunity in the new land.

Montauk was also the domain of failed visions of grandeur during Long Island's Gilded Age. Entrepreneurs and speculators arrived—Arthur Benson's Montauk Association, Austin Corbin's railroad and proposed port of entry, and Carl Fisher's scheme to create another Miami Beach. The Point saw military occupation over 175 years and six wars as well.

Not to be overlooked in Long Island's lively and vibrant history is its crown jewel and most famous landmark, the Montauk Point Lighthouse. Since 1797 its beacon has kept a constant vigil over this major landfall location where treacherous shoals lurk and a steady stream of maritime traffic passes. It has seen the roar of tempests and the mirror-like calmness of the sea, the ravages of war and periods of prevailing peace, plus many changes in commerce, culture, and politics. It has survived everything from hurricanes and erosion to sheer human neglect. Through it all, the light has operated faithfully.

Montauk Point was one of the first lighthouses in the country to be completely planned and built by the federal government. When the sentinel's eight oil lamps went into service in the spring of 1797, their light gave much needed guidance to ships and boats at sea on moonless nights or in stormy weather. By day, the whitewashed stone tower served as a bold white daymark against the brown and green hills. Mariners were grateful to have a landfall beacon that identified perilous Montauk Point. The lighthouse cast a welcome beam several miles at sea for vessels of all kinds heading into harbors along Long Island and into the burgeoning port of New York City.

Montauk Point and its lighthouse are not only a part of the history of Long Island, but the story of America as well. The lighthouse witnessed conflict during the American Revolution, suffered threats from World War II German submarines, and was alert to warnings of possible nuclear attacks during the Cold War years. Adding to these problems over the years were a number of shipwrecks—fewer than before the lighthouse was built, to be sure, but inevitable given the Point's many navigational perils. When tragedy occurred, the lighthouse keepers teamed with the surf men from the nearby life saving stations to save lives and recover property.

With its rich and engaging history and its service to mariners for over three-hundred years, the Montauk Point Lighthouse is a recognized emblem of our maritime heritage. Though the station's keepers are gone and it has been automated to operate self-sufficiently (as have all lighthouses in the United States), it now has a new dual role as both an active navigational aid and a popular museum. The tower was placed on the National Register of Historic Places on July 7, 1969. On July 17, 1976 a bicentennial plaque was placed on the lighthouse by the U.S. Coast

Guard in commemoration of our nation's 200th anniversary. The light station celebrated its own bicentennial in 1996.

Technological advances in navigation, such as radar, global positioning, and other electronic developments, have reduced the usefulness of Montauk Point Lighthouse; yet, it remains a vital link in the nation's chain of navigational aids and continues to serve its intended purpose, guiding seagoing vessels safely to their destinations and protecting the lives and property of those on board. Few other lighthouses in the nation show such a long and diverse timeline of social and technological progress and adaptation to change.

The Montauk Peninsula of modern times has a personality all its own. It's a diverse and pleasant place for those who call it home and a drawing card for tourists from around the world who come to experience the area's natural and manmade qualities: the sounds and smells of the sea, the sparkling beaches and breathtaking views, the fun of beachcombing and fishing, the aroma of freshly cooked seafood dinners, and perhaps even an old-timer's tale about adventures on Montauk long ago.

Montauk! There simply is no other place like it!

For those who love Long Island, lighthouses, and especially the Montauk Point Lighthouse, this book offers a closer and sometimes intimate look at a very old and venerable sentinel of the shore.

The Montauk Peninsula, 1897: (Letters for locations added by author)

A- First House site
B- Second House
C- Third House
D- Montauk Point Lighthouse
E- Montauk Village
F- Old fishing village site
G- Montauk Point State Park
H- Camp Hero State Park
I- Lake Montauk

(Montauk Library)

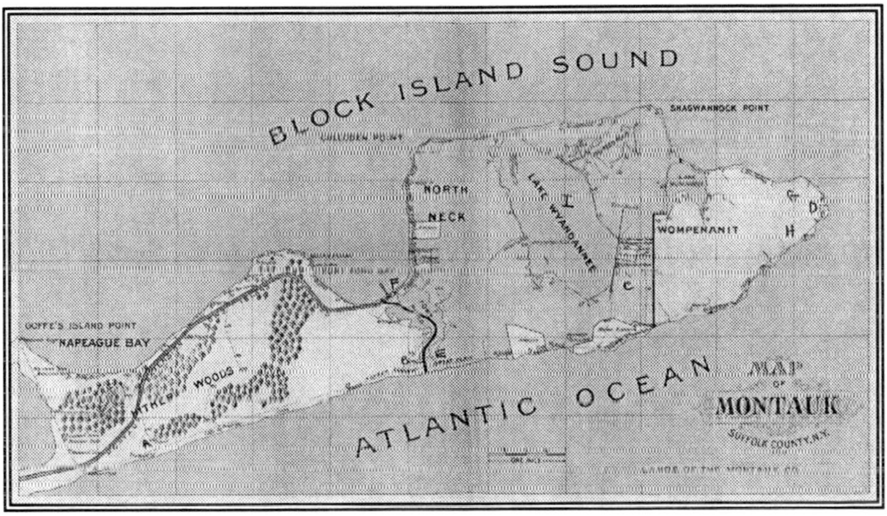

INTRODUCTION
A Brief History of the Montauk Peninsula

From its earliest days of habitation, the desolate and windswept Montauk Peninsula has been home to many people—natives and immigrants, farmers, fishermen, merchants, whalers and sailors, the very poor and the very wealthy. The name "Montauk" is said to mean "fort place high land." The Point's first fort was mentioned in a 1662 deed as Fort Hill at Fort Pond.[1] At the very tip of this elevated land, the federal government later acquired a few acres for a lighthouse. The site of the lighthouse, called Turtle Hill, was known to the Montauketts (the original name of the Montauk Indians) as "Wamponamon," meaning "at the east" or "to the east."[2]

Probably the first European to see Montauk Point was the Italian explorer, Giovanni da Verrazano. After investigating what is now New York Harbor in April 1524, his ship traveled east along Long Island's south shore, bound for present-day New England. Undoubtedly, Verrazano sailed around Montauk Point. Nearly a century later, in 1614, the Dutch explorer Adrian Block came ashore at Montauk after sailing the perimeter of Long Island Sound in his ship, the *Restless*. Where he landed and how long he stayed is unknown. He gave the area the name "Hoeck van de Visschers," meaning "Point of the Fishers," after the Indians he observed there.

As early as 1655, Montaukett chief Wyandanch granted permission to a group of men from East Hampton to lease the land at Montauk. On April 10, 1655 it was agreed that a fence would be built south of Fort Pond.[3] The land was sold to these same "proprietors" a few years later. The influence of the Montauketts declined in these years, hastened by an epidemic that wiped out about 50 percent of the Indian population in the winter of 1658-1659. Transactions with the settlers in 1661, 1670, and 1687 completed the purchase from the Montauketts of what is now the Montauk Peninsula.

In all probability, from 1661 until 1879 the entire Montauk Peninsula was used as pastureland and for fishing by the Montauk Proprietors. As early as 1662, Isaac Hedges was selected to "keep the dry herd at Montauk," and in 1663 twelve men from East Hampton were ordered to Montauk to construct a yard for the cattle and build a shelter for the animal keepers.[4]

Montauk also was suitable for gunning, which became popular in the mid 1800s and continued into the twentieth century. Groups of well-to-do men traveled to Montauk, sometimes from far away places and for weeks at a time, to enjoy hunting, fishing, even berry picking and card playing.

The first three dwellings built on the Montauk Peninsula were named for the order in which they were built: First House, Second House, and Third House. The occupants of each house had important responsibilities with regard to the pasturelands. First House was built in 1744 and replaced in 1798. It was situated between the fork formed by Montauk Point State Parkway and the Old Montauk Highway in present Hither Hills State Park. The responsibility of its keeper was to maintain the common pasture list of sheep and cattle according to their earmarks and ensure certain fences were in good repair. He kept a watchful eye tending the sheep between First House and Second House. First House was destroyed by fire in the spring of 1909.

Second House, built in 1746 and enlarged in 1797, was located on the main road in Montauk village. The resident keeper saw to the tending of the sheep to the west and cattle to the east and made sure they didn't cross over into the opposite territory. Second House still stands in its original location.

Third House was built in 1747 and was replaced in 1806. A wing was added after 1879. Its keeper was responsible for the entire pasture and oversaw the annual livestock roundup each year on June 20, when the cattle were paraded from East Hampton and Amagansett east to Indian Fields. Then, around the first of November, the cattle were driven off and brought back home for the winter months. Third House is located just north of present Montauk Point State Parkway in Theodore Roosevelt County Park

For many years, these three dwellings and the lighthouse at Montauk Point were the only manmade structures on Montauk. By the 1860s all three had been converted into hotels. Guest registers read like a *Who's Who* of the rich and famous. Second House was sold to Mr. & Mrs. David Kennedy in 1910 for use as a summer residence. When they left, the house stood empty until it was purchased by the Town of East Hampton and New York State Historical Trust in 1968. It opened as a museum on June 28, 1969 and continues to be maintained as such by the Montauk Historical Society.

During the era of Camp Wikoff in 1898, Colonel Theodore Roosevelt headquartered at Third House and was visited by his family. A few years later, the virtues of spending time at Third House were extolled in the *Brooklyn Daily Eagle* in July 1901: "Here is the ideal spot for the tired city worker to spend a brief vacation and even he who can only come up over Sunday returns to his labors with new life and vigor and his lungs filled with the ozone that permeates this wild region...He has the lighthouse and the life saving station with Captains Scott and Miller to spin him yarns and he can go to bed tired to sleep soundly in a temperature so cool that a blanket is comfortable."[5]

A rare photo showed First House, ca. 1900. It was built in 1744 and rebuilt in 1798. When cattle were pastured on Montauk, the overseer recorded all cattle on the Common Pasture list. The house was also a welcome sight for weary travelers crossing Napeague. It burned in 1909. (Peg Winski)

By the mid 1700s, trouble with England was brewing. On July 5, 1775 East Hampton reported to the New York Provincial Congress that there were about 2,000 cattle and over 3,000 sheep lying unprotected at Montauk and asked that troops be stationed there to protect them. The request was approved and a company of men under Captain John

Hurlburt was assigned to Montauk and provided with weapons, ammunition and provisions.[6]

In April, 1776 General George Washington advised east-enders that a British fleet consisting of several ships and about 600 men was en route to Montauk. East Hampton Patriot, Captain John Dayton (1727-1825) of the First Regiment of Minutemen in Suffolk County, had a plan. He and forty farmers went to Montauk and, by parading around and around a hill and changing clothes all day, gave the British the impression that a large American army was defending Montauk Point! The ruse succeeded, and the British raided Gardiner's Island instead.

When General George Washington and his troops lost the Battle of Long Island (fought in Brooklyn) in August of 1776, eastern Long Island was left open to attack. At Montauk Point the cattle and sheep were at the mercy of the invading British, since American soldiers could not be spared to protect them. By the end of the year the British occupied the towns of the east end.

During the winter of 1780-1781, a good portion of the British fleet lay at anchor in Gardiners Bay. They were monitoring the French fleet that had anchored near Newport, Rhode Island with the purpose of aiding the Americans. On January 22, 1781 word came that three of the French ships were within striking distance. The 161-foot British ship *Culloden* was dispatched, but a heavy snowstorm blew it onto Shagwong Reef a short distance from Montauk Point, tearing a hole in its hull. The captain, George Balfour, managed to get the ship off the reef at high tide and bring it into Fort Pond Bay, but it ultimately sank off the eastern highland of the bay, then known as Will's or North Neck Point (now Culloden Point). The crew of 600 men was saved but not before they stripped and burned the ship to the waterline to prevent the Americans from removing its seventy-four guns.

Second House, shown below ca. 1900, was built in 1746 and rebuilt in 1797. Its overseer looked after the sheep pastured to the west and the cattle to the east. The house also served as lodging for travelers to Montauk. It was purchased by the Town of East Hampton and New York State Historical Trust in 1968 and opened as a museum in 1969, operated by the Montauk Historical Society. (Montauk Library)

For much of the Revolution the British kept a huge bonfire burning on Turtle Hill at Montauk Point to act as a guide for the Royal Navy that patrolled Long Island Sound. During the War of 1812 the British fleet once again was anchored in Gardiners Bay. Troops attempted to come ashore at Montauk but were repulsed. However, they did make some raids on the cattle herds between June 1812 and December 1814.

The use of Montauk as pastureland by the proprietors

continued throughout much of the 1800s, with no trace of human presence. Settlement did not seem possible in such a remote, lonely, and windy place, but there were men with big ideas. In October 1879, all of Montauk was scheduled to be sold at auction in East Hampton. Arthur W. Benson (1812-1889), a developer, President of the Brooklyn Union Gas Company, and active in the shipping industry, was attracted by the prospect of abundant hunting and fishing for sportsmen at Long Island's east end. On December 1, 1879, he bought at auction from the descendants of the original proprietors "...all that peninsula of land being on the extreme southeastern extremity of Long Island known as Montauk bounded on the North by the Bay and the South by the Ocean" for the price of $151,000. The only properties not included in the purchase were lands occupied by the Montauk Point Lighthouse and the Life Saving Station at nearby Ditch Plain.

Benson's intention was to make Montauk into a posh hunting and fishing resort for the wealthy. Part of his plan included the creation of a private housing development called the Montauk Association on the cliffs overlooking the Atlantic. To that end he acquired the services of Frederick Law Olmsted (1822-1903), designer of New York's Central Park, to do the landscaping. He then hired the famous architectural firm of McKim, Mead and White to construct eight spacious homes for several of his well-to-do friends. The tourist movement in Montauk appears to have begun with Benson's small wealthy community. However, his death in December 1889 dealt a blow to progress in that direction.

In 1895 Arthur Benson's heirs sold 5,500 acres to a group led by Austin Corbin and Charles Pratt. Austin Corbin (1827-1896), who became president of the Long Island Railroad in 1881, envisioned the creation of a Port of Entry for transatlantic steamships at Fort Pond Bay in Montauk. Though interest in this project had previously been rejected by Congress, Corbin made a few trips to East Hampton, making speeches to the townsfolk to convince them of the virtues of extending rail lines eastward from Bridgehampton. The first train reached Amagansett on June 1, 1895. The line was extended to Montauk and in use by December 17 of the same year.

Interest in the Port of Entry plan was revived with the building of the Old Montauk Inn early in 1896 and the building of the first steel pier about forty feet into Fort Pond Bay that August. However, with the sudden death of Corbin on June 4, 1896, the project, which could have significantly changed the course of Long Island's history, was doomed. Once again, the chance for extensive development at Montauk was thwarted.

During the Spanish American War in 1898, many troops contracted yellow fever and malaria while fighting in Cuba. Fearing a possible epidemic, New York and Brooklyn authorities searched for a suitable location for a quarantine center. Colonel Theodore Roosevelt, leader of the Rough Riders that successfully captured San Juan Hill during the war, knew Long Island well and recommended the remote region of Montauk. In July 1898, Camp Wikoff was established on 4,200 acres of pastureland at Indian Fields, Montauk. Nearly 30,000 men sick with malaria and yellow fever were sent to the camp over the next two months. Roosevelt joined them, though not ill himself. He was visited by President William McKinley and other dignitaries on September 3, 1898. The last troops left Montauk on October 9 and by December 6, 1898 Camp Wikoff was officially disbanded.

During World War I, a Naval Training Station was established at Montauk in April 1917 using Napeague Bay and Block Island Sound as testing grounds for torpedoes.

Top—Theodore Roosevelt was photographed on a ride at Camp Wikoff in 1898 after his return from the Spanish American War. (Montauk Point Lighthouse Museum)

Bottom During WW I, a Naval Aviation Camp existed at Montauk. The dirigible hangar, shown ca. 1917, stood where the Carl Fisher Tower now stands on the Plaza. The hangar was dismantled in 1920 and moved to Cape May, New Jersey. (Peg Winski)

An Aviation Camp began operations east of Fort Pond three months later. In October 1917, a Naval Aviation Base was constructed on a 33 acre plot close to the site where the Fisher Tower stands today. It included a hangar for dirigibles.

After several years of relative inactivity on the Point, another more ambitious attempt at development was made. On September 11, 1925 Carl Fisher (1874-1939) bought more than 5,000 acres between Fort Pond and Third House from the Montauk Company for over $1 million. For the lofty sum of $2.5 million he eventually obtained 9,632 acres, including several ponds and miles of beaches and hills. After creating Florida's Miami Beach in the early 1920s, he tried to duplicate his success with Long Island's "Miami Beach of the North." The plan included a port of entry for ocean liners at Montauk (Austin Corbin's 1890s dream).

By 1927, Fisher had built 63-miles of road, created a channel between Lake Montauk and Block Island Sound, and constructed a seven-story office building and the luxurious 178-room Montauk Manor on Fort Hill. A bathing casino, 150-foot swimming pool, 18-hole golf course, 125,000-square-foot tennis building that seated 900, a yacht club on Star Island in Lake Montauk, a polo field and trotting track just south of Third House, and other stylish amenities followed. Fisher also built a new railroad station, lumber yard, and a steam laundry. These developments, in turn, resulted in construction of numerous restaurants and hotels.

Not to be outdone, New York's master builder, Robert Moses (1888-1981), announced plans to acquire land on Montauk for state parks at Hither Hills and Montauk Point. On May 30, 1927 both Montauk Point State Park and the

Montauk Manor opened to the public. Not surprisingly, Montauk Highway, which had been extended to Montauk in 1927, soon was lined with cars. Montauk had its first of many traffic jams!

The Carl Fisher Tower, shown in December 2005, was built in 1927 by developer Carl Fisher as the centerpiece of the new Montauk business center. From its penthouse, Fisher had a panoramic view of his vast properties and entertained prospective investors. The building now houses condominiums. (Author Photo)

In the midst of the extensive development, by May 1926 cattle could not be driven on Montauk for pasture. Montauk's era as a pastureland had ended, though it would be revived briefly in 1936 before ending permanently during World War II.

Montauk's reputation as a summer vacation resort was widely known by the late 1920s. Homes sprouted up in

Shepherd's Neck, a pier was under construction, and plans were set to open Fort Pond Bay to Long Island Sound. Eight-hundred workers were on the job every day during Fisher's heyday. Tudor style homes were built, along with many businesses. However, serious financial problems plagued Fisher's company. After only a few years, construction at Montauk ceased and workers were laid off. Fisher ultimately went bankrupt in 1931. The vision of converting the charming little fishing village of Montauk into another Miami Beach and a port of entry died once again.

More extensive changes occurred with the onset of World War II, as a military presence was felt from the village all the way to the Point. The old fishing village at the north end of Fort Pond Bay had flourished since 1882, but with the arrival of the great hurricane of September 21, 1938 much of it was decimated. What remained almost entirely disappeared in 1943 when the U.S. Navy revealed plans to build a torpedo testing range at the site and gave the village residents thirty days to relocate. Nearby Montauk Manor was used as a barracks and the Fisher office building became officers' quarters.

Gun emplacements were constructed at Montauk Point Lighthouse, and huge guns were mounted in bunkers directed at the Atlantic Ocean on an adjacent 278 acres. The new site was called Camp Hero. Montauk had indeed become a military town.

Camp Hero opened in 1942 as part of a defense network against Nazi submarines. Tunnels connected the four 16-inch and two 6-inch guns that were housed in concrete bunkers overlooking the ocean. They were supported by anti-aircraft and machine gun emplacements at the camp and a short distance west at the Shadmoor area. The camp was deactivated in 1947 and thereafter used by the Army

Reserve for training purposes. In November 1950 the Eastern Air Defense Force activated the 773rd Aircraft Control and Warning Squadron, occupying the western portion of the property. The facility provided basic aircraft mapping information.

Montauk Manor, pictured in December 2005, was opened in 1927 by developer Carl Fisher. It served as a shelter in several hurricanes and housed military personnel during WW II. In addition, it was and remains a tourist attraction. Currently, it houses condominiums. (Author Photo)

Camp Hero was reactivated in 1951 as a subordinate installation under the command of the Army Anti-Aircraft Artillery. It was deactivated again on December 5, 1957 when all property was transferred by the Army to the Air Force and the site was renamed the Montauk Air Force Station. In 1958, Semi-Automatic Ground Environment (SAGE) was installed. It was an automated system for collecting, tracking, and intercepting enemy bomber aircraft during the Cold War. SAGE's large radar dish, a landmark for mariners, was officially commissioned in 1962. With changes in radar technology over the years, the base became obsolete and was closed down in 1981. In February 1984 the surrounding property was auctioned off and the Air Force Station itself was donated to the New York State Parks Department. It eventually opened to the public as Camp Hero State Park in the fall of 2002.

Following the disastrous hurricane of September 1938 and the U.S. Navy takeover of Fort Pond Bay in 1942, the fishing village moved to the northwest corner of Lake Montauk where it thrives today. Here, in 1943, Robert and Mary Gosman opened a chowder and lobster roll eatery, which evolved into Long Island's famous Gosman's Dock Restaurant & Clam Bar. Over the years other businesses emerged around it, firmly establishing the area's credibility as a fishing center. Today, several marinas line the entrance to Montauk Harbor along East Lake and West Lake Drives and on Star Island. The charter fishing business, which got its start in Montauk in 1932, still prospers.

Summer cottages began to appear around the village during the late 1940s. Development of Seaside Shores began along Ditch Plains Road, Miller Avenue, and Seaside Avenue in 1947, followed by Surfside Estates between the churches and the ocean in 1949. Soundview Estates grew along Fort Pond Bay beginning in 1952, followed by Oceanside in 1957, Hither Woods in 1962, and the more upscale Culloden Shores I and II in 1961 and 1963 respectively.[7] Eventually, more and more homes were occupied by year-round residents. Before long, tourists began to visit Montauk in greater numbers and by the early 1960s about one hundred motels and resorts had opened to meet the demand.

CHAPTER 1
The Lighthouse is Built

The long jagged finger of the Montauk Peninsula, ending at the high bluff known as Turtle Hill, seemed a probable site for a beacon. The Montauk Indians were the first to recognize the fact by setting signal fires there to guide their dugout canoes around the Point. During the American Revolution the British kept a huge bonfire burning on the bluff to guide the ships of the Royal Navy.

After the Revolutionary War, the newly formed American government desired to build trade with other world nations. To make the port of New York more readily accessible, hazards to shipping had to be reduced. Montauk Point had a menacing reputation as one of the most perilous locations along the coast, claiming a huge number of sailing vessels annually. Complaints from shipmasters and owners alleged that there were no safe harbors along the entire treacherous south shore of Long Island. Proof lay in the number of shipwreck remains along the beaches from Fire Island to Montauk.

One of the earliest wrecks on record at Montauk was the *John & Lucy*, a ship bound for New York from Rhode Island in 1668. Its disastrous voyage along the shores of Colonial America would typify the experience of many ships, whose masters sailed mostly by the seat of their pants with rudimentary navigational instruments in poorly charted waters. The *John & Lucy*, with a crew of fifteen, first ran aground near Fisher's Island. Re-floated at high tide, it then sailed southeast and ran aground a second time on March 22, 1668 along the Montauk shore.[8]

On November 23, 1701 the sloop *Mary* went aground off Montauk Point. It carried contraband from New York to Canada—cheese, flour, tobacco and shot. From Quebec came brandy, claret, wine, furs, cotton goods, and beads. This information was found in a journal kept on board by John Maher. Since trade goods were not permitted to leave or enter the colonies without first passing through England, the ship was seized by East Hampton's Captain Josiah Hobart (1634-1710), Justice of the Peace of the Town under authority of the Colony of New York.[9]

In 1791 the Treasury Department resolved to build a lighthouse at Montauk Point to serve as a landfall light for ships heading for New York from Europe and as a navigational aid for vessels bound for coastal ports in Connecticut, Rhode Island, and Massachusetts. The authorization to build the lighthouse was passed by the Second Congress on October 24, 1791 and stated, "As soon as the jurisdiction of such land on Montok point in the state of New York as the President of the United States shall deem sufficient and most proper for the convenience and accommodation of a light house shall have ceded to the United States it shall be the duty of the Secretary of the Treasury, to provide by contract which shall be approved by the President of the United States, for building a light house thereon."[10]

On October 7, 1791, Tench Coxe (1755-1824), Commissioner of Revenue, wrote to the congressional delegation of New York for information regarding the purchase of land for the lighthouse.[11] The delegation, in turn, asked the

New York Chamber of Commerce to study the matter and determine the most desirable location for a lighthouse at Montauk Point. The Chamber asserted that Ezra L'Hommedieu would be suitable to survey the bluffs at Montauk Point and submit a recommendation.

Meanwhile, Coxe conducted a survey on his own of well known merchants and ship captains of the day regarding the construction of a lighthouse at Montauk. New York merchant-skipper Joseph Anthony wrote, "I have drove the coasting business through all seasons for twenty years and often reflected upon the settling of a light upon Montague which in fact would be favorable to the trade of all the Middle States—a light upon Montague would give the most universal relief & satisfaction of any spot you culd fix upon."[12]

Captain C. Miller of New York agreed: "If the great object of lights and landmarks is to conduct ships into safety from the Great Atlantic…Montauck light is as necessary as Henlopen or Sandy Hook and the reasoning opposed to it is very frevelus."[13]

William Allibone of Philadelphia noted, "Its elevation is such as makes it a Key to a Great portion of the Foreign trade both to New York and Several of the eastern states and to all the Coasting trade in that quarter." [14]

In addition to letters such as these, there was approval from another business sector. In 1792 the New York Stock Exchange was established, and most early investors banked their money on overseas trade. With shipwrecks so rampant (resulting in the loss of cargo and, therefore, loss of investments) shareholders were eager to support the building of a lighthouse at Montauk Point.

On April 12, 1792, an act was passed by the Second Congress to authorize construction of a lighthouse at Montauk Point. It read as follows:

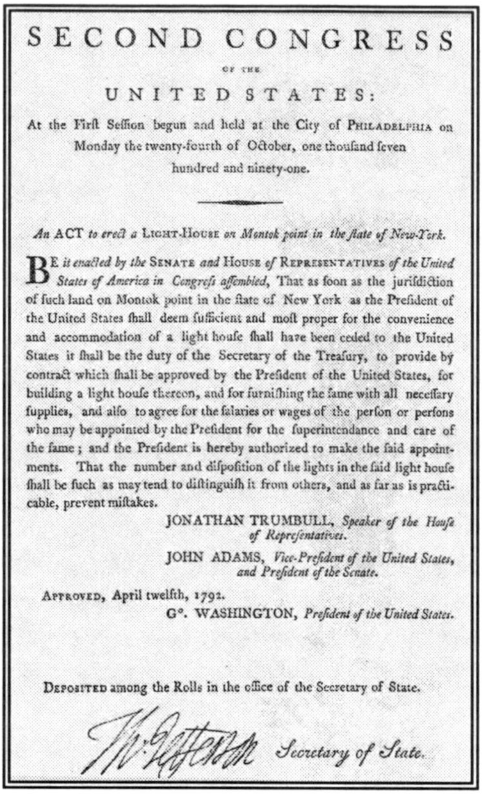

SECOND CONGRESS

OF THE

UNITED STATES:

At the First Session begun and held at the City of PHILADELPHIA on Monday the twenty-fourth of October, one thousand seven hundred and ninety-one.

An ACT *to erect a* LIGHT-HOUSE *on Montok point in the state of New-York.*

BE *it enacted by the* SENATE *and* HOUSE *of* REPRESENTATIVES *of the United States of America in Congress assembled,* That as soon as the jurisdiction of such land on Montok point in the state of New York as the President of the United States shall deem sufficient and most proper for the convenience and accommodation of a light house shall have been ceded to the United States it shall be the duty of the Secretary of the Treasury, to provide by contract which shall be approved by the President of the United States, for building a light house thereon, and for furnishing the same with all necessary supplies, and also to agree for the salaries or wages of the person or persons who may be appointed by the President for the superintendance and care of the same; and the President is hereby authorized to make the said appointments. That the number and disposition of the lights in the said light house shall be such as may tend to distinguish it from others, and as far as is practicable, prevent mistakes.

JONATHAN TRUMBULL, *Speaker of the House of Representatives.*

JOHN ADAMS, *Vice-President of the United States, and President of the Senate.*

APPROVED, April twelfth, 1792.

G°. WASHINGTON, *President of the United States.*

DEPOSITED among the Rolls in the office of the Secretary of State.

Th: Jefferson *Secretary of State.*

Page 36 - As one of his first duties as president of the United States, George Washington authorized the construction of a lighthouse at Montauk Point on April 12, 1792. (Montauk Point Lighthouse Museum)

Be it enacted by the Senate and House of Representatives of the United States of America in Congress assembled, That as soon as the jurisdiction of such land on Montok point in the state of New York as the President of the United States shall deem sufficient and most proper for the convenience and accommodation of a light house shall have been ceded to the United States it shall be the duty of the Secretary of the Treasury, to provide by contract which shall be approved by the President of the United States, for building a light house thereon, and for furnishing the same with all necessary supplies, and also to agree for the salaries or wages of the person or persons who may be appointed by the President for the superintendance and care of the same; and the President is hearby authorized to make the said appointments. That the number and disposition of the lights in the said light house shall be such as may tend to distinguish it from others, and as far as is practicable, prevent mistakes.

The document was signed by Jonathan Trumble, Speaker of the House of Representatives, Vice President John Adams, and President George Washington. Congress allocated $255.12 for the purchase of land for the construction of the lighthouse. It was one of the first lighthouses in the United States authorized and funded entirely by the Federal Government.

Ezra L'Hommedieu (1734-1811), surveyor of the site, was well-connected politically and socially. He was born in Southold and was a noted Revolutionary War patriot who represented New York in the Continental Congress and was an author of the state's constitution. He was widely respected for his integrity and intelligence. His first wife, Charity Floyd, was the sister of William Floyd (1734-1821) of Mastic, Long Island, one of the signers of the Declaration of Independence. Like George Washington, L'Hommedieu was interested in scientific farming and understood land issues. He acted as advisor to President Washington on the construction of the Montauk Point Lighthouse.

A special committee of the New York delegation submitted L'Hommedieu's report to the New York Chamber of Commerce on November 19, 1792. It read:

Gentlemen – I am now on my Return from Montauk point where with the advice of Capts. Rogers, Post and Franks, experienced mariners, and Abraham Miller, Esq., I have fixed upon a spot for erecting a light-house agreeable to the request of the Chamber of Commerce...The hill called Turtle Hill, where the Light-House is to stand, is seventy-five feet above the level of the sea at highwater, and two hundred and ninety-seven feet from the shore. The hill is equally high to the Bank, and the land equally good for a foundation, being to appearance gravel, stone and marl, with clay, but as the Bank is washed by the sea in storms, we suppose it best to set the Building at this distance...

The Proprietors are content to take six pounds per acre for the land, provided the United States fence the same, or such part thereof as shall be improved, at their own expense. They will grant the privilege of landing on any part of their land, and carting through the same, whatever may be necessary for the Light House...Notwithstanding the height of this hill, above the water, there are others at a distance near the sea, something higher, which will make it necessary in the opinion of the gentlemen with me to have the Light House seventy or eighty feet above the top of the hill, so the same may be seen over land by vessels which may be to the westward, near the shore. On the north side there is no obstruction. We could see Plum Island, Gardiner's Island and Fisher's Island very plain.[15]

L'Hommedieu's bill for his services was $18.25.

On March 2, 1793 Congress appropriated $20,000 for

the construction of the tower. The need for Montauk Point Lighthouse was, in some ways, even greater than for other lighthouses in the new nation. While many towers already standing in the United States served to guide ships into major ports, the Montauk Point Lighthouse was intended to be the landfall light for ships approaching New York City from Europe. Coastal vessels also would use its beam to sail around Gardiner's Island and inside Gardiner's Bay, to enter Long Island Sound, and to head eastward from the Atlantic Ocean to harbors at Newport and coastal Massachusetts. It would assist ships through the Race (a swift tidal current in Long Island Sound) to New London, Connecticut.

In April 1795 the Treasury Department was prepared to receive bids for the lighthouse project. By August, Tench Coxe had received four bids:

Abisha Woodward, New London	$32,000
Abraham Miller & Co, East Hampton	$30,000
Nathaniel Richards, New London	$22,500
John McComb, Jr., New York	$22,300

In his proposal to Tench Coxe, Abraham Miller cited several reasons why the lighthouse could not be built for less than $30,000, among them the distance of the site from the nearest settlement, its lack of a suitable harbor for landing materials and a work crew, the heavy surf around the site, and its location on a steep hill with rough ground. These factors, Miller said, inflated the cost of labor.[16]

The contract ultimately was given to John McComb, Jr., since all government work at this time went to the lowest bidder. This was a fortunate turn of events; McComb was a talented builder and the only man with prior experience in constructing lighthouses, having built the Cape

Henry Lighthouse in 1792 at the entrance to the Chesapeake Bay.

John McComb, Jr. was born in New York City on October 17, 1763. His family moved to Princeton, New Jersey until the end of the American Revolution, then returned to New York City. He studied architecture and became a successful designer and builder, furnishing the plans for numerous public and private buildings in New York and the eastern states. He was the chief mason in the construction of such notable New York City structures as St Peter's Church on Barclay Street in 1785 and a townhouse for State Senator Rufus King in 1794. He designed and built Alexander Hamilton's residence, "The Grange" on Convent Avenue in 1802, City Hall from 1803-1811, and Castle Clinton in present Battery Park from 1807-1811. His buildings reflect the Federalist style and were popular with influential Quakers on the east coast. Though his popularity and success was well known, lighthouses were not his primary works. He would build only one other lighthouse after Montauk, at Eaton's Neck, Long Island in 1798. He died in New York City on May 25, 1853 at the age of 89.

Of the other bidders for Montauk Point Lighthouse, Abisha Woodward (1768-1829) would go on to build three lighthouses in Connecticut between 1800 and 1803 at New London, Faulkner's Island, and Lynde Point. The other two bidders had no building experience at all, Abraham Miller being the East Hampton town clerk and Nathaniel Richards a merchant in New London.

On August 11, 1795, Tench Coxe submitted the bids to George Washington and recommended McComb for the job, saying, "This is the same person who built that [lighthouse] on Cape Henry in Virginia. His attention, skill, and fidelity in that case inspire confidence on this occasion. His offer is lower by two hundred Dollars than any other, and moreover includes certain matters designedly omitted in the Advertisement."[17]

Washington approved Coxe's recommendation and on August 18, 1795 Coxe advised McComb via a letter that he had been chosen: "...the President has this day approved the proposals for building a Light House on Montauk Point, as made by you...You will therefore consider this same as mutually binding upon you and the United States."[18] McComb signed the contract six days later.

Henry Packer Dering (1763-1822), Collector of Customs at Sag Harbor and Long Island's first U.S. postmaster, later wrote to Tench Coxe, "From what acquaintance I have had with Mr. McComb the Contractor, I presume the Contract is a good one as he appears to be a very thorough man and well acquainted with the business; but as he will not be constantly here, some occasional Inspections, I should suppose would be prudent."[19]

The only stumbling block to the construction of the lighthouse came from the East Hampton proprietors who had been using the lands of Montauk for pasture since 1661. Their concerns were voiced in a letter from Dering to Coxe: "They did not object to selling the land, but requested some stipulation or proviso that they might at all times have the privilege, right, authority & power to remove & drive off any fishermen or other persons who might trespass on the lands and come there to reside and make deprivations on their property by killing their calves, sheep, cattle, etc."[20]

Also important was the fact that many local merchants and captains (some of whom were proprietors themselves) did not support the idea of a lighthouse at Montauk Point but preferred instead that one be built at Fisher's Island. It was finally agreed that the lighthouse would be established on Montauk with the stipulation that only lighthouse-related structures could be built on the property. That said, the proprietors deeded the land (13 acres total) to the government for $250 on January 16, 1796.[21]

Plans called for the Montauk Point Lighthouse to be 80-feet tall and shaped like an octagonal pyramid with a base of 28-feet diameter, tapering to 16-feet 6 inches at the top. An octagonal iron lantern 10-feet, 9-inches in diameter and 10-feet in height would rest at the top. An oil vault containing nine 200-gallon cedar cisterns and a keeper's dwelling and well were among the details of the contract. A description of McComb's contract (which was almost identical to the plans for Cape Henry Lighthouse) follows:

> *...a Light-House of stone, faced with hewn or hammer dressed stone...of the following form and description.*
>
> *The form is to be octagonal-- the foundation is to be of stone, to be sunk thirteen feet below the bottom of the water table, or the surface of the earth, and to be commenced of the Diameter of twenty-nine feet, from such commencement to the bottom of the Water Table-- the foundation wall is to be thirteen feet high and nine feet thick.*
>
> *Secondly. The Diameter of the base from the bottom of the Water Table to the top therof where the Octagonal Pyramid is to commence is to be twenty eight feet, and the Wall there is to be seven feet thick. The wall of the Octagonal pyramid is to be six feet thick at the base therof, on the top of the Water Table.*
>
> *Thirdly. The height of the building from the bottom of the water table and from the surface of the Earth is to be eighty feet to the top of the stone work, under the*

floor of the Lantern, where the diameter is to be sixteen feet six inches and the wall three feet thick, the whole is to be built of stone, the water table is to be capt with sawn stone, at least eight inches wide and sloped at the top to turn off the water. The outside of the walls is to be faced with hewn or hammer dressed stone, having four windows in the East and three in the West. The sashes to be hung with hinges, and each sash to have twelve panes of glass eight by ten inches.

Fourthly. On the top of the stone work is to be a framed Tier of Joists bedded therein, planked over with Oak plank extending three feet beyond the wall thereby forming an Eave which is to be finished with a cornice the whole having a descent from the Centre sufficient to throw off the Water & to be covered with Copper.

Fifthly. A complete and sufficient Iron Lantern in the octagonal form is to rest thereon, the eight corner pieces or stanchions of which are to be built in the wall to the depth of ten feet. These stanchions are to be nearly three inches square in the lower ten feet, and three & an half by two & an half inches above. The Lantern is to be ten feet high from the floor to the bottom of the dome or roof, and to have a dome or roof of five feet & nine inches in height. The whole space is between the posts or upright pieces, at the angles is to be occupied by the Sashes which are to be moulded on in the inside & struck Solid. Each sash is to have twenty-eight panes of glass, fourteen by twelve inches; a part of the sash on the southwest side is to be hung with hinges for a convenient door to go out on the platform.

Sixthly. The rafters of the Lantern, are to be framed into an Iron loop, over which is to be a copper funnel thro which the smoke may pass into a large copper ventilator in the form of a man's head, capable of containing one hundred gallons. This Head is to be turned by a large weather vane, so that the hole for venting the smoke may be always to leeward. At least eight dormant ventilators are to be fixed in the roof. A large curved air pipe or pipes are to be passed thro the floor, and a close stove is to be provided & fixed in the lantern.

Seventhly. There are to be seven pair of stairs to ascend to the Lantern, the entrance to which is to be by the trap door covered with copper. The building is to be furnished with two complete electrical conductors rods with points. The floors are to be laid with plank of at least one inch and one half in thickness. The entrance to the Light house to be well secured by a strong door hung upon hinges with a strong lock & latch.[22]

In April of 1796, John McComb, Jr. made his first visit to Montauk Point and began planning the construction. According to Henry Packer Dering, McComb proposed to build the tower an additional 50-feet further inland from the site selected by Ezra L' Hommedieu, noting that the bank "wastes away very fast." [23]

During the summer of 1795, McComb detailed requirements for the project in his "Memorandum Book." His list included two lighters (large barges) for transporting sandstone blocks from ships anchored offshore to a landing on the beach and the cost of building a road from the beach to the construction site, plus two yokes of oxen for carting materials. He planned to hire a crew of fifty men, mostly laborers that included masons, carpenters, and blacksmiths.

He also estimated the cost of provisions for the comfort of the workers camped at the Point. One item would keep his workers very comfortable—500 gallons of rum.[24]

The origin of the sandstone in the tower is unknown. However, sandstone quarries in Portland and Middletown, Connecticut, which had been in existence since the 1600s and were within reasonable distance from Montauk, are considered likely sources. Both were located on the Connecticut River about 50-miles west of New London.

In May 1796 a road was built to the site for transporting the building materials and on June 7 construction officially began with the laying of a cornerstone. Some materials came from the lands at Montauk, as noted on May 2, 1796 when it was "agreed to let John McComb have some old dry wood at the point…and allow him to keep two pair of oxen in the fatting field and level a certain hill for his convenience of carting and to get stone."[25]

Assurances as to the sturdiness of the building site were addressed on June 20 in a letter to Tench Coxe by Henry Packer Dering: "The soil is much firmer than was expected and intermixed with a coarse gravel which rendered it so hard that the workmen could scarcely get it up with their pickaxes. From these circumstances there is no danger of the foundation except from the sea's undermining the eminence on which the building is erected as it stands nearer the Bank or cliff of the sea than I could wish."[26]

Work proceeded well and according to plan, as indicated in further correspondence from Dering to Coxe on August 29: "…The Light House erecting on the land is in very considerable forwardness; The weather having during the summer season proved very dry and favorable for building, has not in any way impeaded the work from which circumstance Mr. McComb tells me he shall compleat his contract in all Oct. or Nov. next…by which time I suppose it might be proper to have some person in view to take charge of the light."[27]

Coxe wrote to his agent, Thomas Randall, in New York: "It is expected that the building of the Montauk Light House will now be very soon completed, and it being of importance to have the same lighted as soon as practicable, you will be please to have a set of copper lamps made for a Lantern of 10½ feet diameter...with all possible dispatch."[28]

By October 1796—a mere four months after work began—McComb and his crew finished the tower and started work on the lantern. In a report to Coxe on October 10, Henry Packer Dering noted, "Mr. McComb does his work in a faithful and workman like manner." However, a difficulty that potentially could have hampered the project was noted by Coxe: "...three or four bad gullies around the hill on which the light house is placed where the ground is badly broken by the raines and requires immediate attention in securing it from undermining the foundation of the building."[29] This was the beginning of centuries of erosion-related problems at Montauk Point. McComb had stone walls built across the gullies and filled in the valleys behind them, charging the government an additional $440.66 for the work.

In mid-September McComb ordered the lantern from Robert Boyd & Co., "Black and White Smiths" of New York.[30] Days later Coxe wrote to the Secretary of the Treasury that the lantern was in the process of being set in place and said of McComb: "The Inspector of his builds at Cape Henry & Montauk agree that his work is excellent, & his zeal and exertions are greatly to his credit."[31]

The lantern was completed on November 5, 1796. Three days later, Henry Packer Dering visited the site and reported to Tench Coxe the lighthouse is "together with the

Oil Vault and dwelling house completely finished." Since Dering had not been made aware of the appointment of 63-year-old Jacob Hand as keeper, he "thought it advisable not to leave the buildings without some person in charge of them as they were in an exposed situation & probably would get plundered…I therefore put a young man son of Mr. Hand (Jared) in charge of them until I rec'd your letter informing of the appointment of his father."[32]

Jared Hand would one day become the keeper at Montauk following the retirement of his father. The Hands being 'keepers of the cattle' for the East Hampton proprietors were the perfect choice as lighthouse keepers.[33] In fact, there was a Hand assigned to one or another of the three houses nearly every year from 1774 to 1806.[34]

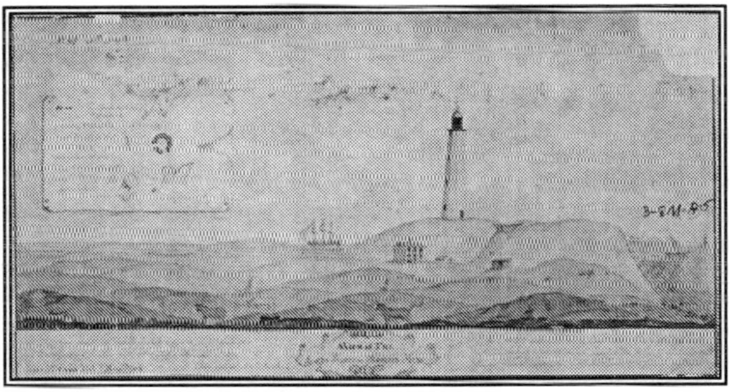

Isaac McComb, brother of Montauk Point Lighthouse architect John McComb, painted this watercolor entitled "A View of the Light House on Montack Point", an accurate representation of the property in 1796. (National Archives)

According to McComb's contract for the lighthouse, provision was made for the building of a keeper's dwelling, which was to be:

> *...a framed House, Thirty-four feet in front & sixteen feet deep with a Cellar under it, the cellar wants to be eighteen inches thick and seven feet high. The first story of the House is to be eight feet & the second seven feet six inches high. The floors to be laid in whole length and nailed through. The stack of chiminies with two plain fireplaces on each floor, one of them large for a kitchen. Two windows below and three above, in front and rear, each sash to have eighteen panes of glass ten by eight inches. The door to be hung and furnished completely. The ceilings and inner sides of the House to be plastered with two coats. All the woodwork inside and out to be well painted and the whole to be finished in a plain and decent manner.*[35]

The house was built at the foot of Turtle Hill to give shelter from the frequent and, at times, harsh winds and to allow for the convenience of a well to be dug nearby. A huge chimney in the center divided the first floor into two large rooms. The kitchen, on the west side of the house, had an oven beside the fireplace and a straight run of stairs to the second floor. Construction of the house was completed on September 22, 1796.

To mark the completion of the entire project at Montauk Point, Isaac McComb, younger brother of John McComb, Jr., created a watercolor of the lighthouse and buildings entitled, "A View of the Light House on Montack Point." Inscribed on the painting was the following description: "This Light House stands 130 Yards from high water mark, the hill is 65' above the water and the Lights are elevated above the level of the Sea, 150 feet, the Oil Vault is 30 feet from Light-House, the dwelling House is 32' above the water, & 160' from the Light House." The inscription also included a site plan that showed the stone dams built across three gullies to halt erosion during construction. The watercolor provided an accurate representation of the original property and structures.

It is interesting to note that McComb's contract did not include the eight lamps for the lantern. Therefore, on September 16, 1796 Tench Coxe requested that Thomas Randall order the lighting apparatus for the lighthouse. It is generally thought that when the lamps were installed they were hung in two tiers, the same as in McComb's Cape Henry Lighthouse.

Tench Coxe also directed Randall, to announce to the public the completion of the lighthouse at Montauk Point: "You will be pleased to publish in one of the New York Papers, that the Light House on Montauk point, at the East end of Long Island, is completely finished, and that it will very shortly be lighted."[36]

With all the praise lavished upon McComb at the conclusion of the Montauk Point Lighthouse project, Coxe immediately asked him to submit an estimate for the building of a lighthouse at Cape Hatteras, North Carolina. The job ultimately went to Henry Dearborn. McComb, however, built one more lighthouse at Eaton's Neck, Long Island in 1798.

The delivery of the lamps probably took place in late November 1796. However, there was an unforeseen delay and a touch of irony in the lighting of the tower. The commissioning of the Montauk Point Lighthouse was intended to reduce the number of shipwrecks around the Point, but on December 10, 1796 Henry Packer Dering reported to Tench Coxe that the ship carrying the oil for the lighthouse "is on shore at a place called Napeague…about 14 miles from the Light House. At this place the vessel was drove on shore in the late violent gale of wind which happened on the night of the 8th instant. The

Oil fortunately is all saved and safely landed."

The same storm shattered fifteen panes of glass in the lighthouse's new lantern, with no replacement panes available. Dering continued: "I have not been able to account for or discover the real cause for the glass's braking but believe it arises from several; some, the sashes not being entirely true, the glass are cut too small & do not bear equally or in every part on the sash—in others, the glass appears so thin that the pressure of the wind breaks them." [37]

According to Richard (Dick) White, chairman of the Montauk Historical Society's Lighthouse Committee in 2006, no one offered to salvage the cargo from the shipwreck and bring it to the lighthouse: "The local people didn't want the lighthouse because the light would help ships find their way at night, and these people made a living off the shipwrecks."

Congress was forced to pay for recovery of the materials and transport to the Point.[38] A new shipment of glass did not arrive until March 1797, significantly delaying the lighting of the tower. In the meantime, the oil was secured at First House.[39]

Since the lantern glass often shattered during violent storms, it was suggested by Henry Packer Dering that keeper Jacob Hand be provided with a diamond to cut glass, since his son "is by trade a shop joiner & house carpenter & will at any time cutt the glass to suit the sashes and putty the same in." [40]

A diamond was ordered about two months later. It would come in handy. Another severe storm struck the lighthouse in April 1799, described by Dering as a "tornado…accompanied with a violent wind and heavy storm of large hail [that] broak more than half the glass out of the Lantern." The lighthouse was "much injured," as was keeper Hand who was in the lantern room during the storm and "was badly cut in the face & hands by the glass."[41]

The actual date the lighthouse was placed in service is unknown. Sources vary, from as early as April 1797 and to as late as November 5, 1797, a full year after construction was complete. Regardless of the inception date, the Montauk Point Lighthouse was one of the new nation's first public works projects. It was also the fifth lighthouse completed by the fledgling federal government. The first four were at Portland Head, Maine (1791), Cape Henry, Virginia (1792), Cape Fear, North Carolina (1796- later rebuilt), and Seguin Island, Maine (1796- later rebuilt). Eleven lighthouses built during the colonial era also were in service when Montauk Point was lighted.

Jacob Hand (1733-1813) was appointed the first keeper on November 4, 1796 and assumed the responsibility two weeks later when he moved into the keeper's dwelling with his wife Abigail Conkling (1734-1805) and son Jared (born 1762). Jacob Hand had been given a vote of confidence in April 1796 from Henry Packer Dering in a letter to Tench Coxe: "I know of no one that would give better satisfaction than Mr. Hand a resident on the land & who I understand has applied. He will be entirely satisfactory to the proprietors of the land."[42]

Yet, in a letter to Coxe five months later Dering appeared to have changed his opinion: "Two applicants have applied from this District a Mr. Hand & a Capt. Willis the former was recommended by the proprietors, but the latter (Capt. Willis) I think will have the preference as being a good pilote on the coast & acquainted with all the harbors & their bearings & distance from the Light as he formerly resided on Block Island and I suppose him better acquainted with the business generally to be undertaken than Mr. Hand."[43]

Dering apparently did not want this change of heart

known to Hand, as he concluded by stating, "I could wish my name not to be mentioned in the preference of Capt. Willis to Mr. Hand…I have nothing further in view than the interest of gov't in my preferring Willis to Hand."[44]

Others vied for the position, among them Ezra Waite of Lyme, Connecticut who wrote to Tench Coxe: "Should you Sir think it proper to give me the appointment requested, I shall be ready at any time to come under the usual obligations for executing the business of that establishment with faithfulness and punctuality and to enter upon the same when necessary. As to my character, ability and to execute the business in contemplation, I would beg leave to refer you to our Representatives in Congress, especially Messrs Coit and Griswold, as they are very particularly acquainted with me."[45]

Another applicant of note was John Seward, who had eight years experience as keeper of the Sandy Hook Lighthouse in New Jersey. William Heyer wrote to Coxe on Seward's behalf in September 1796: "…some time ago, I recommended to you John Seaward as a person capable to keep the light house, last night he was at my home and told me he was ready at any time to attend to that business if he should be appointed."[46]

Three months later Seward wrote Coxe that he had "waited with the greatest anxiety to know the appointment on whether I should be the successful Candidate….I have made my arrangements and kept myself in readiness for the Business."[47]

Jacob Hand, however, kept his appointment as Montauk Point Light's first keeper. Hand's annual salary was $266.66. In the correspondence that cited his pay, it was also noted that "his Grandson shall live with him in the character of an assistant, without further compensation than is above mentioned."[48]

Hand's routine at Montauk Point Lighthouse included many tasks, the most important being the care and operation of the illuminating apparatus. Every evening before dark, he walked to the oil vault where whale oil for the lamps was stored in nine 200-gallon cisterns. He filled a 5-gallon jug with oil, carried it to the tower, and climbed seven flights of wooden stairs to the lantern. There he fueled the beacon's eight lamps, which were displayed in a double-tiered chandelier. Behind each lamp was a 14-inch reflector to intensify the light. Hand kept watch in the lantern all night, making certain the light continued to shine. He trimmed the lamp wicks periodically to keep the flame steady and bright, and cleaned soot from the storm panes.

* * * * * * *

Today Montauk Point Lighthouse holds the distinction of being the fourth oldest lighthouse tower in the United States in continuous operation, behind Sandy Hook, New Jersey (1764), Boston Harbor, Massachusetts (1783) and Portland Head, Maine (1791). It is interesting to note that though John McComb, Jr.'s bid of $22,300 was the lowest one for the construction of the Montauk lighthouse, most other light towers of that time were built for less.

Robert J Hefner, in a study of the Montauk Point Lighthouse prepared for the Montauk Historical Society in 1989, expressed high praise for the quality of John McComb, Jr.'s work:

> *John McComb Jr. had an excellent reputation as a builder and there is every indication that the Montauk Point Lighthouse was constructed to the highest standards of the time. The fact that three out of the four surviving towers constructed by the Federal govern-*

ment before 1800 were built by McComb is testimony to his skill and careful supervision. The Montauk Point Lighthouse was not always well maintained and its present (1989) sound condition is certainly the result of McComb's initial construction.[49]

In November 1797, Henry Packer Dering visited the lighthouse and reported it was "neat & in attentive order, and from observation [Dering had] reason to believe the keeper punctual & unremitted in his attention to the light." However, Dering noted a lack of adequate ventilation in the lantern:

...the light in the first part of the night is very clere and bright & I may with propriety say equal if not superior to any in the U.S. But in the latter part of the night the Glass becomes so smoked that the light becomes dim and dull. I noticed this to the keeper who told me he had before observed it & endevoured to remedy it and in very calm nights had left open the trap door which some what helped the draft. This I told him was dangerous as sparks might fall from the lamps endanger the burning the next story floor. I noticed that the 8 dormant ventilators in the roof were I thought rather small.[50]

In 1799, Dering reported numerous glass panes needing repair in the tower: "...the Lantern will want a supply of one Box of Glass this fall as there is at present no spare glass on hand and there is at least 60 squares now wanting. I propose sending for a Box to New York as soon as the regular conveyance from this place opens which will be in the course of a few days."[51]

Dering's assessments of problems at the lighthouse

were the first of many over its more than 200-year history, but they were not uncommon. Similar issues plagued all American light stations in the early nineteenth century. In the ensuing decades, the excessive frugality of the U.S. Lighthouse Establishment and its inadequate response to problems at lighthouses only increased troubles at light stations around the country.

CHAPTER 2

Lighthouse Developments: 1800-1860

In general, little maintenance occurred at the Montauk Point Light Station during the years 1797-1857. The primary concern was keeping the lantern watertight and maintaining the white daymark on the exterior of the tower, to help mariners recognize it from a distance in the daytime. The illuminating apparatus—the most complex and demanding part of the lighthouse—also required constant care.

Lightkeepers lighted and extinguished the whale oil lamps and kept them clean. Lamp wicks were trimmed and the glass chimneys and reflectors behind the lamps were polished. Keepers cleaned the lantern panes inside and out and replaced broken glass. They also did small maintenance tasks around the station. Substantial repairs were made only after long delays and sometimes not at all. For example, the dome was reported leaking in 1816 but was not replaced until a new set of lamps was installed in 1838, twenty-two years later.

The lantern was re-glazed as needed to keep it watertight and to produce a clear light. Whitewashing the tower to make it recognizable during the day was done by contract, usually once a year. One of the earliest references to whitewashing was in July 1801 in a letter from Henry Packer Dering to William Miller, Commissioner of Revenue:

> *...the Light House under my superintendence will require White Washing in the course of the Summer or Autumn. As the work will probably be done by contract, I request to be informed what the usual expence has been in contracts or for Work of a similar kind on other Lighthouses. The Building at Montauk is as large and high or higher than any other in the United States which will be taken into consideration.*
>
> *We have good Masons here whom I think probable will undertake the Works and execute it on as reasonable terms and as faithfully as else where.*[52]

Documents, letters, and other records for the lighthouse indicate that the keepers' job of maintaining the lighthouse was an endless responsibility. From its inception in 1796 until automation in 1987 there was an endless list of equipment, buildings, and other property that, at one time or another, required repair, whitewash, paint, cleaning, polishing, or fencing. Problems included leaks, rust, rotting wood, dampness, broken windows, and items that simply wore out. At times requests were made for additional equipment and other items, but these were not always honored; necessity and cost being factors. For example, a request in 1871 for a separate building to store wood and coal was denied.

Lighthouse inspections revealed problems not only with the physical property and equipment but with personnel as well. Drunkenness, dereliction of duty, insubordination, and poor work habits were among the issues addressed. It was in the best interest of the keepers, especially after the creation of the rigorous and quasi-military U. S. Light-House Board in 1852, to correct these problems or face discharge from duties.

An addition to the keeper's dwelling was built in 1806 by keeper Jacob Hand and Josiah Hand. This was most likely the kitchen addition built on the north side of the structure. Josiah Hand also was credited with developing a new lamp which was installed in the tower. Henry Packer Dering wrote of his exemplary skills to Secretary of the Treasury Albert Gallatin (1761-1849) stating that young Josiah Hand "...has expended nearly 1000 dollars in enlarging the dwelling House, building a barn and a work-shop, in fencing, gardening, planting, and setting out trees, manuring the land belonging to the establishment &c. He really deserves much credit for his invention of the lamp...It is supposed that it will be a saving of near 400 galls [gallons] of oil in the course of a year."[53]

Josiah Hand's new lamp consisted of a single reservoir, 3-feet in diameter, set on a table. Around it were set thirty-two spouts, each with a wick. This resembled a "spider lamp" built by John McComb, Jr. in 1798 for the Eaton's Neck Lighthouse on western Long Island; it consisted of a 30-inch diameter reservoir with twenty-four spouts around the perimeter, each containing a wick.

Secretary of the Treasury, Albert Gallatin, requested further information about the effectiveness of the new lamp. Dering responded in April 1807: "It gives much better light owing to all the air that is admitted through the ventilators at the floor of the lantern, ascending between the glass and the lamps on every side of the lantern which throws the smoke in the center of the lantern and prevents its lodging on the glass, from which circumstances the light continues much brighter through the night. The lamps burn more free and distinct especially in cold weather."[54]

Despite Dering's praise, Hand's lamp proved to be troublesome, giving off fumes that burned the eyes and preventing lightkeepers from remaining in the lantern room for an extended period of time. On the contrary, oil consumption by the new lamp had noticeably decreased, as reported on two occasions. In July 1809 Dering told Gallatin that Montauk Light "...will not require any oil the next season, so great a saving having been made by the new constructed lamp which I had some years since placed in the lantern."[55]

Dering reported to Secretary Gallatin in January 1812 that the new lamp had saved 1,400-gallons of oil over the previous four years.[56] However, the oil vault, composed of nine cisterns of 200-gallons volume each, was by now in very poor condition as noted by Dering to Gallatin in 1809:

> *...the shed which covers the Oil Vault has gone mostly to decay, and that the boards with which it is covered are become so defective that they will not hold a nail and are frequently blowing off and exposing the arch of the vault to injury from the rains and wet, and that the materials of which the shed was built are generally so much decayed as not to admit of repairs unless rebuilt.*
>
> *...a frame roof with sills or plates lying on the wall and covered with Shingle will not only be vastly more dureable, but much more aconomical and cheeper in the end to the United States than one covered with boards which will require rebuilding once in ten or fifteen years.*[57]

In November 1812 Josiah Hand's lamp was replaced by

a patented Argand lamp developed by retired Cape Cod sea captain, Winslow Lewis (1770-1850). The eighteen Lewis lamps were each backed by a parabolic reflector and produced a steady smokeless flame. But this design also did not measure up, since the lamp and reflector were of poor quality, and the light was less steady and bright than previous designs.

Lewis' lighting system seemed to send the U.S. Lighthouse Establishment backwards, and the ability of the federal government to respond to the problems plaguing lighthouses intensified. It had begun fourteen years earlier with the passage of the Ninth Act by Congress on August 7, 1789, whereby the country's lighthouses were placed under federal control under Secretary of the Treasury, Alexander Hamilton (1755-1804). With his guidance, repairs and improvements were made to existing lighthouses and new ones were constructed. But in 1792, the much overworked Hamilton created the office of the Commissioner of Revenue (the precursor to our modern Internal Revenue Service) and assigned the responsibility for navigational aids to him. The first man to hold the office was Tench Coxe of Pennsylvania.

It may seem odd that a department charged with collecting taxes would manage lighthouses, but since the Commissioner of Revenue also collected duties on incoming ships lighthouses seemed to fall under his advisement. The United States also was small enough at this time for Presidents to become personally involved in matters of lighthouse contracts, construction, and appointment and dismissal of keepers. But as the nation grew, and the responsibilities of the Presidency increased, the details of navigational aids were handed to cabinets. By 1802, supervision had been transferred to the Secretary of the Treasury, Albert Gallatin. In 1813, control reverted to the Commissioner of Revenue, who in 1820 transferred the responsibility to the Fifth Auditor of the Treasury, an accountant named Stephen Pleasonton (1776-1855).

Though known primarily for his role in lighthouse matters, he was also celebrated for another, more heroic deed. As a civilian during the War of 1812, with the British advancing on Washington with the intent of burning the capital, Pleasonton grabbed the Constitution, the Declaration of Independence, and the letters of George Washington, and secured them at a safe location in Virginia. This courageous act was later overshadowed by his inadequate management of lighthouse affairs. Pleasonton's preoccupation with economy and his lack of knowledge about navigational aids was partly responsible for an inferior American lighthouse service.[58]

Excessive penny-pinching meant there was little money for construction of new lighthouses and even less money for repairs and upgrades to existing lighthouses. Contracts continued to go to the lowest bidders, whether they had adequate experience or not, and work often was shoddy and necessitated the rebuilding of towers in only a few years time. Pleasonton relied on Collectors of Customs in local ports to manage lighthouses. Political favoritism dictated keepers' appointments. There were suggestions of scandal, too, fueled by the fact that Stephen Pleasonton relied heavily on Winslow Lewis for advice and awarded him nearly all contracts for lighthouse construction between 1820 and 1840. Lewis also cornered the lighthouse market with his patented but inferior lighting apparatus.

Meanwhile, lighthouses deteriorated, the quality of the lights themselves grew substandard to those of Europe, and lightkeepers, who were poorly paid and virtually unregulated, came and went. Needless to say, lighthouse keepers of the day received little if any instructions and training.

Two examples at Montauk Point Lighthouse serve to illustrate the problems under Pleasonton's administration. On November 27, 1822 Henry Thomas Dering (1796-1854), by now the new Sag Harbor Superintendent of Lighthouses, wrote to Pleasonton and pointed out that Winslow Lewis had supplied the lighthouse with six new burners that were the wrong size for the lamps and that the earlier 17-inch reflectors had been replaced with 6-inch reflectors "indifferently plated" with silver.[59] On January 18, 1828, Dering again wrote to Pleasonton advising that the quality of the whale oil delivered by Lewis was "worse than ever received" and would be difficult to burn.

Surprisingly, Dering reported in January 1826: "The Light at Montauk Point is in good reputation and very generally acknowledged as the best in the United States."[60] However, within ten years the situation had changed drastically. In December 1837 and May 1838, John P. Osborn, the Sag Harbor Superintendent of Lighthouses, wrote to Pleasonton about the tower's leaky deck, decayed platforms, beams and stairs: "These platforms and stairs are the same that were originally put in the house when built 42 years since."[61] In 1840 Osborn reported that the windows and doors in the tower were "decayed and let in the rain."[62]

The criticism seemed to come from everywhere. In 1838, the *American Coast Pilot*, published by brothers Edmund and George Blunt, mentioned the significance of the Montauk Point Lighthouse, noting the light "...is passed by all vessels approaching Long Island Sound from eastward, and is a good point of departure for those leaving the Sound. It is also frequently made by vessels from the southward bound to the northward and eastward, and by those approaching New-York bay from the eastward."[63]

Following these comments was the Blunt's scathing report on the poor job Pleasonton was doing with maintenance of lighthouses in the Third District. They cited the Montauk Point Lighthouse as an example: "... the reflectors are of various figures; there is, in all, no proper way of ventilating the lamp room, and the moisture, mixed with soot from the top of the lantern, freezes on the glass in cold weather."[64]

The Blunts also noted the poor construction of the 1838 keeper's dwelling: "The material, generally, is bad for a work of that kind...but it is said to be according to contract, and they are not to use the best materials."[65]

In response to the *American Coast Pilot* report, Pleasonton had Winslow Lewis refit the Montauk Point Lighthouse in July 1838 with a new lighting apparatus consisting of eighteen lamps with 14½-inch parabolic reflectors. Its range increased to 20-miles. According to Pleasonton, the change "imposed additional labor upon the keeper, and, as this is a Light of the first class and from its situation is one of the most important, I would recommend an addition of fifty dollars to the salary of the Keeper."[66] However, in December of that year, Lt. George Mifflin Bache, in his 1838 report to Congress on Third District lighthouses said of the new installation "the tube glasses in use are too short to project through the holes in the reflectors."[67]

The poor quality of Lewis' lamps frustrated Pleasonton, too. In a letter to Lewis dated April 20, 1846 he said: "I am very sorry to learn that the reflectors and lamps at Montauk Point are worn out, for it was only in 1838 that they were put on new. These lamps & reflectors ought to have lasted 16 or 18 years at least...see that the proper quality of silver is put on the reflector you now make, for it is discreditable to have them worn out in 8 years."[68]

While concerns during the Pleasonton era focused largely on the lighting mechanism, work was needed on the tower as well. Repairs finally were done in 1849, near the end of Pleasonton's tenure and after years of criticism against his administration. He ordered a new lantern (about the same size as the original) and outfitted it with a chandelier of fifteen large brass oil lamps, each fitted with 21-inch silver parabolic reflectors. The cost was $3,300. The panes of glass were 16" x 26", more than twice the size of the previous lantern glazing.[69]

During these years the keeper's dwelling also was deteriorating. Keeper Patrick Gould wrote to Superintendent John P. Osborn in Sag Harbor requesting a more spacious house. Osborn, in turn, described the situation in a letter to Pleasonton in January 1837:

> *The Keeper of Montauk Light had made application to me for a new dwelling house the one occupied by him has been built over 40 years...and is unfit in its present state for his accommodation the chimneys unsafe to remain the cellar wall undermined the floors worn out the ceiling and wall very bad the house leaky and cold and if a new one is not erected the old one must have extensive repairs and nothing would be saved but the frame which is not large enough for this place...Montauk is a place of considerable resort for commercial cities and there can be no other accommodations as the land adjoining is all held by tenants in common and cannot be procured by building purposes- there are few Light House Keepers that require so good a house as the one at Montauk.*[70]

(Montauk Point was a destination for travelers from New York and Long Island during the early 1800s, a fact that did not go unnoticed by Osborn.)

Henry B. Haven of Sag Harbor submitted the lowest bid of $2,830 to construct a new dwelling. A contract was signed on May 23, 1837 and the 38' x 22' two-story structure was completed by June 1838.[71] According to the contract, Haven was directed to make certain the interior surfaces were "lathed and plastered with two coats of good lime mortar" and all the woodwork painted white. The fireplaces were "furnished with suitable Iron cranes. Hooks and trammels—The mantle piece...of cut stone. A flue oven to be built with one of said chimneys with an iron door." The floors were "of good white pine 1¼ inch plank planed and grooved," the windows fitted with "inside folding shutters," and the four-panel doors hung "with good-jointed Butt Hinges."[72]

All but one of the above items was included in the new quarters. Since the adjacent 1796 dwelling already contained a large kitchen addition, neither of the fireplaces in the new dwelling was equipped for cooking.

The contract also included money for a well or a cistern. The builder opted for a well. It was dug just west of the kitchen door of the dwelling. A pump house was built over it in 1890 and survived until at least 1936.[73] Five years after the dwelling was finished, two new lightning rods (conductors) were placed on the lighthouse, plus 550 posts and rails for fencing the property were purchased.[74]

An oil painting donated to the Montauk Historical Society by descendants of keeper Patrick Gould provides a glimpse of the light station during the period shortly after the new quarters were added. It shows the lighthouse from the bluffs to the west and depicts the tower and oil house on Turtle Hill and the "double-dwelling" at the base of the hill. The three-bay front façade of the 1838 structure is seen, along with the three dormers and end chimneys. The gable roof of the 1796 dwelling faces to the north. Just east of the structures is the old barn built by Josiah Hand in 1806.

In the 1848 publication, *List of Lighthouses, Beacons*

and Floating Lights of the United States, the Montauk Point Lighthouse was listed as #108, containing sixteen reflectors visible for 26-miles in good weather and the lantern 160-feet above sea level, built in 1795 (the correct year was actually 1796), and refitted in 1838.[75]

During the Pleasonton era, lighthouse tenders (supply vessels) serviced all navigational aids. Captain Jonathan Howland was the skipper of the Long Island area tender, and he made only one visit to Montauk Lighthouse each year to deliver oil and supplies. On a June 1, 1850 visit to the station, Captain Howland reported: "This Lighthouse, and, in fact, the whole establishment, I must call in good order, and the lighting apparatus clean…Went on shore, made repairs to the lighting apparatus, which were trifling, and left the oil in the casks for the keeper to cart up and pump off, he not having a team, and none to be obtained short of 6 or 7 miles."

Captain Howland reported that an average of about 32½-gallons of oil was used per lamp each year since his last visit on June 9, 1849. This was significant, since the national average was 35-gallons annually.[76]

As Pleasonton squeezed the dollar, he unknowingly sacrificed the quality of the nation's lighthouses and undermined not only the safety of mariners but the U.S. Lighthouse Service mission overall. Historians agree he was a diligent and compassionate government servant, but economy, simplicity, and the excessively frugal and partisan politics of the day steered his course. He was forced, as well, to allocate much of his budget to construction of new lighthouses. During his thirty-two years managing the nation's navigational aids, the number of lighthouses increased six-fold.

Pleasonton's most consequential decision was to delay the adoption of Fresnel lenses, citing their expense and complexity. Introduced by the French lighthouse authority in 1823, prismatic lenses were vastly superior to the lighting system developed by Winslow Lewis. The French physicist Augustin Fresnel (1788-1827) designed a cone of prisms and spherical glass that surrounded a single oil lamp. The lenticular arrangement captured 70 percent of the lamp's light rays and bent them into a horizontal beam. Several different sizes (or orders) of lenses were developed. First and second order lenses were used for major landfall or coastal lights, while third through sixth orders worked well for bays and harbor and river entrances. Both fixed (steady) and flashing lenses were developed.

In 1830 Pleasonton wrote to the French government about their revolutionary lenses. The price tag for a first-order lens, such as a landfall lighthouse like Montauk Point would require, was $5,000. Pleasonton had recently built an entire light station on Long Island's south shore at Fire Island—tower and illuminating apparatus, dwelling, and ancillary buildings—for $10,000. He felt he could ill-afford to spend half his construction budget on optics.

Mariners and Congress did not agree, and in 1838 Pleasonton was ordered to purchase two Fresnel lenses and have them installed in the Navesink Twin Lights in New Jersey. Everyone, including Pleasonton, was amazed by their superior brilliance and beauty, yet Pleasonton continued to use the second-rate apparatus patented by Winslow Lewis. Ironically, an investigation in 1842 by Lewis' nephew, a civil engineer named I.W.P. Lewis, revealed that the old lighting system was not only inferior to the Fresnel lenses but also copied from an English design. Pleasonton objected to the report but assuaged complaints by purchasing two more Fresnel lenses.[77]

By 1851, Congress had heard enough criticism and resolved to take action. A board of military officers convened to study the nation's lighthouse system and to "look into every aspect of the lighthouse establishment, including methods of lighting, all phases of construction, management of the system, effectiveness of the lights, procuring of supplies, the way the lighthouses were operated, and efficiency and economy of operation." Their findings, published in a 760-page report, revealed the shortcomings of the U.S. Lighthouse Establishment and underscored the fact that it fell short in many categories. The result of the investigation was the creation of the U.S. Light-House Board on October 9, 1852.[78]

The nine-member Board included military personnel, engineers, and a scientist from the Smithsonian Institution. The Board's regimented and somewhat martial style, which had been lacking in past decades, brought immediate improvements. Inspectors and engineers were assigned to each lighthouse district (Montauk Point was placed in the Third District) to provide proper supervision. Keepers received training, regular inspections, and awards for superior performance. In the 1880s they began wearing uniforms.

Plans for keepers' dwellings, towers, and lanterns were developed as part of a major overhaul of the entire lighthouse system. A new system was created to classify lighthouses and provide appropriate designs and equipment for each classification. The Board sought the newest and best technology for construction, illumination, and fog signaling. Eventually, every lighthouse in the country would have a Fresnel lens.

The Light-House Board viewed the lighthouse at Montauk as a "...very important light, especially for navigators bound from Europe to New York. It is fitted now with only 15 lamps and 21-inch reflectors for a fixed light. Its reported elevation is 160-feet above the level of the sea, and with a first order apparatus would be seen under ordinary circumstances about 20 nautical miles."[79]

In a report to Congress in 1852, the Board recommended that ten lighthouses be refitted with first-order Fresnel lenses, Montauk Point and Fire Island among them. The report also recommended that a first-order lighthouse be constructed at Shinnecock. The three lights would serve as guiding beacons for ships sailing in and out of New York City.

The Board's priority was the construction of the lighthouse at Shinnecock (also known as Great West Bay and today as Hampton Bays). It was completed in 1856. Plans for a fixed first-order lens at Shinnecock conflicted with Montauk Light, which also displayed a fixed beam. In the Board's report of June 30, 1856 it was "...contemplated to fit Montauk Point Lighthouse with a first order lens apparatus for a fixed light, varied by flashes, at the time of the exhibition of the Great West Bay (first-order lens fixed-light) rendered necessary by the erection of the latter, the apparatus for which is already provided."[80]

On August 19, 1853 Captain Augustus Ludlow Case (1812-1893), the new Third District inspector, visited the Montauk Point Lighthouse. In a report to Thornton Jenkins (1811-1893), Secretary of the Light-House Board, he pointed out that the tower was "...a little cracked and wants some repairs...Reflectors and lamps much out of adjustment but passably clean. Lantern smoked and dirty overhead and badly ventilated...Deck coppered but Rain beats through under it. Lantern heated by small stove with anthracite coal. Oil kept in base of tower and stone vault a few feet from it...Double dwelling house (one brick and the other frame) with outbuildings all want repairs."[81]

Inspector Case visited again in April 1854 and reported to Secretary Jenkins:

The Tower, Lantern, and Illuminating Apparatus were clean and look as if attention and care was bestowed upon them...The Lamps and Chandelier are in very bad order, the first showing decided marks of wilful abuse, or gross neglect, being broken or bruised to such a degree as to render their repair out of a proper workshop impossible. The Chandelier is very slight and cracked, and it would not surprise me to hear of its having broken down at any moment...The ventilation of the Lamp is very bad, there being but two single ventilators in the sides, and the larger one on the dome is so rusted and stiff as to be immovable except in heavy gales...The Lantern is dry- but rain beats through under the deck in every storm, and runs in streams down the inside walls. The wood work was wet and appeared to be rotten on the South, South East, and East faces. The basement of the tower is paved with cobble stones, and is very wet in stormy weather, the door having shrunk so as to admit rain which creates dampness throughout the structure.[82]

Repairs did not take place until 1857 as part of preparations for the installation of the new first order Fresnel lens. With regard to the remoteness of the Montauk Lighthouse and its proximity to any settlements, Case added, "...I would respectfully repeat my former suggestion that an assistant keeper be allowed at all the isolated stations such as this. The nearest house to Montauk Pt is four miles distant, and the nearest place where supplies can be obtained [referring to Sag Harbor] Twenty seven miles. If an accident should happen to the keeper, the lights would certainly suffer."[83]

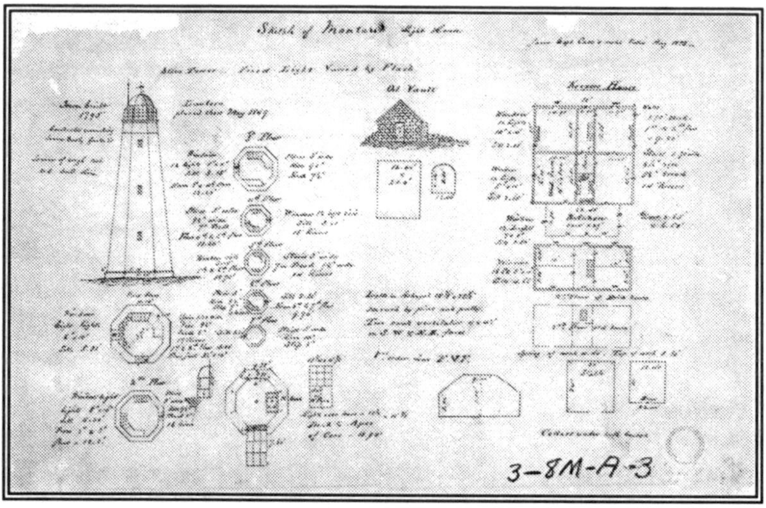

A "Sketch of Montauk Light House, From Capt. Cases's notes taken Aug 1853" provided details about the tower, dwelling, and oil vault. Third District Inspector, Augustus Ludlow Case, visited the lighthouse in August 1853 to examine the condition of tower and dwelling. (National Archives)

Of the keeper's dwelling Case noted, "The House wants repairs about the dormer windows, roof, coping on North end, gutters and windows: the gutter between the two buildings is decayed, and the water runs down between them and is undermining the walls."[84]

Nothing was done for a year and on April 8, 1857 Third District engineer, Lt. J. C. Duane reported: "The Tower at Montauk is badly cracked and will require rebuilding before many years. In placing the new lantern and lens upon it, it will be advisable to use as far as possible such material only, as can be transferred easily to another tower. The expense of refitting this tower will be about

$2,000, this does not include the Lantern."[85]

Duane's recommendation was accepted. Since the Lighthouse Board considered building a new tower at Montauk Point, only minimal repairs were made in anticipation of the installation of the Fresnel lens.

In his monthly Secretary's report to the Board for September 1858, Lt. James St. C. Morton requested $35,000 to construct a new tower at Montauk Point and in April of 1859 he submitted plans stating: "Tower ready to fall— dwelling in bad order— New tower and dwelling required."[86] His plans called for a new 80-foot lighthouse and dwelling resembling those recently constructed at Great West Bay (Shinnecock).

However, by October 1859 the Board was reconsidering the renovation of the existing tower. The change may have been the result of Lt. Morton being replaced by Captain William F. Smith (1823-1903) as Secretary to the Lighthouse Board.

In June 1857 the Light-House Board announced that on January 1, 1858 a new first-order Fresnel lens would be displayed at Shinnecock as a fixed beam while at the same time a new first-order Fresnel lens with a fixed beam varied by flashes every two minutes would begin operation at the Montauk Point Lighthouse.[87] The new lens for Montauk was sent from the French government as a gift, but since its destination was not made known to the Collector of the Port of New York it was placed in a warehouse where "a lover of auction elephants bought it for $70; then sold it to the government for $900 and it was assigned to Montauk."[88]

After several delays and logistical problems, Montauk Point received its first-order Fresnel lens in 1857, exhibiting a fixed white light interrupted every two minutes by a brilliant flash. The lens was manufactured in Paris around

1854 by Henry LaPaute. The light shone from 154-feet above sea level and was visible 24-miles. The apparatus consisted not only of a fixed first-order lens but also a separate eclipser that revolved around it to create the flash. The device revolved at a rate of one revolution every six minutes, so that a flash panel passed a point on the circumference of the fixed lens every two minutes. The eclipser was powered by a clockwork mechanism activated by an 80-pound weight suspended under the lantern deck. The clockworks had to be wound every three hours.

The 1849 lantern was too small for the big lens. Third District engineer, Lt. James St. C. Morton, noted in an April 1859 report that the "roof of the present lantern at Montauk comes down over and hides the upper or inclined third part of the lens."[89] It was clear the tower needed to be renovated to meet the standards of a first-order light station.

In addition, the Fresnel lens required constant monitoring through the night. A single lamp (type unknown but possibly a moderator lamp built by Ira Winn of Portland, Maine) provided the light source. Lightkeepers had to trim the lamp's four wicks every four hours; hence, three keepers were needed to rotate watches in the tower. In preparation for the increased work, a new keeper, William Gardiner, was assigned to the station in June 1857, and two assistant keepers, Josiah Lee and S. G. Bailey, followed in September. The three families shared the station's original 1796 dwelling (designed as a single family house) until the new dwelling was built in 1860.

On January 1, 1858 the Montauk Point Lighthouse, equipped with a first-order Fresnel lens, changed its characteristic from a steady white beam to a flashing light every two minutes. On the same day, 35 miles west of Montauk, the Shinnecock Lighthouse began service as a fixed beam.

These changes set the stage for a famous maritime disaster, since there was no way in those days to notify vessels already at sea of changes in lighthouses or their characteristics.

The ship *John Milton,* captained by Ephraim Harding (1815-1858), had departed from New York in December 1856, picked up a cargo of guano from the Chincha Islands near Peru, and was heading home to New Bedford. On February 18, 1858 Harding recorded running into "strong gales and a thick snowstorm." As the ship sailed eastward along Long Island's south shore in the thick of the tempest, the captain was able to pick out the steady beam of what he believed to be the Montauk Point Lighthouse. He continued eastward for a distance and then turned north into what he thought was the open water of Block Island Sound. Just before dawn on February 20 the *John Milton* crashed on the rocks approximately five miles west of Montauk Point. The entire crew of thirty-three perished. Harding had mistaken the new Shinnecock Light for Montauk Light.

The keeper at the Montauk Lighthouse, William Gardiner, went by horseback to East Hampton to amass a search party. The bodies of Captain Harding and twenty-two others were found frozen along the beach, along with numerous personal items, at a spot known today as Dead Man's Curve. An elderly man, first on the scene, noted years later that the ship "melted like a lump of sugar."[90]

One of the few visible remains of the ship was its bell, set upon two beams projecting from the remains of the bow. With every wave that passed, it "tolled out the requiem of the departed."[91] The bell later was taken to the Presbyterian Church in East Hampton and installed in the Sunday school building. Today it rests in one of the new Gilmartin exhibit rooms in the Montauk Point Lighthouse Museum.

The 1st-order flashing Fresnel lens at Montauk Point was manufactured in Paris by Henry LePaute and installed in the tower in 1857. It stood 12-feet high, was 5-feet wide, and weighed nearly 5-tons. It was removed in 1903 and destroyed not long afterward. Seen here is a duplicate lens from the Fire Island Lighthouse on display at the Franklin Institute in Philadelphia. (Montauk Point Lighthouse Museum)

Eighty years after the wreck, Mary Esther Mulford Miller, author of *An East Hampton Childhood,* recalled:

"The roads from East Hampton to Montauk were badly blocked with snow. But the news of disaster brought many men from Amagansett and East Hampton, men who knew the sea. All the men could do was to pick up the bodies as one by one the ocean washed them ashore, then bring them to East Hampton for burial,"[92]

A funeral service was conducted by Reverend Stephen L. Mershon and many bodies were interred in the Old South End Burying Ground in East Hampton. Miller wrote of the cold February funeral procession, the bodies carried in biers, carts and wagons, "everything snow covered, everything frozen, women looking on from windows of houses and weeping, the church bell tolling and tolling until the last sailor's body had passed through the open gate of death."[93]

The reason so much is known about this disaster is that Captain Harding kept excellent written accounts of his activities at sea. Long Island maritime expert, Benjamin Rathbun, wrote: "Believing that they were practically home free, Capt. Harding had gone below to bring his ship's log up to date, after which he had put it safely away in his sea chest. Although everybody aboard perished and the ship was reduced to little more than match wood, the sea chest containing the ship's log floated ashore relatively intact and was salvaged."[94]

In 1890, an edition of the *Sag Harbor Express* noted remembrances of the tragedy by Dr. Abel Huntington: "My father was coroner and I recollect how a messenger came on horseback the next morning bringing from Montauk news of the fearful wreck and loss of life; and later, just as the dusk of twilight gathered around, how two farm wagons rolled slowly through the snow up to our home and fourteen frozen corpses were lifted out and laid side by side in the carriage house. I remember also what feelings of awe, I went with my father later in the evening and gazed by the light of a dimly burning lantern on the ghostly spectacle."[95]

J. Arter Gould, grandson of lighthouse keeper Patrick Gould, recalled the story of Captain George Hand of East Hampton who was the Wreck Master when the *John Milton* went down. Hand was presented with a canvas bag of money that had been recovered from the beach after the disaster. It was the responsibility of the Wreck Master to keep the property until lawful heirs claimed it. A gentleman from New York soon arrived in East Hampton, claiming to be a friend of Captain Harding and offering to deliver the money to Harding's widow. Hand gave him the money. The man and the money were never seen again.[96]

Another shipwreck that was thought to have resulted from the change in the light at Montauk Point was a schooner that ran aground about two miles east of Amagansett on May 13, 1858. Three of the four people aboard were lost, with two bodies recovered and buried in the South End Cemetery at East Hampton.[97]

Less well known is the plight of the whaling ship *Washington* which had returned to Long Island from a whaling expedition around the same time as the *John Milton*. Its captain, Henry Babcock, also was unaware of the change in lighthouses along Long Island's south shore when he came upon the steady beam of the Shinnecock Lighthouse. Earlier in the day he had taken a reading of the sun and surmised that the ship could not have made Montauk Point so quickly. Being a man of strong will and wisdom, he gave the order to maintain an eastward course. Hours later, the beacon at Montauk was in sight. Babcock had saved his ship and crew from disaster. Ironically, he would later become a keeper at the Montauk Point Lighthouse.

In 1860, William F. Smith, Engineer-Secretary of the Light-House Board, made plans to upgrade Montauk Point

Lighthouse to meet the requirements of a first-order light station. The project was supervised by John Oct, an employee of the Third District. He received his instructions from the Third District Inspector, A.M. Pennock.

Inspector Pennock reported that the lowest bid of $1,000, "for the lumber required for Montauk," came from Marino and Cross of Brooklyn. In addition, he noted that "the parties who furnished the sashes and doors for Fire Island and Great West Bay (Shinnecock Lighthouse) agree to furnish the same for Montauk for $110."[98] Pennock made arrangements for a schooner to deliver the materials from New York and two teams of oxen to haul them up to the lighthouse from the landing. He also hired the necessary labor force.

The *Sag Harbor Corrector* of June 16, 1860 reported on the progress of the construction: "The work of repairing and raising Montauk Light commenced the first of the week. There are now twelve men engaged in carrying out the proposed arrangements. The Lighthouse is to be built 14 feet higher than at present and a new superior lantern introduced. Beside this, it is to be strengthened by thickening the walls. Two new dwelling houses are to be built for the use of the keepers, so constructed however as to form one building. A schooner from New York has already landed a cargo of lumber and returned for a cargo of brick."[99]

One source indicated that over 100,000 bricks were to be used in the project.[100]

Work proceeded steadily. On August 15, 1860, John Oct reported that the stairwell wall, radial walls, and iron spiral stairway were completed and that the next day he would set the iron watch room deck. He then requested "a man from the shop to assist in setting & arranging the Iron Work of Lantern."[101] On August 27 he reported, "I have got the brackets set on the tower and will be ready to set the

Gallery deck by the latter part of this week."[102]

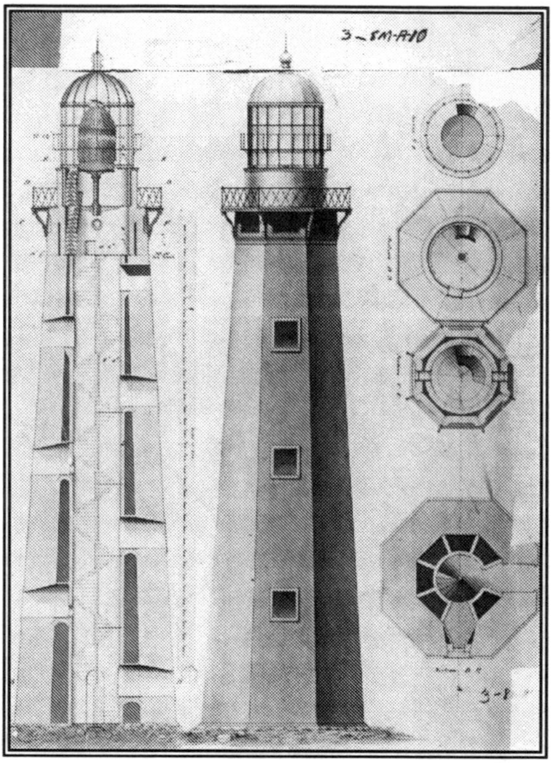

The caption for this image (not shown on the photo) read: "Montauk Light House As altered in 1860". Renovations included a new lantern with iron railings, and replacement of the seven wooden stair courses with an iron spiral stairway held in place with a brick sleeve. (National Archives)

When the tower's new iron spiral stairway was installed, two window openings on the lower east side of the tower had to be bricked up because the stair treads, which were set in the walls, fell against the two windows. The other five windows remained.

By September 26, 1860 Inspector Pennock reported to the Light-House Board: "Montauk thoroughly renovated and new lantern placed. New Dwelling for keeper & assistant and oil room built."[103] The dwelling was ready for occupancy by keeper William Gardiner, his assistants, and their families. It was a two-story frame structure with a wall down the center, dividing it into two equal size apartments—mirror images of each other. Hallways on either side of the wall each contained a front entrance, stairways to the basement and second floor, and a rear entrance to the passageway. Adjacent to the hallway were two rooms, the front room being slightly larger than the back room. The second floor was identical to the first except a small bedroom was built across one end of the hallway. The entrance porch had boxed posts with plinth blocks and caps supporting a cornice.

The "double dwelling" actually housed three families rather than two. In addition, they all had to use one kitchen, located in the south basement. There was a well some distance away in the meadow below Turtle Hill, but it was too far away to meet the station's needs. Rainwater was caught on the roofs of the buildings and directed into a cistern that measured 12-feet deep, 8-feet in diameter, and could hold over 2,700 gallons. It served as the water supply until electricity was installed in 1938.

The keepers moved into the dwelling in September or October of 1860, with the head keeper and his family occupying the south apartment. The first assistant keeper lived on the first floor of the north apartment and the second assistant lived above him.

In order for the Montauk Point Lighthouse to be classified as a first-order light station, it had to meet certain requirements as described in the Light-House Board's

"Specifications for a First-Order Lighthouse"[104] issued in 1861:

1) A first-order lighthouse had a focal plane of 150-feet or more above sea level. Montauk Lighthouse had a focal plane of 154-feet when the Fresnel lens was installed in 1857.
2) A first-order lantern was designed specifically to house a huge first-order lens. The first-order lantern at Montauk was ordered from Ira Winn (1817-1916) of Portland, Maine and shipped on July 3, 1860.[105]
3) A service room just below the lantern housed the pedestal and the revolving apparatus for a first-order lens, and a watch room was required for the keeper to tend the light throughout the night. These components were added to Montauk Point Light in 1860 and increased the focal plane elevation of the first-order lens.
4) The tower had to be fireproof. As part of the 1860 renovation the tower's wooden floors, stairways and windows were removed, an iron spiral stairway, shipped to Montauk on July 6, 1860 by J. P. Morris & Co. of Philadelphia,[106] was installed in a circular brick stairwell. The watch room and service room stairs were also constructed of iron, as were iron decks, casement sashes, and other items. The only remaining wooden components were the interior main balcony doors. In addition to these improvements, an oil house for storage of flammable fuel and a maintenance workroom were built adjacent to the tower.

Since the Light-House Board required that keepers stand watch overnight in the watch room, a stove was provided. Assistant keeper Elbert Edwards, in a letter written on January 6, 1866, noted: "I have a bright coal fire in a red hot stove which makes the room very comfortable during this season of intense cold."[107] A *New York Daily News* article of October 5, 1939 described the keeper's task of "...lugging up buckets of coal for the old-fashioned stove which keeps the watch room heated in cold weather."[108]

On September 26, 1860 it was reported by the Third Lighthouse District that the 1796 dwelling had been demolished. However, the 1838 brick dwelling remained. It would be renovated for use as a barn after a hurricane on September 23, 1869 destroyed the 1806 barn built by Josiah Hand.

With the implementation of these improvements, and raising the height of the tower to 110½-feet with a focal plane 168-feet above sea level, the Montauk Point Lighthouse became a First-Order Light Station.

The U.S. Light-House Board's aim to establish the world's most superior system of navigational aids was a difficult and sometimes bitter struggle. Often at the center of the controversy was the beautiful and highly functional Fresnel lens. Captain Benjamin Rathbun skillfully summed up the issues: "On one side of the controversy stood the Lighthouse Service establishment, riddled with rampant nepotism, influence peddling, bureaucratic bungling and an absolutely intransigent adherence to the status-quo. Lined up on the other side were the Blunt family, publishers of the famous *Blunt's Coast Pilot,* and almost every deep sea American ship-master and owner. The dispute raged for years unchecked but the unquestionable superiority of the Fresnel lens, combined with a change in the top administrators of the Lighthouse Service, won out in the end and the Fresnel type lens was eventually installed in all our lighthouses."[109]

Following the renovation of the Montauk Point Lighthouse, which took place less than a year before the outbreak of the Civil War, a circular plaque was installed in the wall midway up the tower listing the members of the Lighthouse Committee. It contained the names of two future Union generals and a Confederate general and admiral. Brigadier General and topographical engineer, Andrew Atkinson Humphreys (1810-1883), was assigned to the Coast Survey Office when the lighthouse was renovated. He later saw action in several battles for the Union. General Joseph Totten (1788-1864) was chief engineer of the U.S. Army from 1838-1864 and was responsible for the construction of modernized defenses around New York City. Fort Totten, near Bayside in Queens was named for him in 1898. Confederate General Howell Cobb (1815-1868), Secretary of the Treasury at the time of lighthouse renovation, later was promoted to major general in the Confederate Army. Admiral Raphael Semmes (1809-1877) was captain of the *Sumter* and the *Alabama,* making many successful raids on Union cargo vessels during the war. He was assigned to lighthouse duties prior to the outbreak of the war.

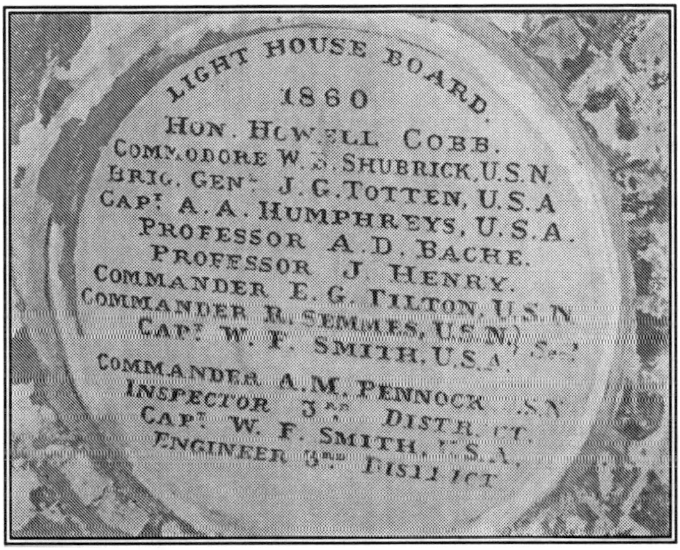

A circular marble plaque set in the stairwell wall opposite the third stairway landing of the lighthouse commemorated members of the Light-House Board and the Third Lighthouse District inspector and engineer involved in the renovation of the lighthouse in 1860. The photo was taken in September, 2004. (Author Photo)

CHAPTER 3

Lighthouse Developments: 1861-1939

Under the watchful eyes of the Light-House Board, the Montauk Point Lighthouse was maintained in good order during the latter half of the 19th century. With three keepers assigned to the station instead of one or two, a more vigilant watch was kept on the light and considerably more work was accomplished. The tower was white-washed annually without outside assistance, and the station grounds were well-groomed. The quarters also were given fastidious care by the keepers' wives. It is not surprising that light stations improved in appearance during this period, too, due in large part to the U.S. Light-House Board's military discipline, training, and frequent inspections.

With so many people living on the station at this time, a garden was essential. A survey of the light station in 1868 included a 90' x 200' vegetable garden located just south of the 1838 building; it was in use for a number of years.[110] A 1928 aerial photo shows an outline of the garden, which had been recently abandoned, undoubtedly due to the many tourists who overran the property each year[111].

Changes also occurred in the buildings at Montauk

Lighthouse. An ice house was added in 1871 at a cost of \$110.[112] In 1888, the renovated tower was shored up with the addition of stanchions, eye bolts, and safety line along the main tower stairway. In the keeper's dwelling, attic windows were installed and separate kitchens were added in the apartments of the assistant keepers in 1893. A year later, an additional cistern was built below the basement of the keeper's dwelling.[113]

With new developments in fuels and lamps, the lighting apparatus was upgraded. A significant amount of maintenance and repair was done on the Fresnel lens between 1871 and 1902. Keeping the light reliably bright and distinct was paramount, but its mission became even more important in the late nineteenth century as thousands of immigrants came to New York from Europe. Montauk Point Lighthouse was their first glimpse of America.

In late 1869 a Funck's Hydraulic Float Lamp was installed in the lens at Montauk Point. It was developed by Joseph Funck, a foreman in the workshop at the Third District lighthouse depot at Staten Island. Through a series of reservoirs, pipes, and a float chamber, a constant supply of oil was sent to multiple wicks. The apparatus was considerably more reliable and self-sufficient than the previous French-designed mechanical lamp. It consumed about 75-feet of wick a year.[114]

By the late 1850s, whale oil had become scarce and expensive, as the population of whales dwindled and ships traveled greater distances in search of them. It was a dirty, foul-smelling fuel, and the Light-House Board began researching alternatives for use in lighthouse lamps. Colza (made from cabbages) and lard oil were burned when whale oil was not available, but they were troublesome too. Colza could not be produced fast enough or in large enough quantities. Lard oil tended to congeal in cold weather and, like whale oil, it gave off fumes and soot.[115]

By 1884 kerosene, or mineral oil, had been adopted for use in many lighthouses, including Montauk Light. It burned cleaner, brighter, and for less expense than previous fuels. The drawback was its flammable nature, which dictated careful storage and handling. In 1890 a separate oil-house made of galvanized iron to house the kerosene was built just east of the oil room. Thereafter, the oil room, which was connected to the tower entrance, served no particular function until 1981 when the Coast Guard used it for a small exhibit of lighthouse artifacts. Since 1987, the Lighthouse Museum has displayed its fine collection of Fresnel lenses in the oil room.

A number of other changes took place in the late nineteenth century. The lantern glazing was completely renewed in 1875. In June of 1876 an inspector's report claimed "the lantern is in need of repairs, several of the bricks have been started by rocking in gales of wind."[116] The glazing was again replaced and in 1896 half the lantern panes were renewed.

The first system of communication between the lantern and the keeper's dwelling, installed in June 1872, consisted of a "speaking tube and gong leading from the watch room to the keeper's dwelling."[117] The first telephone was installed on December 13, 1899 and reached Amagansett.

Though fog was not as serious a problem at Montauk Point as elsewhere in the nation, a fog signal was added in May of 1873. It consisted of a first-class Daboll trumpet powered by two steam engines that sounded a 12-second blast every 50-seconds.

Montauk Point Light Station, as it appeared in 1873, saw the fog signal house under construction (second building from right, rear). (National Archives)

The following are selected annual records of hours of fog signal operation:

748	hours	July 1874-June 1875
1226	hours	July 1875-June 1876
990	hours	July 1877-June 1878

504	hours	July 1890-June 1891
571	hours	July 1899-June 1900
470	hours	July 1900-June 1901
413	hours	July 1902-June 1903
600	hours	July 1904-June 1905[118]

The boilers used to generate steam for fog trumpets often were labor intensive and problematic, and it wasn't long before maintenance on the fog signal was needed. On January 11, 1875 it was noted in the lighthouse journal that a Mr. Sheilds spent a few days at the station to clean and repair the machinery.[119] Mr. Sheilds came many times over the next several years to do work on the equipment.

A fog signal building was added in 1897 to house the engines and compressors that powered the dual fog signal.[120] (The building today houses the automated equipment for the electric beacon and fog signal.) On February 20, 1898 the old Daboll trumpet fog signal was replaced by a first-class dual siren. It was powered by two 10-horsepower oil engines and two Belt air compressors and included two vertical air receivers and two first-class sirens.

Also in 1897 the old "barn" (the 1838 keeper's dwelling) received a new foundation and floor. The original roof, dormers, and rafters were removed. New rafters were installed and a new wood shingle roof with overhanging eaves was laid.[121]

The old equipment from the original fog signal house was removed to make way for the naval militia signal corps that was stationed at the lighthouse on April 11, 1898 as a safeguard during the Spanish-American War. Telephone communication with the office of the lighthouse engineer began April 30, 1898 under an appropriation of money for national defense.[122]

"All the Atlantic seaboard was alarmed over the Spanish trouble,"[123] wrote Long Island author Jeannette Edwards Rattray.

As part of the defense system, a signal pole was built at Montauk Lighthouse for use by the Coast Guard Service. On May 14, 1898, the new telephone was fixed and connected with the life saving station at Quogue. Also on that day nine homing pigeons arrived from Newport to work alongside the signalmen if needed.[124]

The fog signal building at Montauk Point Lighthouse was photographed in July 1934. Note the keeper standing outside the building. (National Archives)

In preparation for use of the signal pole, it was noted in the *Brooklyn Daily Eagle* in June 1898 that "...all the lighthouse keepers and their assistants are busy studying the international code of signals, which they will use in future for communicating with passing vessels when the officers of the Naval Reserve Coast Signal Stations are relieved from duty. The present signal corps will remain on duty during the war, and after that the signaling will be done by the lighthouse keepers and their assistants. A new pole has been attached to the balcony at the top of Montauk lighthouse for displaying the international code signal flags."[125]

While Camp Wikoff was in existence at Montauk, keeper James G. Scott received an almost continuous flow of visitors from the camp at the lighthouse. Each day a group of soldiers would hike or ride to the lighthouse, and Scott would entertain them with stories of shipwrecks and other tales. He was happy to have company and would tell the men as they left, "You soldier boys are always welcome to all I've got."[126]

Colonel Theodore Roosevelt visited the lighthouse on September 6, 1898. His name, and the names of those of his entourage, are listed in Captain Scott's guest log:

> James R Church, Asst Surgeon, 1st USV Calvary, Wash DC
> R H Ferguson 2nd Lt, 1st USV Calvary
> Charles L Ballard 2nd Lt USV Calvary of Troop H. Roswell NM
> Hal Sayre Jr. 2nd Lt. 1st USV Calvary
> Daniel M Goodrich 1st Lt. USV Calvary[127]

On December 30, 1902 the rigging arrived for a wireless telegraph pole and twelve days later the pole was erected. It didn't last long. A logbook entry on June 12, 1903 indicated, "wireless telegraph pole broke and came down." It was replaced two days later. The Marconi wireless station had only a few years of limited success before it was demolished. The wreckage of the old telegraph pole was removed on September 18, 1908.[128]

A new oil house was built in 1904 to store fuel for the generators of the naval radio station.[129] The 8' x 10' brick structure, with a corrugated iron roof and concrete floor, cost about $450. It still stands at the extreme north end of the lighthouse property.

The year 1898 was a busy one at Montauk Point. In addition to many other changes, the Third District engineer, Major David Heap (1843-1910) decided that the two minutes between flashes of the lighthouse beacon was too long and that a span of 15-seconds was more reasonable: "The shorter time the mariner has to wait for the signal the more valuable the signal will be for him," Heap reasoned.

In addition, he recommended that all flashing lighthouses be painted with a distinguishing daymark. For Montauk Point Lighthouse, Heap suggested a brown band on the tower as a "simple and excellent method of denoting by day that the light-house displays a flashing light."

For unknown reasons, Heap's recommendation was not implemented at this time, and the flashing pattern remained at two minutes.[130] But the daymark was added in May 1899, a brown band midway up the tower. (In more recent times the paint used for this characteristic was Benjamin Moore's "Van Dyke Brown.")[131]

The U.S. Light-House Board eventually approved Heap's plan for changing the light characteristic. On December 5, 1901, Major William Russell (Heap's successor) wrote to the Light-House Board warning, "…the revolving apparatus of the 1st order light at Montauk Point, for which changes were recommended, is rapidly wearing out and may break down at any moment." He suggested installing a new lens that would produce the 15-second flash recommended by Major Heap.[132]

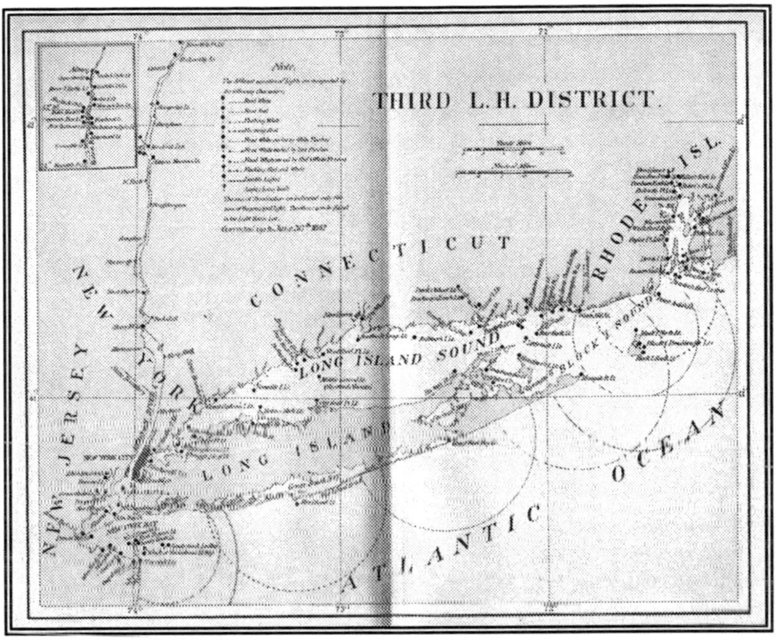

An 1882 map showed the Third District lighthouses and featured 1st-order light stations on Long Island's south shore at Fire Island, Great West Bay (Shinnecock), and Montauk Point. (National Archives)

The new lens, a "3rd order small model bivalve lens," was manufactured by Henry LePaute of Paris and was first displayed by him at the Chicago World's Fair Columbian Exhibition of 1893. It resembled a clamshell and consisted of two 54-inch diameter bulls-eye lenses oriented back to back and equipped with a mineral oil pressure lamp.

In his report to the U.S. Light-House Board on December 16, 1901 Major Russell explained his preference for the new lens: "The present first order white light has an intensity of 30,000 c.p. (candlepower), which is visible in clear weather a distance of 53 miles, in ordinary weather 22 miles, and in misty weather 11 miles. The 3rd order bi-valve lens apparatus gives an intensity of light of 86,000 c.p.; its range of visibility is, in clear weather 64 miles, in ordinary weather 30 miles, and in misty weather 13 miles. This shows a great superiority over the present 1st order light."[133]

Montauk Point Light Station was captured from Turtle Cove, ca. 1903. The Marconi wireless station radio tower was to the immediate left of the keeper's dwelling and the wireless building was at the far left. The wireless structures were removed in 1908. (National Archives)

On January 14, 1902, the Board approved the purchase of the new lens from "Messrs. Barbier, Benard & Turenne, of Paris, France" at a cost of $1460.[134] This same year marked the golden anniversary of the U.S. Light-House Board—fifty years of excellent service.

Only a year later, major change swept the U.S. Light-House Board. Congress was concerned that the Board was growing increasingly militaristic in its handling of light-house affairs, and the scope of its work had become too cumbersome to effectively manage. While many in the maritime industry argued to the contrary, the process of civilianizing and simplifying operations of the Board began when it was placed under the jurisdiction of the Commerce Department in 1903. Total civilian control came in 1910 with the creation of the U.S. Bureau of Lighthouses.

The old U.S. Light-House Board had accomplished much during its 51-year existence. Among its achievements was the issuing of the annual "Light List," which described and showed the location of all navigational aids in the United States. In addition, "Notice to Mariners" informed maritime interests of changes in these aids. No less important was the rigorous organization and efficiency the Board had instituted. Under its administration, the United States had risen from the bottom to the top, with 11,713 total navigational aids in 1910 and a reputation as the best-lighted nation in the world.

The new U.S. Bureau of Lighthouses was headed from 1910 to 1935 by an efficient civil engineer named George R. Putnam(1865-1953). During his tenure as Commissioner of Lighthouses, the number of navigational aids doubled while the number of employees declined almost 20 percent. This was due mostly to the implementation of automated equipment. Like his distant predecessor, Stephen Pleasonton, Putnam was frugal, but he managed to tighten the purse strings without sacrificing quality of service.[135]

On June 15, 1903 the new bivalve lens from France replaced the first-order lens at Montauk Point Lighthouse. The new lens exhibited a flashing white light every ten seconds. (The name "3½ order" would appear later and referred to the interior diameter of lens, which was 750mm, midway between the 1,000mm third-order lens and the 500mm diameter of the fourth-order lens.) The lens stood on a new pedestal that incorporated a roller bearing and clockworks. One of the cells of the tower wall accommodated the 80-pound weight that dropped a maximum of 80-feet to power the clockworks. At the same time, a fourth-order fixed red range light was mounted on the main balcony of the lighthouse to warn of Shagwong Reef, a navigational hazard about 3.75-miles northwest of the lighthouse.[136] The range light remained in use until the light was electrified in 1940.

In 1902, the "List of Lights and Fog Signals on the Atlantic and Gulf Coasts of the United States" gave the following description of Montauk Point Lighthouse:

Characteristic of light- Fixed white varied by a white flash every two minutes.
Order of light – 1
Description of station – White tower with a brown band about midway of its height; white dwelling on hill nearby.
Fog signal building about 100 feet easterly of tower
When established – 1797
When last rebuilt – 1860
Fog signal – 1st class compressed-air siren; blasts 3 sec. alternate silent intervals 3 and 31 seconds.
Remarks – There is a life-saving station on the point, about 750 feet to the southward of the tower.[137]

In 1904, the lens was fitted with a mineral oil "Air Pressure Lamp." On December 3, 1907 this lamp was replaced with a third-order Incandescent Oil Vapor Lamp, or IOV, which greatly increased the light's intensity.[138] The IOV worked similar to a modern day camper's Coleman lantern, using air pressure to vaporize mineral oil and burn it on a mantle. The result was an intense white light and considerable savings of fuel. This apparatus was the last modification of the flame in the lens until the light was electrified in 1940.

A "Description of the Montauk Point Light Station" dated August 10, 1911, indicated that additional living space was needed for the assistant keepers and their families and that the kitchen provided for them was "underground and very damp." In addition, the report referred to the dwelling as being "in a dilapidated condition and badly in need of repairs."[139] As a result, the keeper's dwelling was extended 14-feet to the north in 1912, creating additional rooms for the families. New shingles were installed on the roof, as well as 1860s-style windows throughout the house.

The flash sequence of the light became an issue on the night of October 8, 1919 when the USS *Shubrick* passed the point and noted that the flash "was timed by two stop watches as of twelve seconds interval while the light list shows the light should be ten seconds."[140] A subsequent letter from keeper John E. Miller on November 15, 1919 explained: "...on the night of October 8, 1919 from ten o'clock P.M. to eleven o'clock P.M. we were making repairs to the lens clock works as a pin in one of the cog wheels broke and dropped out of the clock work and this pin head had to be made with a taper to hold the cog wheel in the proper place. While making this pin we turned the lens by hand judging ten seconds intervals of flash as near as possible as we did not use our stop watch as we were quite busy making repairs."[141]

The roller bearing that turned the lens was replaced by a mercury float in 1920. The new apparatus consisted of a tub of high density, low-friction mercury in which the heavy lens rested and could rotate almost effortlessly. At the same time a new pedestal and clockworks was installed. This assembly would remain in use until 1987 (the clockworks were again replaced in 1938) when the lens was removed from the lantern.

An area that was repeatedly exposed to corrosion was the exterior ironwork, especially the railings of the lantern gallery and the main balcony. In 1902, the eighteen stanchions of the lantern gallery were replaced and the main balcony railing was repaired with installation of two new sections.

In January 1922 the main light was described as having 130,000-candlepower while the range light for Shagwong Reef had 3,500-candlepower.[142]

Changes to the lighthouse during the twentieth century were few. In 1923, small concrete slabs were poured in the window embrasures to seal shut the bottoms of the casement windows. This was prompted by rain leaking under the window sashes.[143]

The same year, a report submitted by the district superintendent on August 14, noted: "Iron railing on lantern parapet deck rusted out beyond reasonable repair" and recommended replacement with "substantial galvanized pipe railing." The new railing was not fitted until about 1934. Also in 1934, a central hot water heating system was installed. In 1936 the keeper's dwelling roof received new asphalt shingling.

Most buildings on Long Island were equipped with indoor plumbing facilities by the 1930s, except in some out of the way locations such as the Montauk Point Lighthouse. A May 1933 article in the *East Hampton Star* reported that the lighthouse was functioning quite well without the aid of electricity, because "electricity is fairly expensive and even Uncle Sam does not wish to be extravagant. It is that old standby, kerosene [that] can produce a brilliant light indeed."[144] At this time, the light generated 220,000-candlepower and could be seen at a distance of 19-miles.

The lack of modern facilities at the lighthouse was brought to the attention of the U.S. Bureau of Lighthouses in a November 1937 letter by Meier Steinbrink, a New York City judge:

> *The only water supply that they have is from a well, which is about 150 feet from the house...They have no running water in the house and therefore no provision whatever for hot water....Speaking from a long-time experience with real estate matters...I know that it would be a very simple matter and not at all expensive to pipe the house and connect with the well water, installing an instantaneous hot water heater, which would likewise furnish the occupants with a supply of hot water....Imagine the problem in carrying water in pails from the well up to the house, first, in order that they may have a proper supply of drinking water, secondly, for cooking purposes, and finally, for either bathing or cleanliness. This matter has been the subject of comment from a great many who either visited there with me or from others whom we saw there. The place is immaculately kept and reflects credit on the lighthouse service of the government. I wonder if it wouldn't be possible to have one of your inspectors look into this and see whether or not this could be accomplished.*[145]

H. D. King, Commissioner of Lighthouses, responded on December 2 that the matter was under consideration and work would progress as soon as was practical.[146]

In November 1935 representatives from the Department of Health of Suffolk County conducted an investigation of both the cistern and the well at the site. Results showed the water from the cistern was "highly colored and had a disagreeable taste and together with the...bacterial analysis, indicated that it was unsafe and unfit for human consumption…it seems desirable and advisable that the water supply be obtained in the future from the well which is at the foot of the hill…[and] that the cistern water be boiled if it is to be used for drinking and cooking purposes." In addition it was discovered that the privies at the site were not in the best shape either, not being adequately ventilated and the "brick pits are so deep that it is difficult to remove the material."

A recommendation was made to install a motor-driven pump for the well and modern plumbing in the dwelling. The proposal brought results three years later, when the house was electrified and plumbing was installed at a cost of $4989.60. The 1860 cistern was abandoned.[147]

Due to the great influx of visitors in the summer months, a "Recommendation as to Aids in Navigation" was issued February 12, 1934 by the Bureau of Lighthouses, detailing the need for a concrete road from the property entrance up to the tower: "The direct and most used approaches to the tower are over a dangerous, steep, badly eroded and gullied slope."[148] The roadway leading to the keeper's dwelling was built later that year, with an extension to the renovated garage in 1939.

The 1838 dwelling was renovated between 1937 and 1939 for use as a garage. Among the alterations was the installation of two 8-foot doors flanking the circa 1859 arched doorway on the north side of the building. The overall results of the renovation left no clue that the building had previously been used as a residence.

With increasingly large numbers of tourists coming to the lighthouse, a letter from the Superintendent on General Duty written to the Lighthouse Third District in July 1930 indicated the potential of Montauk Point Lighthouse as a tourist attraction: "Community growing up around this light station. There is a need for it being a show station. Many visitors here and increasing."[149]

However, the thought of the lighthouse grounds opened to the public as a formal attraction was unacceptable to Third Lighthouse District Superintendent, J.T.Yates, who wrote back on July 22, "….no funds will be expended to create a show station at this or other points until more important work is cared for." Even a request to modernize the station was denied.[150]

Assistant keeper George Warrington was pictured operating the incandescent oil vapor lamp during the 1930s. The lamp was replaced with an electric bulb in 1940. (Montauk Point Lighthouse Museum)

A fishing pier was built and dismantled each year at Montauk Point by Frank Tuma, as shown in this 1930s view. Note the Shagwong Reef range light to the left of lantern balcony. It was damaged in the 1938 hurricane and moved inside the lantern until it was removed in 1940 when the lighthouse was electrified. (Montauk Library)

An article in the *New York Herald Tribune* in the late 1930s described life at the lighthouse under the watchful eyes of keeper Thomas A. Buckridge, first assistant John A. Miller, and second assistant George Warrington. The article noted that the station could count on two visitors almost every day. One was the school bus and the other the milk-man, "who drops by from Montauk Village every morning with 3 quarts of Grade B."

The keepers had given thought to starting a vegetable garden, but they realized "it would not have a chance, the way sightseers overrun the place." In spring the men were not overly enthusiastic about their "lawn-mowing chore, made doubly difficult by the rolling terrain," but they stated, "The US insists that its grass be well barbered."

With regards to lighthouse routine, the *New York Herald Tribune* commented: "Some of the brass requires daily polishing, some just weekly. Keepers earned $110 to $145 per month, depending on their position. They make 12-hour shifts in rotation, during which they are directly responsible for the working of the mechanism (the lights by night, the fog horns day and night when necessary). Besides this each man devotes 6 hours daily to cleaning, repairing and polishing, making an 18-hour day. Six hours of every 24 they may call their own, besides 4 full days off each month."

Regarding the lighting mechanism, the article said: "Should [the keeper] be at the base of the tower and trouble develop, a thermostat system would sound a gong denoting that the temperature from the flame inside the light had gone too far above or below its operating limits. Then he would climb up and revolve the light by hand while another member of the crew, summoned by another gong, would undertake the repairs."[151]

Generally about 14,000 to 18,000 visitors came to the lighthouse each year with over 8,000 in the month of August. Assistant keeper Warrington said of the visitors: "So long as they don't get noisy, we don't pay any attention to them."[152]

With the sharp increase in visitation in the 1930s, due primarily to new developments at neighboring Montauk Point State Park and the emergence of Montauk itself, the keepers found it increasingly difficult to attend to lighthouse chores. They were required to escort visitors on the property and up and down the tower. During July and August of 1936 alone, 10,347 tourists came to the lighthouse. This prompted a request by the keepers to hire two workers for the entire summer at the rate of $5.12 per day to help with the housekeeping.[153] The request was granted promptly.[154]

At times the keepers were under pressure to perform their duties, yet were frustrated by brazen tourists. Complaints of misconduct towards the public occasionally were lodged. In one instance, Bureau of Lighthouse Assistant Superintendent, O. C. Luther, responded to reports about keepers at Montauk Point and at the Shinnecock Lighthouse saying: "…during the inspection of Montauk Point and Shinnecock Bay Light Stations I made careful inquiries to ascertain the possibility of 'such an occurrence' at either of these stations. I learned that there are many visitors at each station on Sunday and the keepers have frequent requests for admission to the towers, which are closed to visitors on Sunday. These applicants are treated with uniform courtesy and civility in spite of their sometimes disagreeable attitude and remarks. The keepers deny the charges of being drunk and insulting women."[155]

It is worth noting that the above complaints were written in 1925 during the Prohibition Era, when liquor was not easy to come by and lighthouse keepers were under increased scrutiny for possible involvement with "rum runners."

In 1937 Meade C. Dobson, Managing Director of the Long Island Association, reported a record 18,547 people visited the Montauk Point Lighthouse: "The count is, however, made only of those who enter the lighthouse tower and does not include ten times as many more who visit the Point. It is estimated that considerably more than 100,000 people have already visited Montauk this (1939) summer." Keeper Buckridge attributed the surge of tourists to the pleasing weather and the presence of the World's Fair in New York City.[156]

During the mid 1930s, a rumor began to circulate that

the Montauk Point Lighthouse would be shut down and replaced by a steel tower topped with a flashing signal. This had been the fate of other lighthouses on Long Island—Shinnecock in 1931, Horton Point in 1933, Cedar Island in 1934—all victims of a struggling economy. The rumor was put to rest in a letter from Congressman Robert L. Bacon in 1937: "The proposal discussed is as much news to me as to you. Montauk Point Light Station is an important feature in the system of aids to navigation...I do not find in our files any suggestion that its discontinuance or replacement with any other type of aid has even been suggested."[157]

Following the disastrous hurricane of September 21, 1938, an estimate of $2,197 was submitted for the replacement of shingle roofs on all buildings damaged by the storm, the reason being that it made more sense to replace the badly damaged roofs than to patch them up and subsequently have to deal with leaks.[158]

Repairs were still in progress by July 7, 1939, when President Franklin Roosevelt announced sweeping changes in government that would affect Montauk Lighthouse's future and the future of all lighthouses in the nation. Under the Presidential Reorganization Act of 1939, the U.S. Bureau of Lighthouses was discontinued and its activities were absorbed by the U.S. Coast Guard.

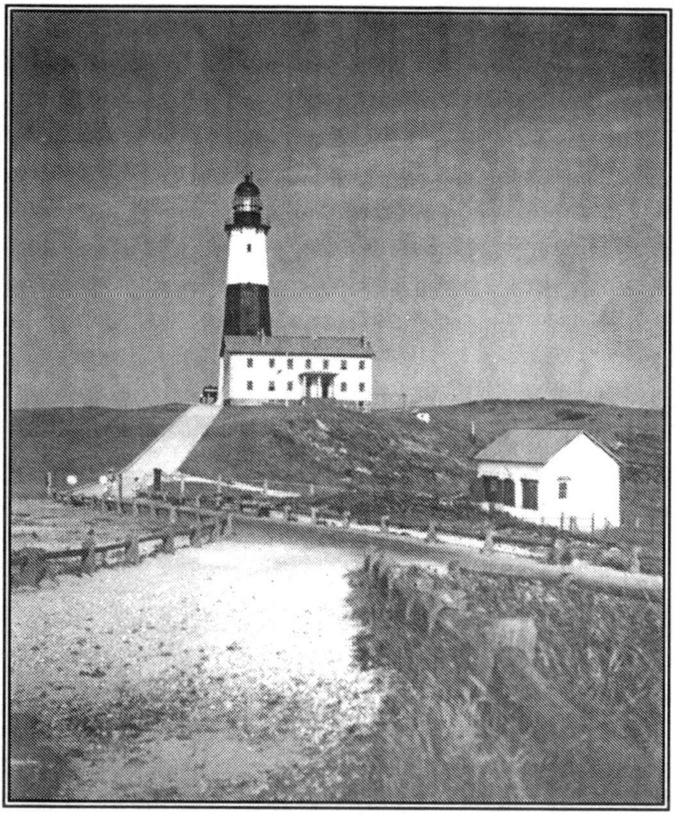

A view of Montauk Point Lighthouse from Montauk Point State Park, ca. 1936 showed several visitors who appeared to be waiting at the gate. In the foreground was the 1838 structure built during Patrick Gould's service as keeper (white building). (Montauk Library)

CHAPTER 4
The Modern Era: 1940-1987

With the arrival of electricity and indoor plumbing in the keeper's dwelling in 1938 and electricity in the tower in 1940, the Montauk Point Light Station entered the "modern era." Keeper Thomas Buckridge recorded in his logbook: "Last day of IOV lamp. To be changed to electric July 1, 1940."[159] A 1000-watt incandescent bulb with 200,000-candlepower replaced the oil vapor lamp and cast a beam 19-nautical miles (22-statute miles) out to sea. At the same time, the Shagwong Reef range light was removed from the lantern.

Fishermen had petitioned for the installation of a radio beacon at the station in 1937, but since only twelve fishing boats were equipped to receive a signal, the Bureau of Lighthouses was reluctant to spend the money. In a May 13, 1937 letter to H. D. King, Commissioner of Lighthouses, from T. L. Bludworth of Bludworth, Inc., the petition was justified, stating that "...practically all of them will equip if and when you act favorably on their request. I am advised that there are more than one hundred small boats represented by the group signing the petition."[160]

However, this was not sufficient to convince Commissioner King. On May 19, Third District Superintendent J. T. Yates replied: "This office doubts the desirability or necessity of a radiobeacon at Montauk Point." He pointed out that signals at Block Island's Southeast Lighthouse and Little Gull Island Lighthouse in Long Island Sound were sufficient to aid ships navigating around or near Montauk Point.[161]

The Department of Commerce issued a statement on June 18, 1937 that offered hope. It stated that a radio beacon at Montauk "would undoubtedly be of considerable value locally to the large number of small craft operating around the point. However, it is considered that there are other needs more urgent considering the service as a whole."[162]

Construction of the steel tower was underway by 1939 and the radio beacon was finally activated in September 1940, primarily to aid vessels using Long Island Sound. Its signal was coordinated with the foghorn, which in 1939 consisted of an air diaphragm horn emitting a 2-second blast every 13-seconds. Emergency generators also were installed in the event of a power failure at the lighthouse.

In spite of these modern changes, some tasks and equipment at the lighthouse remained unchanged. The clockwork mechanism that rotated the flashing signal—in place since the 1860s—still had to be wound by hand every three hours and would continue in this fashion for about twenty more years.

Journal entries in 1941 and 1942 at the Montauk Point Lighthouse reflected the realities of World War II and the eventual takeover of the light station as part of the Eastern Coast Defense Shield. The change resulted in the departure of the civilian keepers. Some examples from the logbook follow:

January 21, 1941: Airplane maneuvers all crew on watch for planes
May 3: Lt. Col. Bray here with a detail. Putting Army radio temporarily
June 6: Detail from Fort Michie here for gun practice
June 7: Coast artillery practically in charge
June 9: "Army occupying everything"
June 11: 242 coast artillery from Fort Michie encamped here for gun practice
December 9: Standing air plane watch. Air plane scare in New York
January 24, 1942: Coast Guard started the first watch at 4 pm
January 25: Standing double watch. Coast Guard in tower, keepers on ground
January 28: [assistant keeper] Warrington moved out
January 30: John A Miller 1st asst Keeper moved out
April 28: Supplies ammunition and rifles arrived by Coast Guard truck from depot
August 14: Changed light from 1000kw to 100kw[163]

The entry for August 14, reducing the beacon's power, was just one way the military attempted to thwart German U-boats known to be cruising the Atlantic. At 100kw, the beacon was not strong enough to silhouette Allied ships passing Montauk Point and reveal their positions to the enemy.

The primary role of the Montauk Point Light Station during the war was surveillance. Its work as an aid to navigation was minor by comparison. Regular logbook entries ended on April 30, 1943, presumably with the lighthouse under full control of the military. Written records are scant thereafter.

In 1943, the average number of men stationed at the

lighthouse was ten and included a few civilians. Air raid drills occasionally were held.[164] The logbook recorded that on April 17, 1944 the tower received a fresh coat of paint.[165] In March 1945 the interiors of the tower and keeper's dwelling were painted.[166] A typical day at the station in June 1945 is described below:

5:14	*Sunrise, turned off light.*
8:00	*Morning colors, crew performing regular morning duties.*
8:15	*Building, grounds, and apparatus inspection.*
8:30	*Crew inspected station.*
9:20	*(several depart the station)*
9:30	*Crew performing routine duties.*
12 Noon	*(men on leave return).*
1:00	*Crew performing routine duties.*
4:00	*Changed dial on lookout time detector; dial properly marked.*
8:00	*Evening colors.*
8:24	*Sunset. Turned on the light.*
8:30	*Inspected station and apparatus.*
	Telephone line tested every odd hour, reception good.[167]

Later records indicate that by the spring of 1946 the military presence at the lighthouse had been drastically reduced, eventually falling under Coast Guard jurisdiction in August. Boatswains Mate First Class (BMC) Archie Jones was placed in charge. (See Appendix B for a complete list of Coast Guard personnel in charge of Montauk Lighthouse.)

With the takeover of the lighthouse property by military personnel, neighboring private lands were sold to the government to make way for the development of Camp Hero.

One such property, located along the cliffs just west of Turtle Cove, belonged to politician Lathrop Brown (1883-1959). An interesting side note concerns a historic windmill on the Brown property, built in Southampton in 1813. It was moved to Wainscott in 1852, where it stood until Brown moved it to his property in 1922 and made it part of his summer residence. The mill was built solidly and survived the hurricane of September 21, 1938 intact. During the war, it was visible just west of the lighthouse on a cliff overlooking Turtle Bend. The windmill later was purchased by G.W. Pierson, a professor at Yale University, who had it moved to the Georgica Association property in Wainscott where he had a summer home. It remains there today.[168]

By 1943 the lighthouse property was well established as a portion of the Eastern Coast Defense Shield. It included Gun Batteries 112 and 113 at Camp Hero, established adjacent to the lighthouse property. Battery 112 was completed on January 24, 1944. It contained two 16-inch guns that could fire a 2,240-pound shell a distance over 25-miles. Battery 113 was built between March 23 and June 5, 1942. It was renamed Battery Dunn for Colonel John M. Dunn. It was over 600-feet long, built of reinforced concrete, and had its own power, water and ventilation system. Like Battery 112, number 113 also had two 16-inch guns. It was deactivated on February 7, 1947 and the guns were removed in 1949.

A Fire Control Station tower was built just east of the lighthouse in 1942 to coordinate artillery fire for the 16-inch guns located adjacent to the property at Camp Hero. As a defense against air attacks, 37-millimeter anti-aircraft guns were mounted on the tower. These weapons also were set up at other locations in Montauk at Ditch Plains, Culloden Point, and Shagwong Point. Fire control bunkers were located at Shadmoor, Hither Hills, and Oyster Pond—all disguised as summer cottages.[169] The lighthouse keeper's dwelling became an army barracks and a separate barracks structure was erected in the meadow just southwest of the lighthouse.

The Fire Control Station was part of the Harbor Defense system in the New York Metropolitan area and Long Island Sound. Built of splinter-proof concrete by the Army Corp of Engineers, it was designated as Location 16 Site 2C of the Harbor Defense of Long Island Sound (HDLIS). Location 16 referred to Camp Hero and Site 2C was one of many sites within Location 16. The exterior of the six-story building was originally covered with camouflage paint. After the war it was painted white. A radar system was planned for the roof to map the surrounding waters, but it was never installed.

The interior of the Fire Control Station had one room per story and contained the mounts and footings for two Azimuth telescopes, one on the fourth level and one on the fifth. The walls contained Ship Recognition Posters to aid in the identification of vessels. Locations of other Fire Control Stations and gun batteries were sketched directly on the walls. The Station managed gun batteries at three sites: Fishers Island, three miles east of Watch Hill, and Camp Hero.

Only Battery #3 Construction 216 at Camp Hero was completed and equipped with two 16-inch guns. The Station was classified as Harbor Entrance Observation Post One, the most important surveillance station in the HDLIS.[170] The guns at Camp Hero were powerful. They could fire a one-ton shell nearly 30-miles. At the time, they were the most powerful guns in the world. Thirteen feet of concrete and 20-feet of soil covered the gun emplacements. All buildings were designed to resemble a quiet fishing village.[171]

Top—The light station was seen in the background, beyond the Lathrop Brown estate and windmill, ca. 1940. The windmill was originally built in Southampton in 1813. Brown moved it to his 60-acre Montauk estate in 1922. The Brown property was acquired by the U.S. Government in 1942 for construction of Camp Hero, after which the windmill was moved to the Georgica Association property in Wainscott where it stands today. (Courtesy of Suffolk County Historical Society)

Right—The Fire Control Tower was shown in September 2001. It was built in 1942 by the military for surveillance purposes, mainly to watch for German submarines during WW II. In addition to the 16-inch guns aimed seaward at Camp Hero and other Montauk sites, the tower was equipped with 37-mm anti-aircraft guns. Today the building is primarily used for storage by the Montauk Point Lighthouse Museum. (Author Photo)

One of the huge 16-inch guns at Camp Hero was shown ca. 1943. Though never fired in combat, guns were fired for practice. The concussion rattled homes and businesses in small Montauk village. (Montauk Point Lighthouse Museum)

The mighty guns were never fired in actual combat but were occasionally blasted for practice. It is said the guns' reverberation shook homes, broke some glass in Montauk, and was felt as far away as Amagansett! Everett Rattray (1932-1980) in his book, *The South Fork* gives a detailed description of how these concrete structures came about:

> *...the parade of five-cubic-yard Colonial Sand and Gravel trucks that rumbled, day and night...toward Fort Hero. They came heavily laden from some quarry far to the west...Through East Hampton and Amagansett they*

roared, the pounding of their wheels cracking chimneys and gradually crumbling the yellowish concrete with which Route 27 was surfaced in those days. Across Napeague Beach they trundled...to be made into concrete and poured into hollows dug in the sand of Montauk Point, concrete for great-gun emplacements.[172]

With the construction of Camp Hero, the Old Montauk Highway from Deep Hollow Ranch to the Point became a dead end road about two miles past Carl Fisher's old polo fields. For the duration of the war the entire property at Montauk Point was off limits to civilians. Coast Guard patrols, accompanied by specially trained dogs, walked the beach twenty-four hours a day.[173]

Near the end of the war, on May 5, 1945, the German sub U-853 sank a large freighter that had sailed past Montauk Point from Rhode Island. Military patrols in the area proceeded to scour the sea in search of the enemy vessel. Historian Joshua Stoff noted: "People watched the search from Montauk Point as if they were watching a circus." The sub was eventually located and destroyed and "…floating debris indicated that the U-853 was no more."[174]

In 1946, the military installation was removed from Montauk Point and the guns at Camp Hero were dismantled. The bunkers remain intact but are overgrown with vines and weeds. The concrete structure that housed the 16-inch gun at the lighthouse property is still visible along the beach at Turtle Cove. In the years after the war, the bunker was exposed by erosion. About 1970 the Coast Guard dug it out and let it fall to the beach. This "conversation piece" intrigues many visitors at the Lighthouse Museum today.

Coast Guard Years

A complete shift to Coast Guard operation of the light station took place in 1946, bringing to an end the era of the civilian lightkeepers. Two or three Coast Guardsmen, usually boatswains and electricians, began tours of duty as keepers. The long family tenures ended, as Coast Guard assignments usually averaged only three or four years, but families still enjoyed the solitude and beauty of the Point.

On December 31, 1947 an unusual event took place at the lighthouse. A New Year's Eve party was held in the living room of the lightkeeper, Chief Archie Jones. Members of the Coast Guard and guests were interviewed by "Vox Pop," advertisers of American Express traveler's checks. Gifts and $50 in traveler's checks were issued to each person interviewed. Jones received a "Stromberg-Carlson radio-phonograph," and his daughter Gloria got "a blue snowsuit set, a Kodak, and a Launderall washing machine for her mother." Coast Guardsman C.M. Jim Lawson, a guest who was stationed at East Moriches and only visiting Long Island for the month, missed his girlfriend. His gift was a "brown tweed suit, topcoat, and materials for a night in New York—dinner at the Stork Club, two tickets for "Oklahoma," supper at the Harem, and $50." The others received equally fine gifts.[175]

The years following World War II were not kind to the Montauk Point Lighthouse and property, as indicated in comments made by Charlie Shoemaker who became keeper in 1954: "When we first got there after WWII the lighthouse had been badly neglected. We sandblasted it down to the bare stone. We started in the spring, pulling hand over hand on a scaffold, just using brute strength to get it done." Shoemaker added that even in the 1950s the Point still seemed remote: "At night, except for the Trail's End, a bar that stayed open late, you wouldn't see a light on in the entire village of Montauk."[176]

A stern-faced Archie Jones, Chief Boatswains Mate (BMC) and keeper in charge of the lighthouse from 1946-1954, was photographed in uniform during his time at the station. (Montauk Point Lighthouse Museum)

With advances in technology, the numerous life saving stations along the coast of Long Island that had assisted with shipwrecks became obsolete. Closures began in the early 1900s, and by 1955 all life saving stations in the area were discontinued. Some were sold or moved, and others simply were abandoned. The only life saving station still in existence is located on Star Island in Lake Montauk, towed there from Napeague.

The worst maritime disaster at Montauk Point occurred on September 1, 1951 when the 42-foot charter fishing boat *Pelican* capsized off Montauk, with the rescue of only nineteen passengers and crew from a total of sixty-four aboard. The boat was overloaded with fishermen and equipment. The weather was poor that day, with strong winds and rough seas, but Captain Edward Carroll launched anyway. Beyond Montauk Point, he decided to head back to port, but his decision was overruled by his naïve passengers.

Later, one of the boat's two engines failed and it began limping back to port with the remaining engine. Unfortunately, as the *Pelican* met the riptide where the Atlantic Ocean meets Block Island Sound, three huge waves struck and the last one capsized the boat. Only one passenger had the presence of mind to put on a life jacket (there were plenty aboard). Some passengers drowned, trapped below deck in the cabin. Other boats in the area were able to rescue a few from the water.

Strangely, the *Pelican* did not sink and was towed to the dock at Montauk, where the horrible discovery was made of ten bodies inside the cabin. Montauk native, Vinnie Grimes, was home on leave from the navy at the time and was involved in the recovery operation at Montauk Harbor. He recalled the grizzly findings in the boat's cabin in *Dark Noon: Final Voyage of the Fishing Boat "Pelican"*, written by Tom Clavin: "When...we were down in the cabin, you could see that these people evidently had an air pocket for a short period of time. They thought they could scratch right through, but hell, there was one-inch planking on the other side."[177]

The search for bodies continued for days, with twenty-eight recovered by September 20. Some were never found. To say that the *Pelican* put to sea overloaded with passengers is an understatement. At the Coast Guard inquiry into the incident, it was stated that the maximum number of passengers should have been twenty and yet sixty-four had gone out.[178]

From the 1960s to the 1980s at Montauk Point Lighthouse, alterations were made to the entrance porch, the original front doorways were removed, and the seven windows installed in 1912 were replaced with smaller ones. The interior floor plan was altered, with most of the early doors removed along with the original trim.

In an effort to strengthen the power of the beacon, the light was dramatically increased from 200,000 to 2,500,000 candlepower in December 1960, making the Montauk Lighthouse one of the most powerful in the region.[179] The flashing characteristic also was changed from the single flash every 10-seconds that had prevailed since 1903 to one flash every 5-seconds. The change in the light characteristic was downplayed by the Coast Guard. Chief Bosun's Mate William Harvey commented: "We just took out the old bulb and reached into the cupboard for the new one and screwed it into place…I doubt if it's a big headline." The new 120-volt, 1,000-watt bulb was ten times more powerful than the old one, yet only about a fifth the total size. The monthly light bill at the time was about $135. [180]

In 1961 a motor was installed in the clockworks mechanism that revolved the flashing signal, finally relieving the keeper of the arduous task of climbing to the lantern every three hours to rewind the clockworks. Two years later the exterior walls of the tower were sandblasted and painted with a waterproof coating. In 1964 new glazing was installed in the lantern (1/4-inch plate glass). It was replaced in the late 1970s with a system of wide stainless steel stops. With the tower used less often by Coast Guard personnel after the "Light Monitor/Alarm System" was installed in 1976, little attention was paid to maintaining the interior tower finishes.

A description of life at the lighthouse was given to the *East Hampton Star* in February 1967 by Boatswain's Mate First Class Kenneth Borrego: "We're actually understaffed. This light calls for a complement of six [there were currently three] and we're expecting at least one more replacement any day now." The men did their own cooking and the monthly food allowance of $77 provided by the Coast

Top—By 1951, Montauk Point Light Station stood close to the bluffs. The State Park building appeared in the upper right by the road. Note the exposed WW II bunker in the bluff at left. (U.S. Coast Guard Archives)

Left—Chief Boatswains Mate Archie Jones was photographed ca. 1950 changing an electric bulb in the 3 ½-order bivalve Fresnel lens. Jones was keeper in charge of the lighthouse from 1946-1954. (Montauk Point Lighthouse Museum)

Guard was considered sufficient.[181]

As far as duties, Bosun Berrego said that in addition to tending the light, "we have radio equipment that beams out a signal and we take care of that. There's the foghorn. We stand watches every night and every three hours we phone in weather reports to the Cooperative Weather Service. We call in temperature, humidity and wind velocity." Assistant George Baltusavich recalled winds of 70-mph during his time at the light station: "We had a fellow taking down the flag that evening and whatever way he was standing, he couldn't get his breath and passed out. We had to go out and help him in."[182]

Bosun Berrego said that the stairs in the tower had to be painted about every eighteen months. He detailed work in the lantern: "We turn on the light half an hour before sunset and switch it off half an hour after sunrise. The light revolves once every five seconds. That way ships at sea can time our lights and tell which point they're looking at. Our fog signal is the same. It blows a two-second blast every 13 seconds. Then for distance timing, we blow a five-second blast every six minutes. Our horn is on an average of 100 hours a month. We switch on the horn when the visibility drops below five miles. The sound can carry five miles out to sea."[183]

Regarding the erosion of the bluff, Berrego said, "It hasn't been too bad lately and with the new parking lot they're building (as part of Montauk Point State Park), they brought over some fill for us and that built the edge back out a bit."[184]

He described the light source, a bulb of the "new long lasting quartziodine type. Rather than being a solid piece of glass, the lens surrounding the bulb is composed of many small pieces arranged like a Venetian blind turned sideways. We have to keep the pieces clean, which is another of our housekeeping jobs. Also we have to wash the windows...Once that wind reaches 50 we don't even come up inside the tower. With a 50-mile-an-hour wind, you can actually feel the tower shake."[185]

He claimed the biggest problem was loss of electric power: "When the power goes out, we switch over to our own generator. And if anything should happen to the electric motor that turns the light, we have a back-up system for that too [the old clockwork mechanism]. It will keep the light revolving for four hours. At the end of four hours, we wind the spring again with that ratchet and she's good for another four hours. If the power goes off and something happens to the generator, we still have the old kerosene lights we can use."[186]

Regarding summer visitors, Berrego said that since their numbers had greatly increased they were no longer allowed up in the tower. However, individuals or groups were permitted by appointment.[187]

Engineman Richard Vanne said in a December 1968 interview, there was always something to scrub, polish or paint at the station in the face of boredom or loneliness: "The Coast Guard's motto is 'If it doesn't move, paint it.' We keep painting the same things all the time." He added, "It's never boring in the summer time [but] during the winter if you hear one car go by you run to the window to see what's going on."[188]

It wasn't always all work and no play for Coast Guard personnel at the lighthouse, as evidenced by entries in Records of Inspection:

November 8, 1966: "Will check into procuring new TV & repairing pool table."
November 21, 1966: "Group is in process of getting new TV for crew's dry room."[189]

Generally speaking, Coast Guard inspections of the light station during the 1960s-1980s resulted in favorable reports. Words such as "excellent, outstanding, exemplary, pleasure to visit," and "keep up the good work," described the staff and the overall station. A particularly glowing report in 1977 referred to the site as a "neat, clean station being maintained by personnel who are interested in keeping a good Coast Guard image at this most important historic site that has served mariners well for a long time."[190]

Sometimes there were surprise visits. On June 17, 1963, Assistant Secretary of the Treasury, James D. Reed, and an Admiral Ross were at the lighthouse. Reed wrote: "Having survived the trip to the top of the light tower, the [tower] was inspected and it appears to be in excellent condition."[191] On August 17, 1968, Paul Foye, Captain of the U.S. Coast Guard, came to the lighthouse: "Visited Montauk Light with family…We enjoyed our visit and greatly admired the station, which is in excellent condition. We deeply appreciate the most cordial reception."[192]

Coast Guard personnel received four-year assignments at the lighthouse. Among the numerous duties, according to a 1983 *New York Times* article, were "using foghorns and radio beacons, plotting courses for distressed ships and checking navigational aids, offshore lights and buoys that are rapidly replacing the lighthouses. Motor pulleys, generators, a paint shed and a maintenance shop are routine checks on the weekly schedule."

In addition to the equipment at the light station, there were search and rescue vessels at the Coast Guard station at Star Island in Lake Montauk. These fell under the supervision of BM1 Gene Hughes, the Montauk Point Lighthouse officer-in-charge in 1986.

By 1986 there was talk of relocating the lighthouse inland due to the severe erosion on the point, but it was superseded by rumors of impending automation.[193] To Hughes, automation wasn't a big deal. "It doesn't take a whole lot to turn on the light switch."[194]

A view of Montauk Point Lighthouse, looking southeast on September 13, 1971, showed its well-groomed grounds. (Photo by John Lehman, U.S. Coast Guard Archives)

In those days Hughes built ship models to fight boredom. He felt that interest in the lighthouse had been declining during the 1980s: "I've been here two years and I have yet to meet anyone who said they were from a historical society." As far as the general public was concerned, Hughes felt most of them were pleasant and courteous, however, "we had to call the police a couple of times. Occasionally a drunk will jump the fence, and we had one guy up here peeping in the windows."[195]

During the time when BMC Frank Abel was lighthouse keeper in the mid 1970s, his days were fairly routine, except one night his four-year-old son Frank "wandered into a room near the tower stairs and...pulled the big switch that turned the lighthouse light off...Of course it set off all sorts of alarms and we immediately got the light back on."[196]

BM1 Paul Driscoll fought off boredom in 1981 by creating a small maritime display in the former oil room and two other areas of the lighthouse. The little museum was open to the public from 10:00a.m. until 4:00p.m. weekdays. Exhibits included beacons, buoys, and other artifacts depicting almost 200 years of maritime safety. Also displayed was a copy of the 1796 contract authorizing John McComb, Jr. to build the lighthouse. A highlight of the museum was the collection of "brass and cut-glass lenses donated...from various navigation towers on the Atlantic coast where the intricate globes were used in the eighteenth and nineteenth centuries." Members of the Coast Guard staff gave guided tours that culminated with a climb to the lantern. To assure the museum tours didn't interfere with light station operations, reservations were required.[197]

The lighthouse crew was mindful of the station's public image. In a Record of Inspection in the spring of 1980 it was noted: "Summer is coming up which means tourists and hard work so you'll really have to buckle down and bust some hump to keep up with everything."[198] The station's continuing role greeting ships and aircraft headed into New York never faltered. In 1981 a huge yellow ribbon inscribed with the words "Welcome Home" was wrapped around the deck below the lantern to honor the return of American hostages from Iran.

Rumors of automation were realized on February 3, 1987 when the Montauk Point Lighthouse's 3½-order bivalve lens was replaced with a DCB-224 revolving airport beacon manufactured by the Carlisle Finch Co. of Cincinnati. The new light was powered by a 1,000-watt, 2.5 million candlepower bulb placed in front of a parabolic mirror. It exhibited a flashing white light at a distance of 24-miles. The beacon also included a backup light. Situated above both the main light and the backup light was a 190-mm emergency lantern with a visibility of 14-miles that could activate in the event of a total power failure at the Point. The old bivalve lens and clockworks were moved to the oil room for use as a museum exhibit.

With automation of the light complete, the Coast Guard era at the Montauk Point Lighthouse came to an end, as did the lightkeeping tradition. The keepers were reassigned elsewhere and the quiet hum and click of self-sufficient machinery replaced them. They would return only for periodic inspections of the beacon or for repairs. For 190 years the lighthouse had been tended by human hands and its walls had protected families. Now, a new era was about to begin.

Since 1972 when Suffolk County announced plans to annex some 45-acres of surplus government property around the lighthouse to a nearby state park, the station had been envisioned as a public place. All that remained was for a group to step forward and make the dream a reality. In 1986, anticipating automation of the lighthouse and removal of the keepers, the Montauk Historical Society approached the Coast Guard with a plan for stewardship of New York's oldest sentinel. Montauk Point Light was about to embark on an exciting new double mission as an active aid to navigation and a museum—a role its Coast Guard keepers had already begun.

CHAPTER 5
Keepers and Life at the Lighthouse: 1796-1885

Anything for a quiet life, as the man said when he took the situation at the lighthouse.

Charles Dickens
"The Pickwick Papers"

From the earliest times, lightkeepers in general did not have the easiest job nor did they experience the creature comforts of modern-day keepers. Pay was low and the work was long and difficult, but lightkeeping was an occupation the public regarded with great respect. Lighthouse keepers provided a benevolent service to mankind, often at great personal risk and sacrifice.

The most obvious occupational hazards were loneliness, isolation, storms and other natural catastrophes, and occasional instances of neglect by the Lighthouse Service. Some lighthouses were situated on remote islands or wave-washed ledges at sea and relied on visiting ships for provisions and assistance. Others, like Montauk Point Light, stood on shore and had access to a town or seaport where they could purchase supplies, find a church or a doctor, and send their children to school.[199] Montauk Point was somewhat isolated in its early years but its lightkeepers found ways to be self-sufficient by fishing and keeping a garden.

Some risks were not so apparent. Noxious smoke, oils, and chemicals permeated the keepers' dwellings and the light towers. Fuels gave off fetid fumes and odors and were highly flammable. Mercury (used to support heavy rotating lenses) was poisonous, and lead paint on woodwork and metalwork posed a risk. The possibility of a fall or other injury added to the mix of daily challenges for lighthouse keepers.

Selection of lightkeepers, early on, was made by the collectors of customs for local ports. In general, keepers came from neighboring towns. Many were retired sailors and sea captains. War heroes and veterans were thought to be reliable and responsible individuals for the keeper positions and often received preferential consideration. There was no age requirement, or special training needed. Until the establishment of the U.S. Light-House Board in 1852 keepers "were not required to be literate, keep records of their work, be able to swim and handle a boat, or undergo inspections."[200] Uniforms did not arrive on the scene until the 1880s. Captain James Scott was the first keeper to wear formal garb at Montauk.

Pay for such a demanding job did not reflect the skills required or the hardships involved, but it began to approach a level commensurate with the military in the late nineteenth century. In the early years, lightkeepers augmented their low incomes by farming, fishing or engaging in other activities such as ice harvesting and lumbering. A few keepers operated stores and businesses. These practices were forbidden after 1852 under the new U.S. Light-House Board, which clearly instructed lightkeepers to refrain from any outside business ventures. The Board felt such activities interfered with lighthouse duties.

Collecting pay was a challenge at remote stations, including Montauk Point Light. District inspectors sometimes delivered pay, but more often keepers had to pick it up themselves. Logbook entries for the 1870s noted that in order for Montauk's lightkeepers to collect their pay, a trip of two to three days to Sag Harbor usually was required. Obviously, only one man at a time could leave the light station to "draw salary."

The early spider lamps created a great deal of work. The oil reservoirs had to be refilled often during the night and the wicks trimmed. Soot built up on all surfaces, especially the lantern glass, which frequently had to be wiped. When Argand lamps were introduced in the early 1800s, additional work was required tending multiple lamps and polishing silvered reflectors. Dirty lantern habits were to blame for poor lights and sometimes even resulted in fires. Reports of poorly kept lights were mostly the result of inadequate training and supervision.[201]

By the mid-nineteenth century, the Light-House Board had improved living conditions for the keepers and introduced better equipment. There were more keepers assigned to each lighthouse and the work was shared. Families pitched in, and wives or grown children might be hired as paid assistants. However, the arrival of the Fresnel lens in the mid-nineteenth century brought increased work—hours of polishing delicate prisms, bull's eyes, and the brass framework and maintaining the clockworks that rotated the lens.

According to lighthouse historian, Elinor DeWire, the Lighthouse Service was so enamored with the look of shiny brass they used it to make such things as oil cans, window and door fixtures, railings, dustpans, and even the buttons on keeper's uniforms.[202] With the regimented operations introduced by the Light-House Board, selection of lightkeepers grew more stringent and their duties more regulated. Brass-buttoned uniforms were intended to foster pride in both the workplace and the work, and polished brass and glass never failed to impress visitors, especially the lighthouse inspectors.

The ocean environment presented lightkeepers with special challenges. Ever present was troublesome salt, sand, and moisture, three destructive elements that constantly threatened light stations. Exposed surfaces required repeated scraping and painting. In some locales, towers were whitewashed annually, with special upkeep of the daymarks. With the advent of better paints, the chore was done less often. At some stations, special crews were hired to paint the tower. At others, the keepers did the work themselves, often rigging up dangerous scaffolds to reach the high walls. A typical arrangement involved a chair slung by ropes over the lantern railing and raised or lowered as needed.

Leisure time, which was less than we might imagine, was spent at various hobbies—whittling, making models, bird watching, hunting and fishing. Reading was the favorite pastime. To educate and edify lighthouse families, stations continually exchanged lending libraries in portable oak cases. A variety of useful and entertaining titles were included. A log entry at Montauk dated October 26, 1891 indicated that a bookcase and forty-five books were delivered to the lighthouse.[203]

From the earliest years, keepers at Montauk supplemented their meager salaries by providing food and shelter for visitors, but for a price. Montauk Point increasingly became a popular spot for dining and overnight accommodations. During the period 1832-1857 keepers maintained a register of visitors. Guests hunted, fished, picked berries, and paid compliments to the wives of the keepers and their Indian assistants for the fine meals prepared.[204] Lodging at the lighthouse ended after the creation of the Light-House Board, since keepers thereafter were not permitted to profit from use of government property. Only shipwreck survivors could be lodged, and their stay was free.

Until the late nineteenth century, vacations for keepers and their families were few and short in duration. When only one keeper was assigned to Montauk Light, he had to make arrangements for someone to keep the station in his absence. Later, when multiple keepers resided at the station, they took leave by turns. With precious little time to socialize outside the light station, visitors were practically the only contact keepers had with the rest of the world. At most light stations, visitors came on Sundays, but at Montauk they were given tours every day but Sunday, the keepers' day off. Often they brought gifts and sometimes a bottle of alcohol, which was forbidden for the keepers to accept or share.

Official instructions were issued as to the proper treatment of visitors. Keepers were to be "courteous and polite to visitors and show them everything of interest about the station at such times as will not interfere with light house duties. Keepers must not allow visitors to handle the apparatus or deface light-house property. Special care must be taken to prevent the scratching of names or initials on the glass of the lanterns or on the windows of the towers." At Montauk in the 1930s, keeper Thomas Buckridge had to keep the privies locked so visitors wouldn't use them.[205]

Light-House Board instructions for stations with two or more keepers (such as Montauk Point after 1852) were divided into two "departments." The first "department" included the maintenance of the lighting apparatus—cleaning and polishing the lens, cleaning and filling the lamp, dusting, trimming the wicks, plus making sure "everything connected with the apparatus and lamp in general was perfectly clean and ready for lighting in the evening." The second "department" involved cleaning the fixtures of the apparatus and the lantern walls, floors, balconies, doors, and windows, plus sweeping tower stairs and passageways from the lantern to the oil storage area. The lens was to be washed every other month with alcohol and polished with rouge once a year. Keepers were required to wear linen aprons to prevent their regular rough clothing from scratching the lens.[206]

Lighthouse keepers did not see themselves as heroic, nor did they have the romanticized image of their occupation we do today. They regarded themselves simply as government employees following orders and providing an important humanitarian service. That their duties sometimes involved personal risk and sacrifice, punctuated by incredible feats of lifesaving, seemed an everyday fact. In the words of Francis Ross Holland, "In essence, the light keeper symbolizes what we think of ourselves as doing in our better moments: when the situation calls for that extra bravery or devotion to duty, we can rise to the occasion and not be found wanting."[207]

Much of the history of Montauk Point's lighthouse keepers is preserved in letters, diaries and journals. They include memories of service during the years when Montauk Point was considered a desolate and inaccessible place. Present Montauk Highway was once a rocky, hilly road. From the Point to East Hampton, the nearest town of size, was a six-hour trip via horse and wagon in good weather. During winter months it was often impassible. Lighthouse occupants no doubt welcomed the arrival of summer travelers. Their existence would remain largely unchanged until the arrival of the automobile.

A list of civilian head keepers who were in charge of the Montauk Point Lighthouse from 1796 to 1943 is found in Appendix A. Appendix C contains a list of some of the lighthouse's assistant keepers. The remainder of this chapter details information on the head keepers who served at Montauk Point Lighthouse.

Jacob Hand (First Keeper: 1796-1812)

Jacob Hand was born in 1733. His wife, Abigail Conklin, was a year younger. The couple had four children—Esther, Jerusha, Jared, and Betsy.[208] When Jacob Hand began his tour of service at Montauk Light in November of 1796, he was already 63-years-old. His salary was $266.66 per year. His wife died in October 1805, midway through Hand's tour as keeper. Only a year after leaving the lighthouse in 1812, Jacob Hand died and was buried in First House Cemetery near the site of First House on Montauk. Some details of his service to Montauk Point Lighthouse follow.

A vote of confidence in Hand's skill and, reliability in the face of insufficient salary is evident in a letter from Henry Packer Dering to William Miller, Commissioner of Revenue, on October 6, 1800:

> *...the present compensation paid the Keeper is actually insufficient for his families support and in my opinion much less than he really merits being a very tidy and attentive man in his business and has got the name of keeping the best light on the Continent.*
> *He has requested me to state to the Secretary of the*

Treasury and Commissioner of the Revenue the insufficiency of his support and that the services he performs are much greater than those of the Keepers of the Light house on Eatons Neck...

I could wish that his circumstances might be taken into consideration and a further compensation allowed that should be equal to other Keepers and enable him to continue his present employment and give a support to his family.

The keeper at present receives the sum of 266 dollars 66 cents yearly and the privilege of ten acres of land to improve.[209]

It was noted in 1804 that Hand was very conscientious in his use of oil. Dering wrote to Albert Gallatin, Secretary of the Treasury: "The keeper is a very faithful and careful man and often grows very fearful and anxious towards the close of the year, that the oil may be expended before a supply may arrive."[210]

In 1806, the Montauk Proprietors claimed Jacob Hand and his son were trespassing on their lands. The proprietors implored the government to remove the keepers from the light station. Henry Packer Dering again communicated with Gallatin:

By the particular request of a number of the Proprietors of the land of Montauk I inclose herewith a petition against the Keeper and Assistant Keeper of the Light house at Montauk Point for trespasses committed on their lands and praying that the said Keepers may be removed and some other person appointed in their stead. Respecting the trespasses mentioned in the Peti-

tion I must observe with my friends Mr. Gardiner of Gardiners Island (one of the signers of the petition) that I have no personal knowledge of any of the trespasses complained of, but have no cause to doubt them, coming from so large a number of respectable characters with many of whom I am personally acquainted.

In case of the removal of the present Keepers of the Light house, the Trustees of the Proprietors of Montauk have requested me to recommend a Capt. John Parsons as a suitable person for their successor.[211]

Dering defended the assistant keeper, Josiah Hand, noting his development of a new lamp and other work done on the property:

The assistant Keeper has laid out and been at great expense on improvement on and about the establishment. It is supposed that he has expended nearly 1000 dollars in enlarging the dwelling House building a barn and a workshop in fencing gardening planting and setting out trees, manuring the land belonging to the establishment &c.

He really deserves credit for his invention of the lamp...It is supposed that it will be a saving of near 400 galls of oil in the course of a year at this light house.[212]

More specifically, Josiah Hand appeared to be the target of the proprietors, referring to him as

...a young man, who may for anything we know do his duty as the keeper of the Light House, but whose

conduct as it relates to our property has at length become injurious and unfriendly to us, and which if we had believed would ever have taken place we should not willingly so conveyed any part of our land to the United States. [He] has committed various trespasses by plowing...mowing and taking off whole Crops of hay and Corn from our Land...and other ways without any just right so to do."[213]

In the face of these charges, both Jacob Hand and Josiah Hand sufficiently defended themselves and were able to remain keepers at Montauk Point Light. In fact Josiah Hand's new lamp (see Chapter 2) was used in American lighthouses for many years.

The gravesite of Jacob Hand (1733-1813), first keeper of Montauk Point Lighthouse, was marked by a plain stone in the First House Cemetery, Montauk. The photo was taken in December 2005. (Author Photo)

Jared Hand (Keeper: 1812-1814)

Jared Hand, son of Jacob Hand, was born in 1762. He married Lucretia Hedges, who was a year younger. She died in 1786 and was buried in the First House Cemetery on Montauk.[214] Hand then married his sister-in-law, Beulah Hedges (1770-1828). They had two children, Beulah and Lucretia. In 1808, Jared Hand's father, then 74, recommended him for the keeper's position at the lighthouse. The senior Hand wrote to Albert Gallatin in 1808:

I have for several years past suffered much from bodily indisposition, and daily feel more and more sensible of the declining state of my health and strength...

My son Jared Hand who lives with me as an Assistant in the discharge of the duties of keeper of the Light House has expended very considerable sums of money on improvements around the establishment by erecting a barn and other buildings and fences for the better accommodation of myself and family...I would through you Sir solicit from the President of the United States the appointment of my son Jared Hand as Keeper of the Light house at this place, the duties of which I am desirous to relinquish provided they may be transferred to him.[215]

A letter written a few days later to the Secretary of the Treasury and signed by several of the Montauk Proprietors agreed with Jacob Hand's proposal that his son take over the lighthouse work:

...[we] take the liberty to express our full and entire

approbation of the application and are desirous that his son Jared Hand may be appointed Keeper of the establishment and pray you Sir to express to the President of the United States our wishes for that purpose.

There has heretofore been some dissatisfaction on the part of the proprietors of Montauk with the conduct of Josiah Hand the former assistant Keeper who has removed into the interior part of the Country.

We recommend [Jared Hand]...with confidence as a suitable character knowing him to be a Man of fidelity and respectability and whose age and other Qualifications of sobriety and steadiness entitle him to the trust that may be reposed in him.[216]

Henry Packer Dering also added his support of Jared Hand for the position:

...I consider him a very suitable person for the appointment, he is a man that has ever sustained the character of an honest and industrious citizen and is a person of decent property, his age I should judge was abut 45 or 47 years—a robust, steady and sensible man, one that has ever given satisfaction to his employees...I have no reason to doubt but will discharge the duties assigned him as a keeper of the light house with attention and honesty.[217]

In spite of the letters supporting Jared Hand, President Thomas Jefferson (1743-1826) responded: "I have constantly refused to give in to this method of making offices hereditary. Whenever this one becomes actually vacant, the claims of Jared Hand may be considered with those of other competitors."[218] These thoughts were echoed by Secretary of the Treasury Albert Gallatin, who wrote to Dering: "The resignation of Jacob Hand as Keeper of the Montauk light house being conditioned on the appointment of his Son as successor; the President does not think it proper to consider such resignation as absolute. Whenever Mr. Hand actually resigns, the claims of Jared Hand will be considered with those of other applicants."[219]

Jared Hand applied for the keeper's position and was found to be the most suitable candidate. He was appointed keeper of the Montauk Point Lighthouse on his own merit on January 28, 1812, replacing his father who was then in his 79th year.[220]

During the War of 1812 a request for permission to purchase "spy glasses" for the lighthouse, for the purpose of observing the movements of British ships, was submitted by Henry Packer Dering to the Secretary of the Treasury.[221] During the war, the British occupied Montauk Point and forced the Hand family off the lighthouse property. Due to its prime location as a landfall light, the British did not harm the lighthouse or its surrounding property. According to Dick White, Chairman of the Lighthouse Committee, "The British in other areas destroyed lighthouses, but they thought this one was beneficial to them."[222]

In advance of the approaching British, Dering wrote to the Secretary of the Treasury: "I saved all the oil and apparatus from the destruction of the enemy by removing them, which will be carried back and reinstalled as soon as the roads are passable."[223] At war's end in 1815, the lighting apparatus was reinstalled and the keepers returned to duty.

Henry Baker (Keeper: 1814-1832)

Henry Baker of Amagansett was born July 29, 1781, one of eleven children. He married Betsey Hand (died August 3, 1849), daughter of first keeper Jacob Hand.[224] Baker was appointed keeper on February 24, 1814 at a salary of $333.33 per year. By the 1820s, Baker and his wife were entertaining and boarding visitors and apparently doing an exemplary job of it. The Montauk Point Lighthouse Museum is fortunate to have pages of a guest register maintained during Baker's service. The following are excerpts from visitors (spellings corrected by the author):

Maj. Timothy Rose of Fireplace Neck, Brookhaven & David H. Miller of Easthampton visit this place Nov. 11th 1823 & took their departure from here the day following.

Mr. A. Folger arrived here the 19th August 1825 from New York via Bridgehampton.

Montauk Register Augt 24th 1825.
(Member of the Rogers and Folger families completing a visit at the lighthouse) "Arrived at this truly delightful romantic and retired point on the 19th ...after a ride of six hours from Bridgehampton, expecting to have taken our departure the following morning, but were detained by a cold and unpleasant easterly storm until the above date. When about to take our leave we cannot refrain from expressing our most sincere thanks to Mr. & Mrs. Baker for their kindness and attention to which [made] our visit extremely pleasant and agreeable with our best wishes for a long continuance of

their happiness and prosperity.

We who have signed our names above visited this truly delightful and retired Point on the 7th of Sept 1825. Sept 8th the weather is rather dull but we are spending our time very agreeable in viewing the works of Nature.

We arrived here before dinner, went to the top of the light-house (which by the by is no easy job), dined and went-away. William B Vandervoort, Albert D Laing August 21, 1830.

A poem was written in the log in 1831—

Came on Montauk
Did not mean to stay
Found such pleasant folks
Couldn't get away

Went to see the Lighthouse
Found it very high
If had not been far from top
Would have reached the sky

Coming down the upper stairs
There had a fall
Which quite put aside
My pleasures all.

By 1832, the district superintendent, John P. Osborn, thought it was time for a new keeper at Montauk. He told Stephen Pleasonton, in charge of the nation's lighthouses at the time, that Baker's son-in-law Samuel Mulford had been handling business affairs for Baker since Baker had become "partially deranged, dejected and melancholy." Osborn recommended Patrick Gould for the keeper's position.[225]

Upon Baker's resignation in May 1832, Felix Dominy (1800-1868) of the East Hampton Dominys, applied for the position of keeper at Montauk. When Dominy learned that Patrick Gould had been appointed to the position by lighthouse superintendent John P. Osborn, Dominy drafted a petition to President Andrew Jackson in which he claimed that the job had gone to someone who was not a resident of Suffolk County or familiar with the area. Dominy asked the President to select a "townsman" who had not sought to purchase "executive patronage." These words being harsh, the final draft of the letter was toned down to recommend Dominy as a "suitable person and well qualified to fill the station &c & [sic] a firm friend to the present Administration".[226] The job still went to Gould.

The Dominy family members were prominent craftsmen and Felix Dominy was a highly competent clockmaker, jewelry and watch repairer, and general metal worker. It was his skill in metal works that earned him a contract to cover the dome of the Montauk Point Lighthouse in copper. The contract was signed on June 6, 1833. Dominy was paid $230 for the job and was permitted to keep the old copper he removed from the dome. The job was completed by July 1834.[227] Keeper Henry Baker did not live to see the new copper-sheathed roof of the lighthouse cupola. He died November 16, 1833 at the age of 52.

Patrick Gould (Keeper: 1832-1849)

Patrick Gould was born March 3, 1799 on the Bridgehampton Road (now Montauk Highway) in Jericho.[228] He married Jerusha Dayton Fithian (June 4, 1804 – May 18, 1879) and began his term as keeper at Montauk on May 9, 1832. During his term, the lighthouse became a popular tourist site for those willing to cross mosquito-invested Napeague in the summer months.

Gould gained fame years later when on December 14, 1856 the brig *Flying Cloud* went aground at Montauk Point. He helped save the crew from drowning in the turbulent seas. A diary of the time stated: "The six men aboard must have perished but for the rockets (or mortar) successfully used in their preservation." Gould was awarded a gold medal for his efforts by the Lifesaving Benevolent Association of New York. The gold medal is currently in the East Hampton Town Marine Museum in Amagansett.

History lists Gould as being "keeper" at the time of the wreck, but since his tenure at the Montauk Point Lighthouse ended in 1849, we can assume he was either an assistant at the lighthouse or, more likely, the "keeper" at the lifesaving station. (Records show Gould was at the Ditch Plains Life Saving Station in 1856.)[229] It was rumored that Jerusha Gould maintained the light during the rescue, but there was no mention of her doing so in official records for the incident.

Gould later was a proprietor at Third House. He bought a house on Toilsome Lane, East Hampton in 1850, which is still in the family. His tour of duty at the lifesaving station ended April 1, 1859. Gould died July 12, 1879 at the age of 80, surviving his wife by only two months. The cause of his death was given as "old age senile." Both Goulds are buried in the South End Cemetery in East Hampton.

Keeper Gould was profiled in an article by his great-great-grandson, Stephen Gould, for the lighthouse museum's 2001 edition of *The Beacon.* It noted that the Goulds entertained guests in their dwelling and were well-liked in the community: "They grew their own vegetables, raised chickens, and fished daily in order to maintain a well-stocked pantry. Indian women helped Jerusha with meal preparations."[230] One of the Gould's most famous visitors was renowned poet Walt Whitman. (See Chapter 9 for an account of one of Whitman's visits to Montauk.)

In the possession of the Montauk Point Lighthouse Museum are pages from Gould's visitor book. A page entitled "Company and Visitors 1833" was written in the lavish script style of the day. Selected samples of entries with dollar amounts follow:

June 7	*David Gardiner Esq. and family $5*
June 20	*Nathaniel Smith Son & Nephue $3*
	Dominy began to board June 10 went home the 20th
July	*Gentlemen from New London $10*
July 14	*Yankees in Sloop James $2*
Aug 13	*Timothy Hedges & family $4*[231]

When Gould requested an addition to the dwelling in 1837, the possibility of using it to accommodate additional guests probably was an incentive. This was reflected in a letter from the Sag Harbor Superintendent of Lighthouses to Stephen Pleasonton, on January 21, 1837: "Montauk is a place of considerable resort for commercial cities and there can be no other accommodations…there are few Light House Keepers that require so good a house as the one at Montauk."[232]

The life of the lighthouse keeper in these times was difficult and keepers probably felt they deserved better salaries. Imagine Keeper Gould's surprise and disappointment when Superintendent John P. Osborn, in a letter dated July 21, 1840 to Stephen Pleasonton, suggested that the pay of the keeper at Montauk "can with propriety be reduced $50. The present salary is $400…and altogether the most desirable situation in this District with the land and other privilege attached."[233]

In March 1841 Montauk Point was the scene of an unusual event. It served as the finish line of a wagon race. Isaac Willets of Hempstead made a sizable wager of $600 with Gilbert B. Miller that he could drive two mares from Brooklyn to Montauk Point in 24-hours while pulling a 300-pound wagon. Willets left Brooklyn at 6:00 p.m. on March 5 and completed the 140-mile trip in 23:02-hours, despite riding through a snowstorm for the final two hours! He recorded his arrival in the logbook at the lighthouse: "5:02 pm, March 6th." [234]

Mary Esther Mulford Miller (1849-1938) recalled a visit with Gould: "…one glorious trip with Father to see Cap'n Patrick T. Gould, the lighthouse keeper. Cap'n Gould had taken me up into the light, step by step for one hundred and eighty steps[235] until I looked beyond the sea. 'Nothing between me and Europe?' I asked. Cap'n Gould handed me a spy glass. 'Can you see it, little Mary Esther?' he said. I have never seen Europe, but oh, the good times I have had looking for it!"[236]

A mystery that occurred near the end of Gould's time as keeper was reported on March 3, 1849 in the *Long Islander* when "six dead bodies, all males, were found on the north shore of Montauk Point on the 3rd inst. A Coroner's Jury was called but nothing appeared to show from whence they came, or who they were. A boat was also found at the same time, on her keel and ready for use." The unidentified bodies were buried in Amagansett.[237]

An interesting letter written in 1850 to Stephen Pleasonton from the Superintendent of Lighthouses for the District of Sag Harbor indicates that Keeper Gould had become overly attached to the Montauk Light Station. The new head keeper, John Hobart, was visited by Patrick. Gould "at various times, since he (Hobart) has had charge of the Light, removed from the dwelling house, fixtures belonging thereto, and that he will probably continue so to do. He has also removed some appurtenances to that building which, I presume he claims as his private property."[238] Pleasonton responded on June 24 that keeper Gould "…should not have been allowed to remove any of the buildings from the Montauk Light without satisfying you that they were erected by him at his own expense."[239]

Two sons of Patrick Gould, Alexander (1835-1885) and Theodore, were born at the lighthouse and later enlisted to serve the Union cause in the Civil War. Theodore Gould, however, died from typhoid fever soon after enlisting.[240]

John Hobart (Keeper: 1849-1850)
Silas Loper (Keeper: 1850)

John Hobart, born 1804, was the keeper of Montauk Point Lighthouse from October 29, 1849 – August 17, 1850. Silas Loper followed Hobart as an interim keeper from August 17, 1850 – November 25, 1850 until a new man was appointed. Loper earned a salary of $350 a year, but only drew three months income.

Little is known about either man. Hobart, according to

East Hampton citizens, didn't go far for fuel to keep warm during the one winter he was keeper of the station. Townspeople noted on December 13, 1849 that Hobart "applied for the right to get his Fire Wood from the Point Woods which was allowed on condition that he pay $15 to the Trustees for such right for one year."[241]

Jason Terbell (Keeper: 1850-1857)

Jason M. Terbell was born in 1807 and became head keeper at Montauk Point Light on November 25, 1850. He earned $350 per year by 1855. Problems with Terbell were noted in early 1857 and may have lead to his removal from the station. As detailed by the Light-House board on April 8: "...absence of the keeper of Montauk Point Light House for the last six weeks without authority."[242] The Light-House Board did not tolerate absences or dereliction of duty. As a result, Jonathan Payne was selected as temporary keeper on April 30, 1857, and on June 12 William Gardiner was appointed as the new keeper.

During Terbell's service at the lighthouse he maintained a register of visitors, which included the following entry from a satisfied guest: "Epicurean Dinners served at Montauk. Bill of fare: October 17, 1854: Wild Goose, Broiled Chicken, Fried Oysters, Raw Oysters."[243]

Terbell died in East Hampton on October 22, 1882, aged 75.

William Gardiner (Keeper: 1857-1861)

William Gardiner was born in 1807. He was appointed

keeper on June 12, 1857 with a starting salary of $350. He requested an increase to $500 in October 1858.[244] A higher rate of $550 was requested and considered by the Light-House Board in 1859 since "it [Montauk] being a light of the 1st order and the salaries of keepers of all lights of that order range from $550 to $600."[245] The extra $50 was not approved, however, and Gardiner's salary was raised to $500 on October 15, 1859. He was transferred from Montauk on May 13, 1861.

The dissatisfaction of lighthouse authorities with the practice of taking in overnight guests, which began at Montauk a few decades earlier, finally came to a head in December 1857 when, during Gardiner's tenure, the Light-House Board wrote to the Superintendent at Sag Harbor, alleging "...that the keeper of Montauk Point Light House repeatedly violated the instructions and regulations of the Department by entertaining boarders for pay in the dwelling house at that station and in vending intoxicating liquors on the government premises...You will please call upon the keeper for explanation which if not satisfactory will result in a recommendation for his dismissal. The regulations are explicit on theses points."[246] So ended the lively era of Montauk Lighthouse as a resort destination.

During Gardiner's time at the lighthouse, rumor circulated that a slave ship was scuttled off Montauk Point on September 18, 1858. Nine Portuguese sailors were rumored to have deliberately wrecked the ship after being paid off in a slave voyage. They left in haste for New London, Connecticut, which made their actions even more suspicious. Another famous wreck during Gardiner's term was the *John Milton,* which met its demise off Montauk Point on February 20, 1858. The ship's ordeal is described in detail in Chapter 2.

Apparently, one of the keepers at the lighthouse during

these years had some good fortune with his fishing rod. It was reported by the *Long Islander* on October 1, 1858 that while fishing on shore the keeper caught a "monster sea bass" weighing 42½-pounds![247]

An interesting article about Samuel G. Bailey, Gardiner's assistant in 1858, appeared in the *Brooklyn Daily Eagle* in 1888. The article revealed that Bailey had "...lost a Government order for one quarter's salary. It was supposed to have been swallowed up in the sea. A few days ago William H. Cook, of Bridgehampton, was tossing old cans into Mecox Bay for oyster spawn to cling to. One of the cans would not sink. It attracted Mr. Cook's attention, and upon investigation he found it sealed up, but apparently empty. He proceeded to open it to gratify his curiosity. The only thing it contained was Mr. Bailey's lost order."[248]

At one time William Gardiner owned a boarding house on Main Street in East Hampton where he was famous for his oyster suppers and banquets.[249] This building later became the famous Sea Spray Inn and was relocated to the shore near Main Beach in 1902. It was destroyed by fire in 1978.

William Gardiner died on March 1, 1880 in Bridgehampton at age 73.

Joseph Stanton (Keeper: 1861-1865)

Joseph Stanton was born in 1804 and took over duties as head keeper at Montauk Point Lighthouse on May 20, 1861, though he was not officially appointed until December 27, 1862.[250] He married Elizabeth Havens Cooper (1815-1892) and fathered eight children. A son, Rear Admiral Oscar F Stanton (1834-1924), had a distinguished career in the U.S. Navy. Joseph Stanton's starting salary at Montauk was $550 per year. The few years he spent at Montauk appear to have been uneventful and he resigned his position on December 12, 1865. He died in 1866.

Jonathan Allen Miller (Keeper: 1865-1869 and 1872-1875)

Jonathan A. Miller, born in The Springs, a small hamlet north of East Hampton, in 1834, served in the navy during the Civil War and lost an arm in a battle while aboard the *Onida.* He was discharged as a result of his injury and began work at Montauk Point Lighthouse as an assistant keeper on October 13, 1864. He was promoted to head keeper on January 1, 1865 with a salary of $700 a year.

As head keeper he indicated in his journal that supplies, wood, oil, and other items were transported to the light station by steamship. On November 24, 1874 an entry read: "Cistern dry; got our wash water from the Money Pond."[251] (This pond, located just north of the lighthouse property, was allegedly the location of treasure buried by noted pirate Captain Kidd.) Miller served dual roles as both keeper at the lighthouse and at the life saving station located at Montauk Point. He was transferred from the lighthouse on May 13, 1869 but returned for a second stint as head keeper (again at $700 a year) from December 3, 1872 until October 15, 1875. Members of the "Custom collection District of Sag Harbor" had petitioned for Miller to return, citing his Civil War injury and that he "deserves recognition from the government."[252]

Miller married Margaret Burke (1839-1909) on March

27, 1856 and they had fourteen children.[253] Miller was the first of three family members to serve at the Montauk Point Lighthouse. His son John E. Miller later served as head keeper, and in the 1930s a grandson, John A. Miller, was an assistant keeper to Thomas Buckridge.

A humorous story related in 1938 by Mrs. Everett King, daughter of keeper Miller, told how she played with two young Montaukett Indians whom she referred to as "Dink and Dank." The three children played at the lighthouse on Saturdays when the young Indians brought "…along their bows and arrows, which they would shoot down from the top of the lighthouse, whenever they could sneak up past my father. One day Dank slid down the lightning rod on the outside of the tower, only to be greeted by my father (who was a stern man) at the base. The last we saw of Dank he was streaking over the hills for Indian Fields."[254]

Mrs. King also spoke of her family's dealings with a Montaukett named Stephen Talkhouse, who had a great reputation for being a superior walker: "My father…often gave Steve a lift with him in his carriage behind a fast team of horses. Once when Steve was in a hurry he refused to ride; my father was indignant at his impertinence. But upon reaching East Hampton, there sat Steve on the porch of Al Payne's store, fanning himself with a palm leaf fan."[255]

On September 1, 1875 the lightkeeper recorded that "…a flock of black ducks flew against the lantern of the Lt House broke out one Storm pane. Three of the said ducks was found at the base of the Light-House by the keeper J. A. Miller who was on watch at the time of the accident."[256] Such occurrences were not uncommon during the spring and fall months when thousands of birds passed the lighthouse each day on their seasonal migrations.

An interesting sequence of events involving problems with personnel at the lighthouse took place over several months in late 1875. In an initial letter from keeper Miller, dated August 26, 1875, to Third District Inspector Commodore Stephen Trenchard, Miller wrote of problems with his two assistants: "...I find the first assistant L. L. Bennett had the watch from 8 to 12 PM on the 17th…he clames there was no fog during his watch more than a mist over the Sea did not think it was thick enough to run the Engine the moon and Stars being in sight most of the time…William G. Bennett had the watch from 12 to 4 the same night he Says there was no fog in his watch. The above is the Statement of the two assistant keepers. So far as the truth of this goes I am not able to Say as I have had former ocations [occasions] to doubt their words…"[257]

On the same day, Miller wrote another scathing letter about his assistants to Commodore Trenchard: "I feel it to be my duty to report my two assistant keepers as not being fit men for this Station as I find by close watching I can not trust eather one of them in thick & foggy weather besides being carless and negligent they cannot comply with the rules and regulations of the Lt House Board I truly think Sir If I had men of my own choice there would be less reports about this Light & fog Signal Station."[258]

On August 30, 1875 Commodore Trenchard wrote to the Board: "In view of the fact that during last summer other complaints of neglect were received against this station, the Inspector approves the Keeper's recommendation for the removal of the Assistant Keepers."[259]

Mr. W. S. Havens, Collector at the Sag Harbor Custom House, felt the blame lay with Miller. He justified his claim in a letter dated September 27, 1875:

I have letters of dismissal of both assistant Keepers of Montauk Point Light, both reliable sober industrious men and very attentive to their duties better assistants cannot be found anywhere in the district in my belief....if the Keeper will speak [the truth] about the men he will say so but I could hardly expect him to do that. Miller is not a proper man for that office and ought to be removed for inattention to his duties nearly quite one third of his time he is reported absent on his private business...I believe the Judgment of General Woodruff his assistants have always complained of him as one too inattentive to duty...I hope this district will be not much longer dishonored by such a person as Keeper of one of our Good Lights.[260]

Based on Havens' letter, Commodore Trenchard changed his position, as evident in a letter dated September 30, 1875: "The Superintendent of Lights at Sag Harbor writes to me describing Mr. Jonathan A Miller...as a person of very indifferent character indeed. He has received two reprimands from the Inspector, on the subject of keeping boarders, which added to other matters apparently trifling in themselves, gives weight to the complaints of the Superintendent...Miller's removal also is, therefore, respectfully recommended. The case of the assistant Keepers was decided upon its merits."[261]

Keeper Jonathan A. Miller was transferred from Montauk on October 15, 1875. In response, Miller wrote a four-page letter to the Light-House Board on October 19th:

Gentlemen I just received yours which was enclosed a copy of the complaint sent by the Collector at Sag Harbor. I would that you could know the unjust feelings that the Collector holds towards me it commences back at the time of my appointment he used every means in his power at that time to have Captain Bennett appointed and I never knew the cause. My prede-

cessor, Mr. Ripley had one of the same assistants L L Bennett which he said he would not have on any condition only he found a very good woman in his wife: when they hired help in boarder time; but he was finally discharged and come to me and I very foolishly had him reappointed. William G Bennett, L L Bennett brother was forced upon me against my will by the Collector and two brothers of their stamp is very unpleasant to live with...The Collector says that I am not a proper person for the office I now hold: he says I have been absent about one third of the time & now that is false. I have stood every watch that belongs to me; this last summer on one occasion I had an opportunity to make a few dollars by carrying a party to Fort Pond which is ten miles from here: I gave the 1st assistant 2.00 to stand my watch in case I did not come back in time: I did get back in time and stood my watch and gave him the two dollars also. Again during the month of september I went to East Hampton for a carpenter to do some work for this Station, at the same time there was four men fishermen wished to ride off with me I took them along for which I received 5.00; this is the extent of any carrying company off or on Montauk this summer....The complaints are all through animosity and spite from the assistants through the collector...I believe I know my duties as regards Lighthouse Keeping; and shall try as I always have done to do them. I sincerely hope and trust your honorable body will carefully consider and investigate this matter and try me a spell longer.[262]

Miller went on to suggest the appointment of Nathan O. Hedges and George E. Miller as first and second assistant keepers,[263] but in December John Donnelly of West

Troy, New York and James Carr of Providence, Rhode Island were selected. However, by early 1876 they were gone, as reported by Inspector A. C. Rhind in a letter of February 25: "...John Donnelly...was compelled to resign as he found he was unable physically to do the work. Carr...was unable from sickness to accept the place and was never sworn in."[264] Perhaps Miller's suggested candidates would have been a better choice.

Inspector Rhind later wrote that keeper Miller was not treated fairly, since the aforementioned letter from Miller "was not received here till after his removal and therefore not sent to the Board. The man was not given a chance to refute the charges against him."[265] Regardless, Thomas P. Ripley became the new head keeper and life went on at the Montauk Point Lighthouse.

One of Miller's assistants was his nephew, Elbert Parker Edwards. Born February 23, 1843 Edwards served in the Civil War and after his discharge in May 1865 went to work on the family farm on Brick Kiln Road near Sag Harbor. Not finding farm life sufficient to support a family of ten, he was hired by his uncle as an assistant at the lighthouse. Edwards arrived at Montauk Point on January 3, 1866, and after only three days, penned a letter to his family, describing life there:

> *I am well pleased with my situation. I am now seated in my little 'watch room'. I have a bright coal fire in a red hot stove which makes the room very comfortable during this season of intense cold...The Governing Apparatus attached to the Flash Clock is humming merrily away and serves to keep me company. Above, the splendid Light House Lamp is burning brightly and flashing its rays far out upon the ocean. I have just been out upon the balcony which surrounds the tower.*

> *The night is dark but far away I can discern twinkling like stars, the distant lights on the Connecticut shore, Block Island, Plum Island and several others. Far beneath me, the surf is dashing upon the rocks with a dull surging roar and here I am penning these lines 200 feet above the sea. Quite an elevated position isn't it... I have become acquainted with the duties of my new position and take my regular turn at watching the light. I am in a fair way to become an expert Light Keeper.*[266]

Edwards served for only about six months. A diary he kept during this time gave a description of activities at the lighthouse. He went skating with Miller's daughter, played dominoes with Miller in the evening, went fishing or duck hunting daily, and occasionally took a 45-minute walk to visit Mr. Stratton, the nearest neighbor. Edwards read a great deal while on watch in the tower and wrote numerous letters. He frequently caught lobsters along the beach and cut wood and ice for storage.[267] Edwards later married Abby Tuthill and lived for a time in East Hampton.[268]

Edwards' father was physically unable to maintain his farm and relocated the family to Connecticut. Elbert Edwards took over the farm hoping to make it a success, but he soon moved on to a variety of other jobs, including selling brooms in Sag Harbor, working in a hospital in Hartford, Connecticut, and painting carriages. He ended up as a salesman in Ashtabula, Ohio. He worked hard to support his family, a factor that may have contributed to his early death, just two days shy of his 31st birthday on February 21, 1874.[269]

Another of Jonathan Miller's assistants, William G. Bennett, was injured at the lighthouse on August 5, 1875 while working with the fog signal. He was "caut in the machinery of left-hand Engine. His foot badly injured will have to lay by for some days." He was back on duty on August 23.[270]

In later years, Jonathan A. Miller was assigned to the Gardiner's Island Lighthouse. He was the last keeper there, serving from July 1893 until March 1894. The land around the lighthouse on Gardiner's Island was eroding at such an alarming rate during the 1890s that the Light-House Board was forced to abandon the station. It eventually collapsed into the sea about 1895 and was not rebuilt. Miller was transferred to the Rockland Lakes Light near Rockland Lake Landing, New York in September, 1894. He didn't have any better luck at his new assignment. The caisson-style sentinel was built on a poor foundation scoured by Hudson River currents and soon began to lean noticeably.[271]

Miller died October 29, 1915 at the age of 81.

Thomas P. Ripley (Keeper: 1869-1872)

Thomas P. Ripley was born in 1821 and became keeper at Montauk Point Light May 13, 1869. His salary was $700 a year. During his time at the station, he was visited by the famous Civil War correspondent, journalist, and author George Alfred Townsend, who wrote a poem in the guest register about the beauty of Montauk.[272]

An example of the extent of the keeper's authority was illustrated in a matter addressed by Ripley to the U.S. Light-House Board in January 1872: "As my assistants seem to think they are entitled to a portion of the premises for garden purposes without my assent, I take the liberty of asking your Honor to please inform me whether or not the premises belonging to this Station are under my immediate controll so far as my assistants are concerned. Trusting your Honor will excuse me for troubling you with so trivial an affair."[273]

Probably one of the first photographs taken of the Montauk Point Lighthouse, this view was dated August 1871. Notes on the bottom of the photo were made by an archivist in the Third Lighthouse District. (National Archives)

Keeper Ripley resigned as keeper on December 3, 1872, possibly because of discontent with his assistants and the district's unwillingness to act on his complaints. He died on June 10, 1888 in Sag Harbor at the age of 67.

Jared Wade (Keeper: 1875-1876)

Jared Wade was appointed head keeper on October 15, 1875 and arrived to take keeper Jonathan A. Miller's place on October 24. His salary was set at $700 per year. During an inspection in mid-November 1875, Wade was cautioned that log entries "should be written up with pen and ink and not with pencil" and was told to "make all the entries clear and plain and note everything of consequence."[274]

On February 2, 1876 Captain Henry Huntting and Lieutenant Bateman arrived to tend to the Life Station (a rare reference to the Life Saving Station at Montauk Point). Less than two weeks later, first assistant John Donnelly, who had just arrived in January, left the station due to illness and was replaced by L. L. Bennett. [275] After serving only about five months, keeper Wade resigned and left the station on March 22, 1876.

Henry Babcock (Keeper: 1876-1885)

Henry Babcock was appointed head keeper on March 2, 1876. His salary was $700 per year. As mentioned in Chapter 4, Babcock was the commander of the ship *Washington,* which he safely navigated around Montauk Point in 1858 shortly after the light's signal had been changed from a steady beam to a flashing beam.

Examples of keeper activity at Montauk Point Light while Babcock was in charge were recorded in the station logbook and by visiting writers of the day. Babcock's assistants traveled to Sag Harbor or East Hampton for food and other purposes. They also received their pay at Sag Harbor.[276] On December 1, 1876, Babcock left the station at 8:00 a.m. to pick up supplies and did not return until 4:00 p.m. three days later. Assistant keeper Stephen Topping left on December 6 at 6:00 a.m. to have the wagon repaired. He did not return until December 10.[277]

Sometimes other matters caused the keepers to leave for extended periods of time. On March 4, 1876 William Lugar went to Sag Harbor for the burial of his father. He returned five days later.[278]

While Babcock was keeper at Montauk Point, around 1884 or 1885, a story about strawberry picking was included in the lighthouse logbook. It involved two boys, Everett J. Edwards, age 13, and his cousin Clinton Edwards, 19. One summer day while they were catching bluefish, and since the "...wind was pretty strong and the fishing poor...they anchored just inside North Bar. Another sloop, owned by two boys doing just what the Edwards boys did that summer, was anchored close by. It was beneath the dignity, Father said, of Captain Clint to go strawberrying, but Father did, with Court Rose off the other boat. They picked six quarts in no time on Point Hill, northwest of the Light, and got the Keeper's wife to make them a shortcake. They had supper with the Lighthouse family and topped it off with shortcake. It was the best meal he ever had in his life, Father said. The captain was mad when the boys returned: The combination cook-mate ashore, filling up with shortcake—it was mutiny."[279]

The crew of the life saving station at Montauk Point saw some activity during Babcock's term, when on December 10, 1876 they "rescued and landed" the crew of the smack *David Prague* out of New London.[280]

In general, the Montauk Point Lighthouse had a stellar record with regard to maintaining the light. However, there were occasions when the beacon failed or did not send a flashing signal. One instance was reported on January 29, 1881, during Babcock's term, when an inspector noted the light was not revolving between 3:00 a.m. and 5:00 a.m. on January 28 due to the keeper not winding the clock-work.[281]

Henry Babcock was transferred from Montauk on September 10, 1885. He and his family left the station for Sag Harbor on October 16, having shipped his "House Hold goods for Sag Harbor" the day before.[282]

CHAPTER 6

Keepers and Life at the Lighthouse: 1885-1943

James G. Scott (Keeper: 1885-1910)

Probably, the most noted and documented civilian keeper at Montauk was James G. Scott. Though his parents were both born in Scotland, Scott was born in Durham, England on May 16, 1840. He came to the United States about 1858 and settled in Holtsville, Long Island. At age 19, Scott began a long career in the Lighthouse Service, interrupted only by a short term of duty with the Union Army during the Civil War.

Scott's first Lighthouse Service assignment was as a cook and mate on the Stratford Shoal Lightship, off Connecticut. In 1867, after his war duty, he rejoined the lightship crew. In 1877, Scott was appointed second assistant keeper at Stratford Shoal Lighthouse in central Long Island Sound and the following year he was promoted to assistant keeper at Stepping Stones Lighthouse in western Long Island Sound. In 1880 he returned to Stratford Shoal Light as head keeper.

On September 26, 1885, James G. Scott transferred to the Montauk Point Lighthouse as head keeper, a position he held for 25-years. His salary was $700 per year, raised to $720 on November 1, 1888. The detailed records he kept of activities at Montauk give a clear picture of life there from 1885 until 1910.

Scott was the first lightkeeper at Montauk to wear an official uniform. Insignia changed several times before the Coast Guard took over lighthouses in 1939, but rank always was shown on jacket lapels and length of service appeared as stripes on the sleeves. A mannequin depicting James G. Scott in uniform is on display in the Montauk Point Lighthouse Museum, along with personal items and documents.

Scott kept copious and detailed records of events. Some examples include:

- *January 9, 1886: A snowstorm and heavy gale blew down the kitchen chimney and the well house. Scott appears not to have been too concerned as the next day's journal entry shows him shoveling snow, fishing for eels and gathering driftwood!*
- *April 22, 1886: We planted the garden and on June 6th caught the first striped bass. Visitors came that day from the Montauk Association clubhouse.*
- *June 15, 1886: The family went strawberry picking*
- *April 18, 1887: Seven crane were sighted in Flag Pond.*
- *November 24, 1887: A Mr. Barns of East Hampton and Mr. Burling, editor of the East Hampton Star, came for a visit. And the next day, keeper Scott killed a pig.*[283]

Captain Scott married Margaret Stanton in Miller Place, Long Island on April 6, 1869. She was born in Liverpool and came to the United States in 1860. She was ten years Scott's junior. They raised a family, but sources do not confirm the number or names of the children. Some of the children were: Anna (1870-1885); Emily (born 1876 and later the wife of James M. Strong of East Hampton in 1896); David (1878-1878); Walter (1884-1898); and John (died 1885).[284] Only Emily survived to adulthood.

A series of tragedies befell the Scott family. Anna died of scarlet fever at age 15, "carried to the Light by survivors of a wreck. John, six, died of appendicitis; the doctor, new to the area, lost his way en route to Montauk and the child was dying when he finally arrived."[285] Young John Scott's illness and death was recounted in the lighthouse logbook:

> *February 14, 9 am: Keeper went after [medicine] for his sick child*
> *February 16: Keeper left station for Dr. 4 pm. Keeper returned 8 pm*
> *Keepers son John Clitz Scott*
> *February 17: Dr. visited this station at 10am*
> *February 18: Keeper and wife left station to bury child*[286]

Another son, Walter Scott, enjoyed writing his name in the visitor's book. One entry in huge red ink stretched across an entire page on September 15, 1896. Sadly, the boy drowned at age 14 while sailing with a friend in nearby Money Pond. The friend, "shaking with fright, walked up to the Light and hung around the kitchen door. Mrs. Scott said: 'It's dinner time. Where is Walter?' The boy replied 'Oh, he's drowned.'" Captain Scott recovered his son's body and took him to an undertaker in East Hampton.[287]

A letter of recommendation for Scott from Thomas Morrison, Bureau of Accounts, Department of State, was sent to Frederick Rodgers of the U.S. Navy in 1889 in response to problems Scott was having with his assistants.

Morrison stated that Scott "...has been in the Light House Service for many years, and as I understand given entire satisfaction...He is a sober industrious man struggling along to maintain his family, and would not intentionally violate any rule or regulation of the Service...It appears from all accounts that immediately upon taking charge at Montauk, he was and is still opposed by his assistants. They said he did not belong on that end of the Island, he had no right to come there, and have I am informed made it exceedingly unpleasant for him and his family ever since."[288] In addition, one assistant, Thomas Gurnett, was noted as being "a drunken fellow [with a] vile tongue."[289]

Montauk Point Light Station, shown in 1884, was devoid of trees and scoured by wind and rain. (National Archives)

Barbara Borsack, active in civic affairs and a member of the multi-generation Strong family of East Hampton, recalled that her great-grandfather, James M. Strong:

> *...took the carriage on regular trips to the Montauk Lighthouse while he was courting the keeper's daughter, Emily Scott, who would become his wife. Blacksmithing [a family business for quite some time] was hard, physical labor, and the trip took hours. So on the way home he would simply point the horses in the right direction (only one good road on and off Montauk in those days- the beach!) and climb in the back to sleep. The horses would make the long trip back on their own, neatly turning north at Hook Pond and proceeding on right into the barn when they reached home.*[290]

During the winter of 1895 the courtship between James Strong and Emily Scott was difficult. In order for Strong to reach the lighthouse, he had to hitch his horse to a sled and wrap himself in a lynx blanket. In April 1994, almost 100 years later, James Strong's great-grandson married Sag Harbor schoolteacher Julie Niemiec at the lighthouse and presented the Lighthouse Museum with James M. Strong's lynx blanket![291]

Borsack spoke of her great-grandmother Emily Scott Strong's days at the Montauk Point Lighthouse:

> *The landscape was quite different than it is now. There were few trees to obscure the view and you could see for miles when you stood on the lighthouse steps and looked west...Company became a cause for great celebration in the winter, when the family was eager for any opportunity to catch up on news from the rest of the world. On rare occasions they would catch sight of a*

wagon or carriage working its way toward them, inching across the wilderness of what is now the hamlet of Montauk. At such times they would busy themselves preparing food for the unexpected company. They were able to have a complete meal on the table by the time the guests arrived, complete with a freshly baked cake for dessert.[292]

Shipwrecks still occurred and the survivors "would be put up at the lighthouse and they would become members of the family for as long as they were marooned there." This sometimes lasted for weeks. One group of castaways included a woman who was the captain's sister. She became friends with the keeper's daughter, Emily Scott, and at their parting presented her with a "beautiful amethyst ring which had come from some foreign port, and which Emily passed down to one of her granddaughters many years later along with the tale."[293]

Another wreck of note occurred on December 18, 1887 when the two-masted schooner *Lewis King*, carrying dates and pipe-clay, ran aground a mile southwest of the lighthouse. The captain, H. C. Farham, apparently mistook Montauk Lighthouse for the light at Watch Hill. The crew of five and one passenger came ashore unassisted. Keeper Scott did not notice the wreck until a member of the crew appeared at the station. Even the crew of the Ditch Plains Life Saving Station was unaware, since the vessel had landed in an area beyond their jurisdiction. The cargo of dates turned up on dinner tables on eastern Long Island towns for months afterwards. After lying on the beach for a few years, the schooner finally broke apart in November 1890.[294]

Borsack described mail delivery as an exciting event. During months when the trails were passable, mail was brought by wagon to Third House and Emily Scott and her mother would go on foot to pick it up: "It was a four-mile hike once a week to fetch it, and that was a good day's effort over such hilly terrain." In winter the crew of the life-saving station would leave the mail at Halfway House, a distance of two miles from the Point. "However," Borsack said, "the cold wind that always blows across Montauk must have made it seem much farther to walk."[295]

Excerpts from the lighthouse logbook during the years 1888-1910 give a clearer picture of life at Montauk during the Scott years. Note the many assistant keepers that came and went over the years:

- *August 31, 1888: Charles Z. Miller, first assistant keeper, was replaced by Joseph Mulligan. A Mr. Davis and Thomas Garnett were second assistants in rapid succession.*
- *August 2, 1889: Generals John McAllister Schofield, A. Mordecai, and Abbott came for a visit. (General Schofield [1831-1906] was a noted Civil War general who saw action in numerous battles, including Atlanta under General William T Sherman.)*
- *September 2, 1889: Some young friends of "keeper's little girl Emily were detained at the Light two days because of the weather." A new second assistant "gunned and fished and wouldn't work" so he was relieved shortly.*
- *During 1890 David E. Johnson became second assistant. Ducks struck the lighthouse, damaging the lantern glass.*
- *In 1891 New York Governor David B. Hill (1843-1910) visited the lighthouse. Freeman Douglas joined the staff as second keeper, and a chimney on the keeper's dwelling blew down in a heavy storm.*

- *September 18, 1892: A Mr. Bennett became the new first assistant keeper.*
- *February 24, 1893: Significant ice fields around Montauk Point.*
- *In 1893 Charles L. Mulford became second assistant.*
- *October 5, 1893: Grass was cut on Flag Pond and members went to pick strawberries.*
- *March 10, 1895: An eclipse of the moon was noted, beginning at 4:20 pm and ending at midnight. Mr. King was second assistant at the time.*
- *January 29, 1897: a snowstorm of 18 inches, the deepest in ten years, fell at Montauk Point.*
- *March 31, 1897: Harry Scott became the new second assistant.*
- *In 1899 keeper Scott's daughter and son Willie came for a visit.*
- *April 12, 1899: Mr. Theodore Conklin plowed the Point gardens.*
- *October 29, 1903: Miss Cook and Charles O. Gould were married in the lighthouse. [Records indicate that this was the first wedding at the site since 1828 when Samuel Millford and a Miss Baker of East Hampton were wed there.][296] The newly installed Marconi wireless was put to use when it "began to flash the news of the nuptials to the lighthouse at Newport, R.I., and the keeper there sent back his wireless congratulations." Gould was the grandson of former keeper Patrick Gould and his father had been born at the lighthouse, which was a reason why the wedding was held there.[297]*
- *November 26, 1903: John Miller became the new first assistant.*

- *May 1, 1904: Raymond Onsel came as second assistant.*[298]

A return to the early days when overnight guests were common at the Montauk station almost occurred in 1892 when John Jacobus, U.S. Marshall for the Southern District of New York, asked permission for his friend Isaac Terrell to stay at the lighthouse, Terrell being a friend of the Scott family. The Light-House Board refused, sticking firmly to established policy.[299]

Captain Scott found time to be away, as indicated by an entry of November 21, 1904: "William Baker came for a few days to take the keeper's place." Baker was the son of one of Scott's early assistant keepers, William Alonzo Baker. The elder Baker was born in Noyack on April 5, 1836 and was involved in the whaling business out of Sag Harbor before entering the lighthouse service. He served as an assistant under Scott from 1889 until 1891 and died November 12, 1899 at the age of 63. His son, William L. Baker (1860-1929) also heard the call of the sea, serving 37-years in the Life Saving Service on Montauk at the Ditch Plains and Hither Plain Stations. The younger Baker not only stood in for Keeper Scott from time to time, but was officially appointed an assistant in April 1908.[300]

Several events of interest were recorded in the logbook in the early twentieth century. The weather in the winter of 1905 was so frigid that on February 18 ice was visible along the shore to a distance of about a quarter of a mile at sea. On November 7 Scott left the property to perform a civic duty: "Voted Republican ticket." A partial solar eclipse was noted on June 28, 1908.

It was reported in 1906 that hundreds of ducks and geese crashed to their deaths against the lighthouse after flying into the blinding light of the Fresnel lens. The impact was so intense that "some times the birds are found with their necks and wings broken." In addition, migrating songbirds collided with the light, sometimes as many as a hundred in a single day.[301]

Montauk Point Lighthouse was captured on film from the Atlantic Ocean in 1891. A hand printed caption on the bottom attributed the image to N.L. Stebbins, Boston. (National Archives)

Keeper Scott's 8-year-old grandson, Willy Strong, came to visit the lighthouse in 1906. Walking around the property the morning after a heavy storm, Willy Strong and his grandfather came across a duck that had apparently died after crashing into the lantern glass the night before. Keeper Scott had the duck stuffed for his grandson, who kept it as a lifelong remembrance of his grandfather's work at the Montauk Point Lighthouse. In 1992, Willy Strong's son, Bill Strong, donated the duck to the Lighthouse Museum where it is now displayed.[302]

On September 7, 1908, a Mr. Lee arrived at 8:00 p.m. from New York by automobile, making the trip to Montauk Point Lighthouse in eight hours. From there he went to the Montauk Inn. Nine days later, the first official automobile run to Montauk Point took place, sponsored by the American Automobile Association of America with forty vehicles completing the trip.[303] Captain Scott received a gold medal when the participants reached the lighthouse.[304] The excitement quickly died down and the station returned to normal. A few weeks later, on November 9, 1908, carpenters began dismantling the defunct wireless station dwelling house.[305]

Years after leaving the light station, Captain Scott's daughter Emily Scott Strong recalled aspects of her father's life at Montauk:

> *In the first ten years father was at Montauk, he had no leave without paying his substitute out of his own pocket. He never had an accident caused by neglect of duty. It was a lonely life and a hard one for our mother.*[306]
>
> *Thousands of sheep were pastured on Montauk then; when the snow was deep they would sometimes eat poisonous laurel leaves and die. Then father skinned them and cured the hides, to make rugs; they were nice and warm to step out of bed on, mornings when the thermometer was down below zero. When the bricks of our stoves gave out father would repair them with Montauk clay; it lasted a long time. In storms, thousands of birds*

would strike the Light; after one storm we counted 300 yellow warblers dead on the beach. Sometimes ducks would strike the light with such force that they were cut in two.[307]

Her opinion of Montauk Point: "I thought when we arrived that Montauk Point was the lonesomest place I had ever seen. But looking back, I feel that some of the happiest years of my life were spent there."[308]

During the keepership of Captain James G. Scott, Montauk Point Light Station was a picturesque rambling of buildings- evidence of its many activities. Photo ca. 1900. (Montauk Library)

Legend surrounds the light station too. Indians told of a medicinal spring in the vicinity of Montauk Point, its exact whereabouts long unknown. One source might have been "that tiny thread of clear, cool water coming out of the cliff a stone's throw from the lighthouse, which Captain James

Scott…considered better for him than the cistern water commonly used at the Point." His grandson, William Strong, recalled "fastening a pail below the spring every night and scrambling down the bank to bring it up full, early in the morning."[309]

When Captain Scott wasn't tending to lighthouse affairs, he pursued other interests, among them recording the many types of birds he observed at Montauk Point from 1890 to 1910 and forwarding the information to William Dutcher of New York, a naturalist with the National Audubon Society.[310] Scott also corresponded with a neighbor, Samuel H. Miller, he had befriended in the 1860s while in Miller Place. In a letter dated April 5, 1886 Scott spoke of the changing seasons and his children:

> *It tis now April and I think Spring is near at hand and things will soon be puting forth there leaves & Flowers. there is not eney trees on this Point but good pasture for Stock. About ½ Mile from the Light there is a Long Swamp there the trees grow. Lots of Small wild fruit on this Point such as strawberry, Sumer grapes…Plenty wild fowel duck & geese. At Present about two Miles from this Light there is a Beautiful Lake and at Present there is…about two or three hundred geese and 10 or twenty Men in Camp on the Lake from Amagansett and hunting them….Emily & John wishes to tell you they have found lots of very nice indian Arrow Heads, three Bords made in shape of Hearts, all full of Arrow Heads of all shapes and colors and sizes. allso we have got a very nice Hair Seal Skin Cured which we Captured on the Beach. With Best Wishes to all we Remain yours truly Mr. & Mrs. James G. Scott.*
>
> *PS: if you have eney garden Seeds to Sell, Send us*

a small quantity by mail.[311]

During his 25-years at Montauk Point Lighthouse, Captain Scott appeared to "keep a good light." However, an inspector wrote to Scott that on December 15, 1909 "the light in your charge was out from 5 pm to 5:25 pm…[It is requested] that you submit a detailed explanation as to why your light was extinguished."[312] Scott responded on December 20 that his first assistant reported the light was out "on account of or because the vaporizer stopped up with carbon and took 25 minutes to put in a new vaporizer or exchange vaporizer."[313]

Not long afterward on February 24, 1910, the light was again out for a period of 45-minutes. Captain Scott said this was caused by oil overflowing in the vapor lamp. The inspector considered this an unsatisfactory reason and replied: "You are informed that in order to maintain an efficient vapor light, the lamp should be constantly attended and you will in the future see that the provisions of Paragraph 64, Page 13, of Instructions to Light-Keepers, 1902, are strictly complied with."[314]

During Captain Scott's last years at Montauk, tensions arose between him and first assistant Evard Jansen, who felt Scott was too old to adequately perform his duties as head keeper. In May 1910 the Light-House Board offered Scott a position at the New Dorp Lighthouse on Staten Island—a smaller and less critical light for navigation. Captain Scott declined.[315] Four months later he was replaced.

Suffering from diabetes for years, Scott died on October 31, 1910 in East Hampton at the age of 70. His name lives on at Montauk Point in "Scott's Hole," a spot on the shore north of the lighthouse where he used to pull up his boat.

In the winter of 1903, a view of Montauk Point Light Station and its numerous outbuildings included the tall signal pole to the left of the tower. The pole was part of the new Marconi wireless station. It stood only five years before being dismantled. (Photo by Hal Fullerton, Courtesy of Suffolk County Historical Society)

John F. Anderson (Keeper: 1910-1912)

John Frederick Anderson was born in Sweden on December 25, 1859. He immigrated to the United States and eventually settled in Providence, Rhode Island. His career at Montauk Point Lighthouse showed a steady progression of responsibility and earnings. He was appointed as second assistant keeper at Montauk Point Lighthouse on November 1, 1906 at a salary of $450 annually. He was promoted to first assistant keeper on January 5, 1908 and received $500 per year. On October 1, 1910 he took over for Captain Scott as head keeper with an annual salary of $720.

Anderson's first assistant in 1910 was Joseph F. Woods, previously stationed at Race Rock Lighthouse in Long Island Sound. The second assistant was William A. Baker of East Hampton, who had transferred to Montauk from Block Island in 1908.

On May 13, 1911, keeper Anderson's performance was evaluated and recorded in a Department of Commerce and Labor Efficiency Report. His scores were high, with a rating of 90 (out of a possible 100) for "Quantity of work" and 85 for "Interest manifested in work." The report described him as a "reliable man. A little apt to unexpected things but subordinate."[316]

In August 1911, the Department of Agriculture requested permission for J. A. Weber to visit the light station for the purpose of studying bird migration. Permission was granted, providing Weber did not interfere with lighthouse activity.[317]

A few months later in November 1911, Anderson wrote to the Third District Inspector's office concerning a problem he was having with one of his assistants:

As I reported to the office on October 28th, 1911 that the [assistant keeper]...installed a woman with a child as his housekeeper. On the 2nd of Nov. he took her from the station by order of the Inspector. Since then he has received a letter from the office that he could have a relative act as housekeeper but to day he brought the same woman here again, I have heard that he has told outsiders that it is his second cousin, but he told me the first time he brought her here that he did not know the woman, and this time he did not say a word to me about bring her here. The story goes that she has one of the worst reputations of a woman on this end of Long Island, and if such a person is to reside on this station my family refuses to stay with me, so I respectfully wish that this matter will be taken up for consideration, as he is contrary in everything that he will not listen to me. Further I wish to state that I have told him time and again to keep his quarters clean but it doesn't seem to matter to him.[318]

Possibly, Anderson exaggerated or misrepresented his assistant's situation, since in May 1912 he was transferred to Cedar Island Lighthouse near Sag Harbor where he had no assistants. Five years later he was transferred to the Princess Bay Light Station on Staten Island and from there to Watch Hill Lighthouse, Rhode Island in November 1922. His final transfer was to Block Island North Light in June 1923. He retired from the lighthouse service in January 1926 and died July 10, 1937 at age 77.

A mustached and dapper John Frederick Anderson (1859-1937) stood for a formal portrait during his tenure as head keeper of Montauk Point Lighthouse 1910-1912. (Montauk Point Lighthouse Museum)

John Ellsworth Miller (Keeper: 1912-1929)

John E. Miller, whose family was from East Hampton, was born in England on May 2, 1863. He married Mary Alice Ledwith (died June 17, 1930) on October 4, 1887. They had six children, including Jonathan A. (Jack) Miller,[319] who would later become an assistant keeper at Montauk Point Light.

John E. Miller was the son of former keeper Jonathan A. Miller. He worked as a Brooklyn police officer for 23-years before taking the position of head keeper of Montauk Point Light on May 16, 1912. During his time at the station, World War I broke out. A reference to the war was noted in the lighthouse journal on July 24, 1917: "Naval Reserve arrived."[320] (Additional information on the station during World War I can be found in chapter 3.)

Poet Charles Hanson Towne (1877-1949) visited Montauk Lighthouse in 1921 and wrote of Miller: "The present keeper has been there nine years, and his assistant told us that last winter, in a heavy storm, they were virtually cut off from the world for three months, and he and the keeper's young daughter trudged through drifts of snow to Promised Land, nine miles away, for groceries and other supplies, and had, as one can imagine, a hard time of it. This young assistant, Mr. Kierstead, had been slightly shell-shocked in the war, and he found the quiet life at the point soothing to his nerves."[321]

An interesting and somewhat unflattering look at Captain Miller, his family, and life at the lighthouse was portrayed in a lengthy letter sent by assistant keeper Phillips

Channell to his father Arthur in Rutland, Vermont on November 16, 1920:

I have four rooms on the ground floor of a two story house, and it's well made too. Hardwood floors, a new stove and I get my coal for free. I've six tons in the cellar. It's also piled full of four foot wood. I get my oil for my lamps free and two lamps furnished and things are not like they are made to day but solid, solid brass lamps brass dust pan good brooms mops soap and rags. My rent is free. I'm furnished all the paint I need.

I get $83.95 a month and can do pretty well on that I guess. Of course it's seven farmer miles over the bleakest country to a small fisherman's town...There isn't a tree with in a thousand miles I guess small hills all sand and covered with cranberry bushes that grow about a foot from the ground, some times higher. It's a regular no-mans-land the second with water, water every where.

There isn't any thing a person can hunt, there are rabbits, fox, coon, mink, muskrat but you can't see them to hunt, there are so many bushes. The old man traps them and lets them rot, too darn lazy to skin them. Of course there are fish and fish.

Let me tell you the wind does blow here when it gets started. We have plenty of fresh air here.

There is the Head Keeper and as first Asst, his son then I come in on the end. Father and son are not usually stationed together. But these two are. Any way it's the damdest family of the whole dam family.

We will begin with the old lady, she of course is Irish and she is at times, most times, off her noodle, she hits up the joy juice when she can get it, and if she gets her hands on it, the old man's out of the game and that starts things agoing. She really is about the most ignorant person I have ever had the pleasure to run across, she talks in spurts and gurgles and the brogue on top of it all. And her nose is so red she makes me think of Mrs. Squires.

The old man is a retired policeman and truly walks like one, he is cranky at times good natured once in a while and dam onary all the time. Every dog knows him for miles around and avoids him by at least half a mile. He has an automobile some one gave him which he can't drive, but likes to look at, two boats which he never uses, rods, guns, and every thing a man can think of. He had rather have them rot than sell or give them away.

[The son] by nature was intended to be a beach comber by trade. He weighs about two hundred pound and his eyes stick out about an inch he is so darn lazy his wife I guess always done his work for him, at least she says she has.

We stand watches as you may guess and I call him to relieve me, I never go up to his door intending to wake him up enough to come to the door with out having a block of wood. My shoes won't stand the jar.

His wife used to answer my racket and stand his watch rather than wake him up. She has had to stand him on his feet to wake him up and before he is fully awake he dreams he is in the bathroom and sort of discolors the ceiling for me.

...I've met all kinds of people and of all colors but I never run across such a mess of people that needed a wet nurse in my short young life.

The light and the lens revolve to the right with the sun and are run by a clock works under neath which is in turn run by a drum over which a weight and wire runs. The weight has a place to run in up and down the side of the tower. And requires winding and looking after every three hours. The lens are of French make as was the old clock works which were taken out last month and they worked on ball bearings while the new clock works and base revolve on a mercury float which they claim is more accurate. The lens are quite large being about four feet round. They are rib shape and made to reflect the light to the center of the lamp upon a more powerful lens.

We have two quite large kerosene oil vapor engines to compress air for two sirens for fog.[322]

An examination of some 1920s log entries during Miller's management of the lighthouse reveals consistency. Each day's entry began with the degree of wind velocity and its direction and concluded with whatever had to be cleaned, washed, scraped or painted that day. Mixed in were periodic inspections of the site. All in all, it was a terse and typical depiction of the monotony and redundancy of chores at a lighthouse. In addition, records were kept of the comings and goings of lighthouse staff members, as well as outside people—family and visitors or mechanics, carpenters, contractors, and laborers who performed necessary repairs.

Some of the assistant keepers who were transferred away from Montauk during Miller's time were: William Follett to Cedar Island Lighthouse on September 29, 1917; Phillips Channell to Stratford Shoal Lighthouse on April 13, 1921; Harry Bell to Robbins Reef Lighthouse off Staten Island, New York on October 29, 1923; James Kirkwood to Stratford Shoal Lighthouse on November 24, 1928.[323]

By World War I, the time required for a keeper to go off the site to take care of business matters was usually less than 24 hours—considerably less than the 3 to 8 days needed in Montauk Light's early years. An entry on November 12, 1916 indicated that a keeper left the lighthouse to pick up groceries and returned at 3:00 p.m. the following day. On November 25, 1916 a keeper left at 12:20 p.m. for a doctor's appointment and returned at 4:00 p.m. the following day.[324]

Regulations stipulated that the U.S. flag be flown daily, and this fact was mentioned in the logbook on special occasions. On February 12, 1914 the entry read: "flag flying from 8 am to sunset on account Lincoln birthday." On January 20, 1914 the death of Admiral George Dewey was acknowledged with an entry indicating the flag was flown at half mast from 8:00 a.m. until sundown.[325]

The passing of a dirigible over the lighthouse was an amazing and beautiful sight. On June 23, 1919 it was noted that the "British dirigible R34 passed this Station at 7 o'clock this AM about 2 miles North of Station on a westerly coarse from overseas (the first dirigible that crossed the Atlantic) time in crossing 4½ days 12 minutes or 108 hours and 12 minutes."[326]

Rough weather caused damage at the lighthouse at various times during keeper Miller's service. On December 8, 1917 he recorded: "at 7:45 this pm the staging and chimney was carried away by the SE gale and lodged against the NE side of main dwelling breaking one window on lower floor and tearing several shingles from the building, also damaged leader pipe and cellar doors."[327] Then on January 21, 1918: "James S. Van Riper, mason arrived… to rebuild chimney to dwelling which was blown down January 12, 1918 during the South East gale at 7:45 am."[328] On January 25, 1928: "during the heavy SE gales at 2:20 this am, the two chimneys on the west of the dwelling was blown down, also a section of the front porch roof carried away."[329]

Keeper Miller and his staff had some unusual visitors on January 24, 1925. Astronomers from the U.S. Naval Observatory in Washington, D.C. came to the lighthouse to observe a total eclipse of the sun.[330] Montauk Point was several degrees of longitude east of the Capital, allowing scientists to observe the eclipse for a longer period of time.

Lighthouse keeper John E. Miller (1863-1932) was photographed ca. 1925. Miller was head keeper at Montauk 1912-1929 and went through interesting times during the tumultuous Prohibition years. Note the insignia on his hat and lapels. (Montauk Library)

There was a distinctive change in handwriting in the logbook for January 23, 1926, where it noted that a keeper left the Station at 5:00 p.m. He did not return until April 16. The keeper was "sick in Southampton hospital."[331] It is possible it may have been Miller himself.

Life at the lighthouse during Prohibition was challenging for Miller. The east end of Long Island was a lively place during this period and the lightkeepers were suspected of collusion with "rum runners." In January 1925 concerns about possible illegal alliances touched off an investigation. It began with a telephone conversation between the Coast Guard and the officer in charge at the Ditch Plains Life Saving Station. The keeper at the lifesaving station claimed to have heard rumors that during a severe storm on January 20 two ships thought to be involved in the rum running trade had landed at Montauk Point. He immediately telephoned the lighthouse to speak with John E. Miller but was told Miller was unable to come to the phone. The officer left a message for Miller to call back, but Miller never did. The Ditch Plains crew checked the area around the point but found no sign of wreckage.

A letter from District Superintendent S. R. Sands of the Coast Guard, dated January 22, 1925 and marked "Confidential," was sent to the Superintendent of Lighthouses in Washington, D.C.:

> *On the 21st instant [Chief Boatswain's Mate] Warner was informed that a boat belonging to Joseph La Chelle of Montauk, N.Y. laden with approximately 500 cases of liquor stranded near the light on the 20th instant, that the boat was broken up but the cargo was saved...He again called the Lighthouse and was told by Keeper Miller's son that a boat came on the bar near there yesterday but had gotten off (This, he states, was impossi-*

ble owing to the heavy sea that was running). Warner then questioned Miller...and asked why he did not notify the station? His reply was 'that we are not supposed to notify you, we have no orders to that effect.' Mr. Warner advises that he visited Montauk Point this date, that the auxiliary craft IMPERIAL of New York of 19 25/100 tons...was found stranded and badly damaged about ½ mile N.N.W. of Montauk Point and about 1/8 mile west of Shagwong Reef, and that the LINNIE BELL...came ashore in the immediate vicinity and was a total wreck. He further states there is every evidence both the boats were laden with liquor and that he was so informed by a person in the vicinity whom he questioned, but who would not divulge his name.

It is inferred from reference (a) that at least two of the light-keepers assisted in unlading the craft and possibly storing the liquor...It is also apparent the members of their families were aware of the conditions that existed and would not give Mr. Warner the information he desired. It is also reported that Keeper Miller of the light has previously been connected with the illicit landing of cargoes of liquor in the immediate vicinity...In any event this office would request that, if possible, the personnel now at Montauk Light be transferred and that they be replaced by persons who will cooperate with the Coast Guard in enforcement of the law and in reporting wrecks where our crews may be of assistance.[332]

On February 10, 1925, W. F. Ockenfels, First Assistant Superintendent of the Third Lighthouse District, went to the Montauk Point Lighthouse to interview the keepers regarding their alleged failure to report the grounding of the two vessels. Head keeper John E. Miller was interviewed first. Excerpted portions of the transcript follow:

Q: Did you receive any telephone call on the morning of January 20th, particularly from the Coast Guard Station?
A: Yes, I did.

Q: Will you explain the nature of the call.
A: He rung up about two wrecks here.

Q: When did you first learn that there were wrecks on the beach or point?
A: I saw them that afternoon, after the message.

Q: Did you then call the Coast Guard and notify them of the fact?
A: No. The First Assistant explained to him. I just heard about them running ashore, first one boat then the second.

Q: What boats were they that came ashore on the 20th?
A: I think one was name Imperia and the other was named the Linnie Bell; that was one of those on the bar, a small boat.

Q: Both came ashore early in the morning of the 20th some time?
A: Yes sir.

Q: What time of day was it that you found they were there?
A: About the next afternoon. There was a regular blizzard the 20th. Could not see.

Q: And what assistance was rendered these two boats that came ashore?
A: I understood that Captain Joe Clark, he and his son-in-law, Hedges, helped the people off.

Q: Who was this man that you say assisted the boats?
A: His name is Captain Joe Clark, fisherman down on the beach near where the boats came ashore.

Q: You mean so far as you know that is all the assistance they received?
A: That is all I know of.

Q: Do you know what the business of these two boats was?
A: Well, I heard that they were in the liquor business.

Q: Was there any evidence of the liquor business present when you went down?
A: No sir.

Q: Who was it salvaged the cargo? The owner or residents of the Point?
A: The residents of Fort Pond. The owner did not look after it at all. I guess it was too rough for them.

Q: Did you salvage any of the cargo yourself?
A: No. I wish I had a chance. No. I did not have a chance.

Q: Did either of the assistants salvage any of the cargo that came ashore?
A: No sir. I am positive of that. [333]

Similar interviews were conducted with Second Assistant James Kirkwood and First Assistant John A. Miller. A follow-up interview was conducted with head keeper Miller, of which a portion follows:

Q: Do you know Keeper Miller of any occasions at any time when you or one of your assistants have rendered any assistance or done any work in connection with the handling of liquor?
A: No sir. Not to my recollection.

Q: Not to your recollection is your answer?
A: No, they didn't do it.

Q: You know they either did or did not?
A: Sure; no, I don't know of their ever having done any such work.

Q: Yourself included?
A: Yes.

Q: Never had anything to do with that traffic?
A: No sir."[334]

On February 14, 1925 a response from the U.S. Bureau of Lighthouses to the District Superintendent stated that as a result of the interviews the following conclusions were reached:

1- ...the Keepers at the Light Station had no knowledge of any boats running ashore or being in distress prior to the receipt of telephone information on January 21st

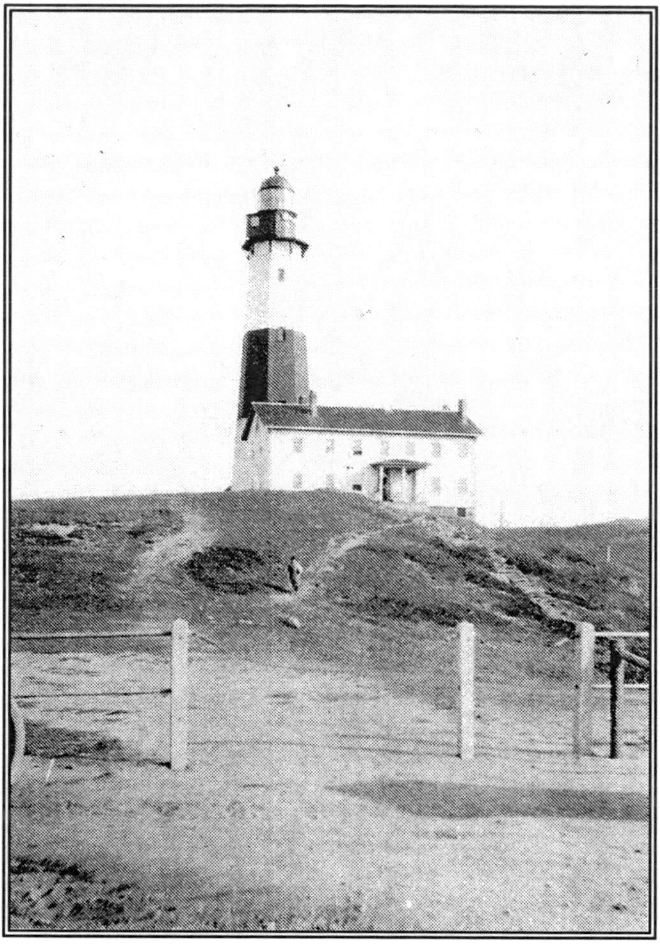

Montauk Point Lighthouse, shown in 1923, had a look of isolation after many of its outbuildings had been removed. (Peg Winski)

2- *...the claim of Keepers that they had no previous knowledge of the matter is apparently correct, they stating it was impossible to see any distance from the station on account of heavy snow or blizzard, which is corroborated by the station records for January 20th, which state there was snow, and fog signal in operation from 7 A.M. to 7 P.M.*

3- *...all three Keepers were on the station on January 20th, and did not visit the boats ashore until January 21st after receiving information from the Coast Guard Station, the Keeper and First Assistant having gone down on the 21st and the Second Assistant two days later, to see the wrecks on the beach, at which time there was nothing but the hulls of the boats and some empty liquor cases which we also saw on the beach*

4- *All three keepers deny, and there was no evidence or information obtained to show that any of the Keepers assisted in handling liquor from the boats ashore*

5- *...Keeper Miller...did not show a proper spirit of cooperation, or even common courtesy in failing to call up the Coast Guard Station after being requested to do so.*

It was also concluded that the two boats referred to were not visible from the station (except from the tower) because of the hilly terrain between the lighthouse property and the beach area. It was recommended that keeper Miller "be cautioned to exercise greater care and use better judgment in responding to telephone calls from the Coast Guard

Station".[335] An additional letter from the Lighthouse Service on February 19 reiterated its position on the matter and stated it would "closely observe this station and the Keepers in the future for any evidence of collusion with the liquor traffic or intentional violation of the regulations of this service".[336] And finally on March 3, 1925, in a letter from George R Putnam, Commissioner of the Bureau of Lighthouses, it was stated that "…it does not appear that the lighthouse keepers are implicated."[337]

In the process of developing land adjacent to the lighthouse for Montauk Point State Park, Long Island State Park Commission President Robert Moses wrote directly to George R Putnam about a problem regarding lighthouse practices. His June 14, 1926 letter stated: "It has come to our attention that the lighthouse employees are in the habit of dumping their garbage and other refuse in a manner which we consider to be a public nuisance. This garbage dump is offensive and harbors a large colony of rats."[338]

Keeper Miller responded on June 24 in defense of a longtime lighthouse practice: "…it has been the custom here for years to throw what small amount of garbage we have over the bank on to the beach which is lighthouse property and as a rule the high tide generally washes it out to sea. I cannot see where there is any basis for this complaint as this is the first time any attention has ever been called to that effect."[339] Miller's defense though true, brought to the Bureau's attention an out-of-date, unhealthy practice. On July 6, 1926 the Bureau responded to Robert Moses saying the lighthouse keeper had been advised to come up with a more effective means of disposing of garbage.[340]

Keeper Miller gave a guided tour and interview to a reporter for the *East Hampton Star* in 1927. He claimed that the view from the lighthouse was so spectacular that "at night you can see the lights of Block Island, Watch Hill, Stonington, Race Rock, Gull Island, New London, and a few others. All told there are eleven lights within sight of this one." On clear nights, he claimed the light was visible for 25-miles but government inspectors had seen the light as far as 35-miles away.

The light was 136,000-candlepower at the time and burned 2-gallons of kerosene each night. Miller said, "when my father [Captain Jonathan A. Miller] was here the old light used to burn five gallons a night." He also noted that each year the tower was whitewashed and the daymark received a fresh coat of metallic paint, due to the severe winds and the effects of ice on the bricks.

When Miller showed his guests the foghorn apparatus, they were amazed: "Into a spick and span engine room with two engines—one in case of emergency—we were led. All this just to blow a fog siren, we wondered! This was the greatest surprise of all. Engines, compressors, intricate apparatus; and all for the single job of blowing a fog horn! After a highly technical explanation by the captain that was wasted on this writer we learned that all this machinery went into the blowing of a fog horn with a three-second blast; a silence of three seconds, followed by another three second blast, and then an interval of thirty-one seconds. This schedule would then be repeated, because just as every lighthouse has its identity mark with its periodic light flashes, it is known to mariners by its timed fog signal."

Captain Miller related the story of the total wreck of the *Madonna V*, a rum runner that ran aground 5-miles west of the lighthouse in 1924. Locals made quick work of recovering the contents of the vessel. A few days later the ship's flag washed ashore near the lighthouse and Miller kept it "as a souvenir of a most memorable work."[341]

John E. Miller died in Springs on February 28, 1932 at

age 69 and was buried in Calvary Cemetery in Queens, New York.

Thomas Buckridge (Keeper: 1930-1943)

Thomas Buckridge, born in 1874, took over as keeper at Montauk Point Light on January 1, 1930, having been transferred from the Race Rock Light off Fisher's Island. He was the last civilian keeper at the lighthouse, replaced by Coast Guard personnel in 1943.

His father, John Nind Buckridge, fought in the Civil War and lost a leg in battle, but afterwards served over 52-years at lighthouses. No doubt his son grew to love the service and chose it based on his father's experience.

Thomas Buckridge began his service at Execution Rocks Light in western Long Island Sound and then transferred to Race Rock Light. Both sentinels sat on rock foundations in open water. Transferring to Montauk Point Light must have seemed like coming ashore from a ship. Buckridge's second assistant, Jack Miller, had quite a history at the lighthouse, with both his father and grandfather being past keepers.

Of life at the lighthouse, Mrs. Buckridge said, "It isn't so lonely. We have many friends at the village and there are church and other affairs. Then the people who come here to see the light make things interesting."[342] Interesting indeed, since some visitors caused problems by grabbing "souvenirs," such as shingles right off the keeper's dwelling. Nevertheless, keeper Buckridge greeted everyone with a friendly smile.

Generally speaking, lighthouse keepers were diligent in their efforts to maintain an organized and tidy station, but sometimes there were problems. An inspection of the keepers at Montauk Point on June 12, 1931 revealed that while the overall condition of the station showed improvements under keeper Buckridge, the "Attic and basement of barn [were] in general disorder. All kinds of stuff said to belong to 1st Asst. Miller in heaps and piles all thrown together." The report indicated that Buckridge's assistant keepers were "slow workers." This was reflected in the efficiency grades: Buckridge 95%, 2nd asst. George Warrington 80%, and 1st assistant Jonathan (Jack) Miller 75%.[343] According to Buckridge's daughter, Margaret Buckridge Bock (born 1919), 41-year-old assistant keeper Miller, who was from nearby Springs, never accepted the fact that he was not appointed head keeper at Montauk and "was often antagonistic toward my father and did not make life easy for him."[344] This may help explain Miller's lack of orderliness.

Second assistant keeper Warrington's son, George Washington Warrington III, gave a sense of the strictness of the inspections when he wrote in the 1930s: "Keep your fingers off the white paint—the Inspector is coming!" He recalled in a 1990 interview that learning to recognize when conditions were right to activate the fog signal and also how to sleep when the foghorns were blaring were challenges.[345]

In 1996 Bock recalled the wedding of her sister Elizabeth (1913-2004) at the lighthouse on May 15, 1938 and also how strict their father was about operating the light station: "It was a small wedding. No champagne or anything like that. Not in my father's lighthouse. He never allowed drinking of any sort…The wedding took place in our living room which is now a museum."[346]

A briny scene at Montauk Point Lighthouse, taken from Turtle Cove in July 1934, showed swimmers on the beach and the jutting point behind them. (Photo by R.C. Smith, U.S. Coast Guard Archives)

Bock described various aspects of life at the lighthouse in the 1930s when she was a teenager:

The keepers worked in 12-hour shifts- 12 on and 24 off, plus every morning except Sunday they worked from 8 am to noon doing maintenance work. The tower was whitewashed every year and the maroon identification strip was painted every two to three years. These jobs were done with scaffolding that no one really enjoyed.

There was always painting to do, engines to clean and oil, visitors to take up the tower and clean up after, lawn to mow, etc. The tower was open every day except Sunday from 10-12 and 1-3. It was the responsibility of the keeper on duty to walk up and down the stairs with each group of visitors. Often in the summer, because of the thousands of visitors, one keeper would remain at the foot of the tower letting in the visitors at intervals and another keeper would stay up in the lantern [a practice carried on by tour guides at the museum today]...Sometimes, the visitors were fun and broke the monotony of our semi-isolation. At other times they were "pains in the neck". Some of them try to rip shingles off the house for souvenirs.

Before the light was automated, it took about ½ hour to light it. It had a mantle similar to that of a Coleman lantern which had to be handled gently to prevent it from breaking. Then, the weights had to be wound to make the light revolve. The lenses were carefully cleaned to make sure they were free of dust and fingerprints. The visitors were not allowed to touch the lenses, but someone always managed to when the keeper was talking to someone else.

There was...a red warning light at the level of the walk-around. When ships could see this, they knew they were in danger of going ashore at Shagwong Reef.

Nobody has any conception of fog unless they have lived at the Montauk Lighthouse. Sometimes, the fog engines would run steadily for a week to ten days. All the pictures on our walls would be crooked. When the horns finally stopped, it would feel as though the world had suddenly come to an end.

There were a few shipwrecks while we were at Montauk, but the most exciting one was the Comanche which came ashore right at the point with a group of party fishermen. Fortunately, no lives were lost. We made coffee and sandwiches for them, and some of them came into the house to "dry out".

In the spring, the migrating birds, attracted by the light, would crash against the tower to their deaths. One year I buried over 100 of these birds.

Garbage collection? Unheard of! The papers were burned and the garbage can was thrown over the bank. In fifteen minutes or less it was all gone-- disposed of by the scavenger gulls.

The new highway (Montauk Point State Parkway) was built while we were living in the lighthouse. A favorite walk was to go as far as the Third House on the new road and return on the old road-- about six miles. No wonder I was skinny then. We still used the old road sometimes, especially to treat our guests to the "thank you ma'ams", an inexpensive roller coaster type ride created by the rolling hills and the correct touch to the car accelerator.

In the 1930's, the WPA put in a cement road at the lighthouse. Dad used to say that the men spent more time leaning on their shovels than digging, but it was a big improvement.[347]

Two ship disasters were noteworthy during the Buckridge years at Montauk. The first occurred on July 14, 1935 when the 189-foot motor tanker *Raritan Sun* struck rocks between the Point and Ditch Plains. Its cargo of petroleum seeped out through a gaping hole. All crewmen on board were rescued, ten in all. For a time there was concern that the oil would have a disastrous effect on area fishing that season, but it soon cleared away.[348] The incident was reported by keeper Buckridge, indicating appropriate actions taken by the lighthouse crew: "The Tanker RARITAN SUN is ashore about three miles southwest of station. She grounded about 4:30 pm in thick fog, which came in with southerly wind. Second Assistant Warrington on watch. He had the fog signal going about 4:10 pm, as soon as we could see any indication of fog from here...There is considerable complaint that the sirens cannot be heard to the southwest when there is any wind at all from that direction."[349] Six days later the vessel was re-floated without incident. The problem with the fog signal was addressed by the Bureau of Lighthouses.

The fishing smack *Mary P. Mosquito* was wrecked at Montauk on November 26, 1936 with thirteen men and a dog, all rescued by the Coast Guard.[350]

With the onset of war in Europe in 1939, visits by the Coast Guard beach pounders from the Ditch Plains station increased. According to Margaret Buckridge Bock, they walked to the lighthouse and later worked four-hour shifts there as lookouts. When the United States entered the war, the lighthouse property was taken over by the Coast Guard, with Mrs. Buckridge moving for a time to Amagansett and then to Essex, Connecticut. Keeper Buckridge continued as a civilian keeper at Montauk until the spring of 1943. He was transferred to the Saybrook Breakwater Light at the entrance to the Connecticut River, where he retired in 1944.[351] He died in August 1955 at the age of 81.

* * * * * * *

By the late twentieth century, the responsibilities of

lighthouse keepers had diminished with modernization and automation and were mostly unnoticed by the public. Today they seem archaic in comparison with high-tech navigational equipment and methods. Between the 1960s and 1990s, lighthouses rapidly lost their keepers as the sentinels were equipped to operate self-sufficiently. Only in recent years has the public realized what a colorful and unique occupation lightkeeping was and how critical to the lighthouse milieu the keepers were—maintaining the stations in apple pie order and being on hand to help a mariner in distress or to greet visitors.

Historian William S. Pelletreau acknowledged with eloquence this time-honored profession: "The soldier and the statesman protect the national honor and the person and property of the citizen, and their acts are performed in the gaze of the world. But the quiet man who trims and lights the shore and harbor lights, and watches them through the long night watches lest they fade out and bring death to sleeping voyagers upon the great waters, stands his vigil for all humanity, asking no questions as to the nationality or purpose of him who he directs to safety."[352]

CHAPTER 7
Erosion at Montauk Point

Other than weather and neglect, erosion is the arch enemy of many lighthouses.* Precipitated by the actions of wind and water, especially during storms, erosion has undermined and toppled many lighthouses. Slowing or preventing its effects was a large concern of the U.S. Lighthouse Establishment and continues to challenge lighthouse preservationists today. Many lighthouses built in the eighteenth and nineteenth centuries at an assumed safe distance from the sea now stand perilously close to the waves. Their builders were unaware of the problems erosion would cause or thought the towers would not stand long enough to suffer the consequences. Sturdy Montauk Point Light has defied the odds, but not without travail.

An ominous warning of the erosion problem at Montauk Point was presented as early as November 19, 1792 by surveyor Ezra L'Hommedieu, (see Chapter 1) who chose to set the lighthouse nearly 300-feet inland: "…as the Bank is washed by the sea in storms, we suppose it best to set the Building at this distance."[353]

Other reports followed. About 1820, W. W. Mather, a geologist from Ohio, wrote to the State Legislature:

> *The coast of Long Island on the south side, from Montauk Point to Napeague Beach, a distance of three miles, is constantly washing away by the action of the heavy surf beyond the base of the cliffs, protected only by narrow shingle beaches of a few yards or rods in width. The pebbles and bowlders of the beaches serve as a partial protection to the cliffs during ordinary tides in calm weather; but even then, by the action of the surf as it tumbles upon the shore, they are continually grinding into sand and finer materials, and swept far away by the tidal currents. During storms and high tides the surf breaks directly against the base of the cliffs; and as they are formed only of loose materials, as sand and clay, with a substratum of bowlders, pebbles, gravel, and loam, we can easily appreciate the destructive agency of the heavy waves, rolling in unbroken from the broad Atlantic. The road from Napeague Beach to Montauk Point, which originally was some distance from the shore, has disappeared in several places by the falling of the cliffs; thus is the ocean ever encroaching on the land.*[354]

David Gardiner, writing about East Hampton, remarked in 1840: "During the violent storm of September 1812, and that of a subsequent period, every considerable inroad was made upon the cliff, and by the ordinary effects of the tides and rain, it is gradually wearing away…The road which was originally some distance from the edge of the cliffs, has already disappeared in many places from the inroads of the sea, and stumps of trees are found on the north side below low water mark."[355]

Charles Parsons of Brooklyn, New York noted in 1871: "The sea is silently eating its way toward the tower, and this will soon compel a removal to the higher ground west."[356]

Long Island historian Richard M. Bayles noted the erosion problem in 1873: "The ceaseless action of the surf upon this point, directly exposed as it is to the angry beating of the Atlantic, is slowly but surely wearing it away. It has been estimated that altogether about two acres of the surface of this peninsula is by this means torn down and washed away every year."[357]

In his *Recollections of Curious Characters and Pleasant Places*, written in 1881, Charles Lanman noted: "It seems to me that the lighthouse itself is not on a secure foundation, and it may have to be rebuilt in twenty or thirty years."[358]

A group of hearty souls from Brooklyn hiked to Montauk Point in 1889. The lightkeeper, James G. Scott, informed them that the light station suffered the:

> *...ravages of the ocean on our island, which kept battering against the place and tearing away earth and stones. It carries the former out and the rocks, becoming imbedded in the sand, remain there. This depredution has been going on for an endless time-- so long, in fact, that some people remember when the easterly point was over half a mile further out than it is as present. And in proof of this there is only about six feet of water for over one mile from the present point. The ocean's present inroad is about one foot a year, and at this rate it will swallow up enough of our land to necessitate the removal of the lighthouse in about twenty years, so near it is to that building at present.*[359]

Author Martha Bockee Flint described Montauk Point in 1896 as "...the defiant finger stretched out to sea...still constantly yielding to the fierce surf which breaks at the base of its jagged cliffs."[360]

This view of Montauk Point Light Station in 1878 showed the mounded outline that gave Turtle Hill its name. (Montauk Point Lighthouse Museum)

Early in 1928, the effects of erosion at Montauk Lighthouse were documented in a letter from Gilbert H. Edwards of Montauk to Congressman Robert L. Bacon. Though exaggerated, it brought the problem to the attention of the government. Edwards stated: "This lighthouse is slowly but surely being undermined by the Atlantic and is said to have stood two hundred feet from the edge of the bank in less than fifty years past. But at the present time it is less than twenty feet from the edge of the bank which…is almost perpendicular."[361]

In response, a survey was conducted at Montauk Point by Associate Lighthouse Engineer, O. C. Luther. Correspondence from the Bureau of Lighthouses in March 1928 described recent measurements and observations at the Point: "The distance from the tower to edge of bank is 175 feet; the distance from signal house to edge of bank is 125 feet…The erosion of bank is caused by heavy rains and not by the Atlantic Ocean."[362]

O.C. Luther's 1928 assessment of the rate of loss fell short: "The edge of bank is moving in at the rate of six inches per year…The 175 feet of land between tower and edge of bank will afford ample protection for same for the next 200 years." Montauk Point as we know it today (the actual point of the Point) is some 60-feet from the base of the tower.[363]

Edwards' information may have exaggerated the problem, but Luther's underestimated it!

An equally interesting survey published in the *East Hampton Star* in the 1920s concluded there had been significant erosion at Montauk Point and other nearby locations for nearly 300-years, but the rate of erosion was considered to be "so gradual as to be negligible and is not apparent in any given generation".[364]

An *East Hampton Star* article in 1933 noted: "Ten feet of rock and sand have disappeared into the sea from Montauk cliffs this season. Mr. Buckridge [keeper] has seen it break off the point, little by little, as lashing seas attacked the shore. Every year the point grows smaller…but people are not yet thinking seriously of moving the lighthouse back."[365]

In a 1938 article written for the *East Hampton Star* by renowned East Hampton historian Jeannette E. Rattray, the tower was "…less than 140 feet from the edge of the sheer cliff…the sea has eaten away the bank through the years. People who know something about such things claim that the light will last only about fifty years longer; then something will probably be put in the water to take its place".[366]

In an attempt to prevent erosion of the fragile bluff from human intrusion, a fence was built in the early twentieth century to keep visitors off the cliffs. However, it was extensively destroyed in 1941 and subsequently relocated nearer the lighthouse.

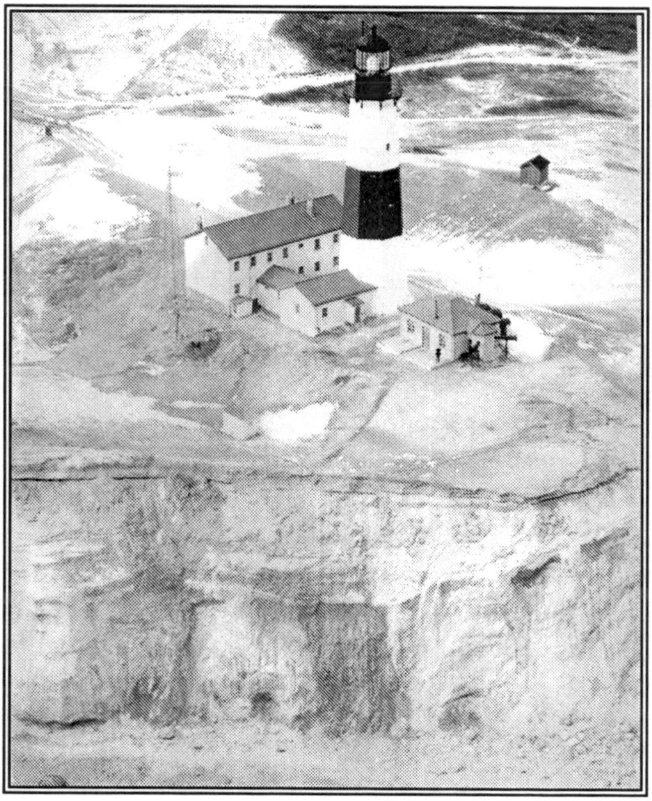

By 1941, when this Coast Guard photo was taken of Montauk Point Lighthouse, it was much nearer to the edge of the bluff than when it was constructed in 1796. (U.S. Coast Guard Archives)

A 12-foot bite was taken off the bluff during a storm on November 22, 1944. At this point, the lighthouse stood approximately 105-feet from the edge of the bluff.

When first illuminated in April 1797, and considering the rate of erosion at the time (more than a foot per year), the lighthouse was predicted to stand for 200-years. By 1940 it had become apparent that in less than a century the bluff would erode and undermine the lighthouse. The tower's future was in jeopardy and something had to be done soon to halt the effects of the erosion. The large foghorns that stood on the ground at the cliff's edge compounded the problem, for when they sounded the resulting vibrations and concussion caused sections of the bluff to crumble.

Around 1945-1946 the Army Corp of Engineers took the first step when they installed a 700-foot-long stone revetment along the beach below the cliffs. The horns were relocated farther inland next to the fire tower. However, the early 1950s brought several severe storms and hurricanes that caused waves to wash over the seawall and eventually collapse it.

I.M. Lewis, Chief Boatswain's Mate at the lighthouse in 1958, commented: "...the light is not going to fall into the ocean next week...But we are watching the steady erosion, keeping track of it, and it's going to cost the Government an awful lot of money one of these days if the erosion doesn't stop." At this time, for safety reasons, the public was no longer permitted on lighthouse property.[367]

The ensuing years were filled with apathy. Advances in technology began replacing lighthouses in many locations and it was assumed the same fate awaited Montauk Light.

The stone revetment (above), completed by the Army Corps of Engineers to control erosion, was visible along the beach in this image, ca. 1946. Also apparent was the scouring effect of waves. Note the army barracks at far left, a remnant of the military's presence during WW II.

At left, the steady progression of erosion due to numerous storms left its mark on Montauk. Severe weather also had begun to break down the stone revetment when this image was taken in the early 1950s. (Greg Donohue Photos)

In October 1967 the Coast Guard announced that the lighthouse would be replaced with an automated beacon by 1972 and that surveyors were inspecting various sites in the vicinity for the new light. The plan was for a steel tower topped by a self-sufficient light fixture. In addition, the fog signal was slated to be transferred to the Montauk Coast Guard Station at Star Island in Lake Montauk. It was emphasized that the old tower would be preserved as an historic monument.[368]

A spokesperson for the Coast Guard stated that it was a waste of taxpayer's money to save the lighthouse and that if the tower was to be preserved funding should come from a preservationist group or historical society. However, action by the Coast Guard was taken to fight the erosion problem, as noted in a Record of Inspection for January 20, 1967: "More fill is being obtained from Tufano's Construction Co. to be placed on bluff."[369]

At this time the erosion problem at the Montauk Point Lighthouse came to the attention of the public. Dan Rattiner, editor of two east end publications, the *Montauk Pioneer* and *Dan's Papers,* brought the plight of the Montauk Lighthouse to the public in graphic fashion when he displayed a photo of the old Shinnecock Lighthouse falling to the ground after it had been destroyed by the Coast Guard in December 1948.

He created a contest to come up with ways for saving the Montauk Lighthouse and staged a "Montauk Point Lighthouse Light In" in August 1967. Some 1,500 people showed up in support of saving the venerable old tower, and a preservation movement was born. By the summer of 1970 the Coast Guard completely reversed its plans to replace the lighthouse with a steel tower and instead looked into ways to halt the erosion. Public outcry surely played a role in the decision.

The Coast Guard further acknowledged that "erosion is the greatest problem here and the steps to control it will have to be monitored carefully."[370]

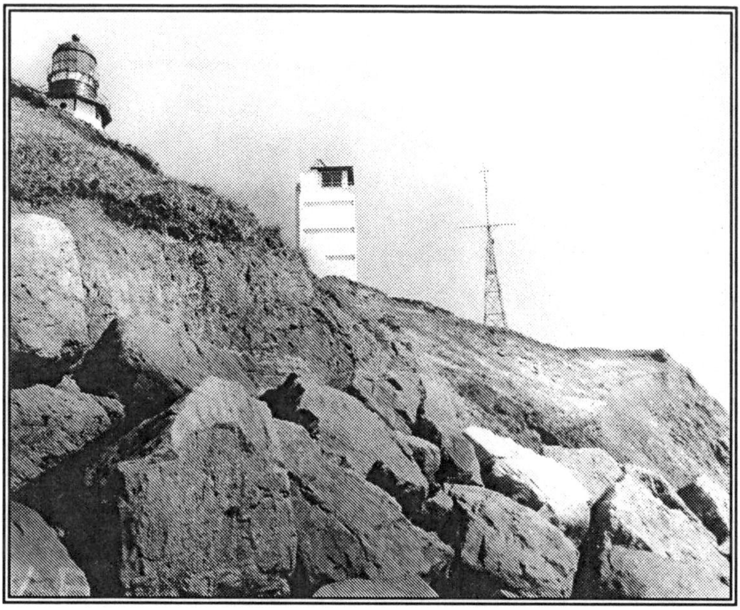

The top of Montauk Point Lighthouse and the fire control tower loomed over the bluff at the Point on May 19, 1958. The stone revetment installed by the Army Corps of Engineers appeared in the foreground. (Montauk Library)

Beginning in 1968, references to the erosion problem began to appear regularly in Coast Guard inspection forms. It was noted on November 15, 1968: "Visited unit following storm of 12 November. Damage to structures minor. Erosion at base of cliff exceeds 10' in some areas. Pictures of new erosion taken this date."[371]

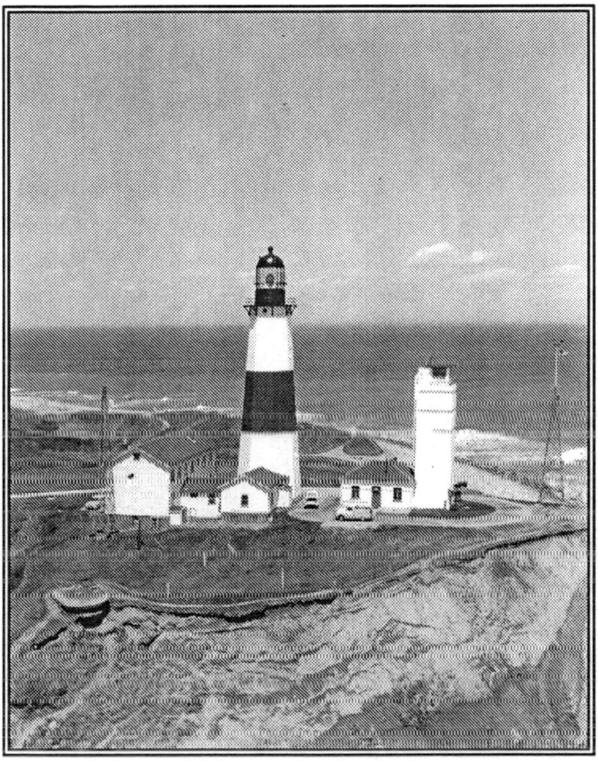

Montauk Point Light Station, pictured in 1961, showed increased erosion around the WW II bunker at left. The steel weather tower sat perilously close to the bluff's edge. (U.S. Coast Guard Archives)

Giorgina Reid's "Reed Trench Terracing"

In 1969, New York City resident Giorgina Reid (1908-2001) heard about the erosion situation at Montauk Point Lighthouse and immediately contacted Dan Rattiner. Her communication marked a turning point in the fledgling effort to save the lighthouse.

In 1969, a landslide that damaged the stone revetment and severely exposed WW II bunker on the cliff below lighthouse, was visible. This was about the time Giorgina Reid approached the Coast Guard with her reed trench terracing plan to save the lighthouse from the effects of erosion. (National Archives)

Giorgina Reid was a textile designer and professional photographer, not an erosion control expert. But she personally experienced coastal erosion after she and her husband, Donald Reid, purchased a two-bedroom cottage about 50-feet from the edge of the cliffs overlooking Long Island Sound in Rocky Point, Long Island. Neighbors warned the Reids to prepare for damage to the cliffs from coastal storms. The couple saw the effects of erosion firsthand when a nor'easter struck the area on March 6-8, 1962, carrying away about 18-feet of shoreline between their home and the sea.

The Reids were at their Jackson Heights apartment during the three-day storm. When the weather subsided, they headed to Rocky Point and found their home damaged, with much debris scattered over the beach. Donald Reid thought of selling the property while there was still property to sell, but his wife did not want to lose their dream house. As the cleanup began, Giorgina Reid noticed pieces of lumber and reeds along the beach with sand piled up behind them. The rubble gave Reid a simple but effective idea for controlling bluff erosion.

Gathering the debris, Reid began to work on the bluff below her property, terracing it by stuffing reeds behind the lumber and packing them tight with sand. Support stakes held the lumber in place, and the sand allowed growth of vegetation. The reeds prevented the sand from leaching out and the hollow stems provided organic matter and water retention for plantings. The bluff was stabilized so that land was not carried away as heavy rains washed down each terrace level.

When the 100-foot embankment was complete, another nor'easter blew in in June 1963 and dumped about 4-inches of rain in only 8-hours. The bluff remained intact. Giorgina Reid patented her "Reed Trench Terracing" method and in

1969 wrote a how-to guide on erosion control called *How to Hold up a Bank*. Her success in Rocky Point gave her credibility when she approached the Coast Guard that same year about working on the eroded bluffs around the Montauk Point Lighthouse. Coast Guard personnel were reluctant, however. They wondered how a 61-year-old woman with no engineering experience or funding could succeed in saving the Montauk Lighthouse when other efforts had failed.

Above, a smiling Giorgina Reid paused from her work on the bluffs at Montauk Point to admire the view. (Montauk Point Lighthouse Museum)

Top—A ca.1972 photo by Peter Beard showed the terracing work (center and right) begun by Giorgina Reid in 1970. The unworked bluff at left showed signs of severe erosion. Portions of the old revetment were visible at lower left.(Greg Donohue)

Bottom—By 1977, terracing work was well underway on the eastern bluff of the light station. A fence along the top of the bluff prevented residents and visitors from falling over the edge. (U.S. Coast Guard Archives)

This page—The steep angle of the southwest bluff face forced a modification and upgrade of the terracing method. The bluff had to be sculpted by hand to create the appropriate slope angle for terracing. Each level of terracing was lined with acrylic filter cloth that prevented loss of silt and soil. Treated lumber was held in place by 6-foot heavy gauge metal posts drilled into the earth. (Greg Donohue Photos)

The lighthouse had been declared a National Historic Landmark on July 7, 1969 and the Coast Guard, thinking they had nothing to lose, granted Reid permission to start a pilot erosion control project funded by local donations. A letter to Reid from Captain G. H. Weller of the U.S. Coast Guard, dated October 7, 1969, included several cautions, including a warning about the danger of working on the cliffs: "[the] soil is so loose in many parts that it can give way under the weight of a person." Permission to work on the property could not "...be assigned to anyone else and may not involve any expense to the Coast Guard." The government reserved the right to revoke this arrangement at any time and for any reason. Giorgina Reid signed the letter on October 11, 1969 and prepared to begin work.[372]

The Montauk Point Erosion Control Project officially was launched on April 22, 1970—also the first Earth Day celebration—when Reid began to work on the bluff around the lighthouse. With tremendous dedication in the face of adversity, she would continue to do so for the next sixteen years. Her husband brought her to Montauk as often as possible so she could work with volunteers. Sometimes she worked alone, trying to stabilize the bluff as quickly as possible. By the end of the first summer, Coast Guard engineers from Governor's Island were so impressed they voted unanimously to continue support for the project. However, it was understood that terracing alone was not the total solution. Nature soon confirmed the fact. Following a heavy and damaging storm in February 1972, the Coast Guard installed a gabion wall to act as a protective foundation at sea level for the terracing above it.[373]

While the job of carving a stable slope angle into the cliffs was difficult enough, it was equally arduous working with insufficient funding. Reid succeeded in stabilizing the eastern bluff of Turtle Hill by 1985, though she broke a leg in the process. In a 1973 interview she described her method as based on gravity, common sense, and the laws of God. It was, she added, "absolutely infallible."[374]

As time passed the Coast Guard grew more interested in the erosion project, noting in one report: "Erosion is the greatest problem here and the steps to control it will have to be monitored carefully."[375] In September 1971, as part of an inspection, the officer in charge of the station was instructed to "fertilize and water new plants and maintain better control over the project to insure a better crop of plants."[376] Giorgina Reid's relationship with the Coast Guard warmed during these years. On July 24, 1972 she met with Coast Guard members and "expressed her satisfaction with the construction to date as well as the cooperation she has been receiving."[377]

A 1984 *Newsday* article described Giorgina Reid as "…this mite of a woman, with rimless glasses and short brown hair, with a personality on the cusp of charming and crusty…in her khaki slacks and sensible shoes, once, twice, three times a week on the steep 80-foot bluff on which the lighthouse stands. On her hands and knees, for five or six hours a day, she has graded the steep bluff into terraces; supported the terraces with upended, one-by-fours; dug deep trenches alongside the boards; filled the trenches with hollow reeds and covered it all with sand."[378]

As of 1984, Reid had accomplished all the work at her own expense—about $35,000 to $40,000—because she was unable to obtain funding from federal, state or local authorities. Even finding a work force was a struggle. At the start of the project in 1970 Reid had seven volunteers, some well-meaning but most ineffective. "We asked them all to bring sacks of reeds" she said. "They didn't know what reeds were so they brought straw instead. Useless. And the girls came because they thought they'd meet guys." Other helpers over the years were little better, in Reid's opinion:

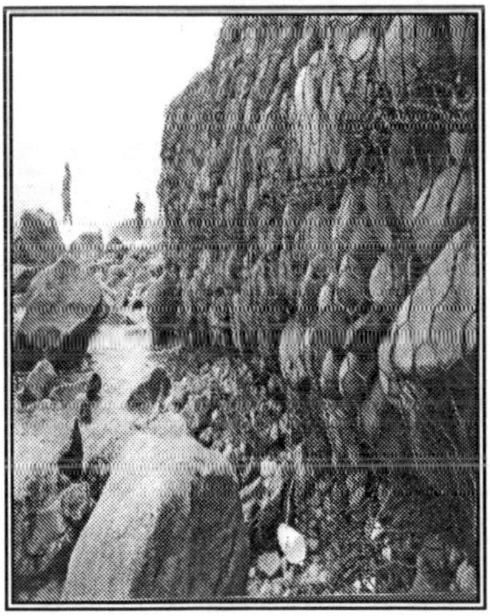

Top—Terrace plantings consisted of Cape American beach grass, hard fescue, and clover-self-sustaining vegetation that protected the bluff face by controlling runoff and holding soil in place.

Left—A Coast Guard gabion wall built in the 1970s provided good toe protection until the powerful "Perfect Storm" of October 1991 tore it apart. (Greg Donohue Images)

"They do it wrong. I have loads of pictures of people doing it wrong." Proof lay in a pile of 1' x 3's—the wrong size for the project—discarded at the base of the cliff.[379]

It was said that when Giorgina Reid rode into Montauk

and saw young people loitering along the street she pulled over and shouted that she had work for them to do at the lighthouse. A former tour guide at the lighthouse, Vinnie Grimes, who operated a service station in the village, always provided free fuel for Reid when she came to town.

As the erosion control effort continued, the media became more and more interested in Montauk Point and Giorgina Reid. The project grew into something more than just a fight against nature. In 1985 Montauk Light's keeper, Petty Officer W. Gene Hughes, underscored the importance of halting the erosion when he told the *New York Times*: "Montauk Point is no longer a point. It's more of a stub."[380] But Reid's work was hampered by a "lack of financing and poor communication between the two governments with jurisdiction over Montauk Point."[381] The lighthouse property was federally owned, with the land directly around it and on the eastern bluff maintained by the Coast Guard. The north and south bluffs and land to the west were under the jurisdiction of the Office of Parks, Recreation, and Historical Preservation for the State of New York. Reid believed: "Geographically, Montauk Point is a unit. It should be stabilized as such."

Although the Coast Guard assisted Reid in her efforts, little support came from the Long Island State Park Commission. According to the commission's regional director, John Sheridan, combating the erosion problem was "not one of our priorities," adding that the commission didn't "have the appropriations to fix the bluff, nor have we requested it." He further stated that there were more important projects to address, among them improvements at Jones Beach State Park and Bethpage State Park.

The major concern at the time was the south bluff. Its edge was some 35-feet from the border with federal land and about 100-feet from the tower. Giorgina Reid felt: "The continuing erosion on state property threatens the finished work on Coast Guard property." She continued to push for funds to terrace the south bluff, an effort she estimated would cost $50,000 through the Montauk Point Erosion Control Project.[382]

Keeping the public off the bluffs was helpful, according to Petty Officer Hughes. His solution to the erosion problem reflected his frustration with the public: "Put a fence up across Montauk Highway on the east end of town and don't let anyone in here for 50 years."[383]

In the midst of ongoing work and the turmoil over raising funds, around 1983 the Coast Guard entertained the possibility of moving the light inland—a complex and costly procedure. But the expense, coupled with talk of automating the light, quickly squelched the idea.[384]

The southwest bluff face proved difficult to terrace due to its near vertical slope. To meet this challenge, Giorgina Reid sculpted the bluff face by hand in order to create the proper slope angle for terracing. Her method of terracing, while effective on portions of the bluff that afforded gentler slopes, were modified and upgraded on steep slopes to ensure a better chance for success. A combination of self-sustaining plantings, including Cape American beach grass, hard fescue, and clover, were used. They effectively controlled runoff and stabilized the soil.[385]

For her dedicated work, Giorgina Reid was honored at the Montauk Point Lighthouse on September 12, 1986. She was presented with a proclamation and a letter of commendation signed by President Ronald Reagan in recognition of her efforts to control the erosion at Montauk Point. (See Chapter 10 for more information.) She retired in 1987 and died in 2001 at age 92.

Erosion Efforts Since 1987

In 1987, following automation of the lighthouse, the Coast Guard leased the keeper's dwelling to the Montauk Historical Society whose members established a museum in the building. With the light station now a public museum, it was vitally important to complete the erosion control project. An awareness and funding campaign was begun. Soon, federal and state funds were made available, as well as donations from the private sector and money raised from public concerts. Since 1990, the combined efforts of the Coast Guard, the Army Corps of Engineers, the Long Island Office of Parks, Recreation and Historic Preservation, the NY State Department of Environmental Conservation, and the Montauk Historical Society have succeeded in stabilizing the bluffs around the Montauk Point Light Station. Support was welcomed from any source, including a 1989 advertisement in *Newsday* that stated: "We'll Donate $3 to the 'Save the Montauk Lighthouse Fund' When You Order Home Delivery of Newsday."

By 1989 the lighthouse reportedly was approximately 75-feet from the edge of the bluff at its closest point. According to an article in *Newsday* in February 1989, "the bluffs 120-feet south of the lighthouse are falling into the sea at a rate of at least a foot a year...and, in some places, considerably quicker, with ravines appearing as storms have washed away huge sections of the bluffs." Lighthouse Museum director, Dana Brancato, warned: "We're in real danger of falling into the sea. In ten years, who knows? We might be at the edge."[386]

When the subject was raised about possibly moving the historic tower further inland, it was rejected. Brancato said: "The expense of moving it would be horrendous. And in the long run, even it you moved it back 300 feet, what would be the point? The erosion would still go on. And away from the ocean, it wouldn't be a lighthouse at all, just some sort of tourist attraction."[387] Lighthouse Committee Chairman, Dick White, felt the time was at hand to raise funds for an erosion control system, because in three to five years the effects of erosion would threaten the tower itself. Where the funds would come from was uncertain. White doubted support would be forthcoming from state or federal coffers, and he didn't think the Montauk Historical Society would be successful in raising the needed money.[388]

On January 3, 1990 the Montauk Historical Society took over the Erosion Control Project and began to aggressively seek funding. A boon to the effort was celebrity interest in the lighthouse. Popular singer, Paul Simon, arranged the first "Save the Lighthouse" concert on August 30, 1990 with guest singer Billy Joel. It raised $265,000.

In December 1990 members of the Army Corps of Engineers scurried over the rocks at Montauk Point to assess the condition of the bluffs and their ability to withstand severe weather conditions. They met with the Coast Guard and the Montauk Historical Society to plan ways to obtain $500,000 in emergency federal money to protect the lighthouse. In order to be eligible for the funding, the engineers had to show an emergency need. Approval and the release of money had to come from the Army Corps of Engineers' division office and headquarters in Washington, D.C. Faced with at least a year's wait, Dick White said, "I understand that the wheels of government turn slowly. Hopefully the good Lord will look kindly on us and not overturn the work that's [already] there with a big storm."[389]

After examining the gabions, rusty and weakened wires were discovered in spots. Part of the breakdown was the result of the constant action of the ocean, but also from people walking on the 44-year-old structure. John Anselmo, Coast Guard engineer and designer of the gabions, noted, "They've taken quite a beating." In 1993, the Coast Guard planned to armor the gabions and part of the bluffs with huge boulders, linking them with the seawall. The federal government budget allowed $200,000 for the Corps to study ways to protect the bluff. Anselmo responded to the funding, saying, "I'd like to see as much money as can go into stone. It has been studied to death."[390]

The work of the Erosion Control Project was put to its first test rather quickly and severely. On August 19, 1991 Hurricane Bob washed out about 50-feet of rubble and terrace on the southeast side of the bluff. This storm also began to destroy the Coast Guard's gabions, which had served as a foundation for Giorgina Reid's terracing. Sections of gabion/terrace work were lost, especially on the north side. The southeast area was "constructed" out of old road concrete, a temporary fix that was slated for removal as part of the first phase of the rehabilitation in 1991-1992 because it was considered unstable and dangerous.

In October 1991 the fierce Halloween coastal storm destroyed about 50-feet of the gabion/terrace work on the north side of the Point, eroding back the bank about 30-feet. Repair work was spearheaded by Greg Donohue of the Lighthouse Committee in conjunction with the Coast Guard and Army Corps of Engineers.[391]

Hurricane Bob and the Halloween storm actually helped save the lighthouse by focusing attention on the need to halt any further damage to the Point. New York Senator, Daniel Patrick Moynihan, procured $625,000 for the Coast Guard "…to repair and upgrade the standard of protection for the Lighthouse." In four months all details were worked out, permits and approvals were obtained, and work proceeded.[392]

Top—A portion of the gabions destroyed during the three-day nor'easter of October 1991 was photographed in ruins. The storm threw its worst fury over barrier beaches of Long Island.

Bottom—The stone revetment was reconstructed after the October 1991 storm, with approximately 28,000-tons of stone. The photo was taken ca. 1992. (Greg Donohue Photos)

This 1960s aerial of Montauk Point shows the U.S.A.C.O.E. revetment and the untouched bluff face before Giorgina Reids pilot project on the eastern slope.

Aerial view before Montauk Point's erosion control efforts: A 1960s image showed only the U.S. Army Corps of Engineers' stone revetment around Montauk Point. (Greg Donohue)

Following a two-year $350,000 federal study by the Army Corps of Engineers, it was determined that a rock seawall of about 28,000-tons could protect the lighthouse from erosion for at least 50-years. A stone revetment, similar to a 320-foot section of revetment built in 1992 by the Coast Guard at the tip of Montauk Point, could successfully prevent any erosion from heavy storms such as the nor'easter of December 11, 1992. The cost was $10 million.[393]

It was emphasized that if money was unavailable for the construction of the revetment, the lighthouse could not be moved because its historic value would be compromised in a new location. Eugene Brickman, chief of planning for the Army Corps' New York district office, said, "…the lighthouse and the surrounding area has archeological and historical significance as a cultural and historical site and it should be protected where it stands."[394]

Funding support for the erosion project came from Rep. George Hochbrueckner and Sen. Daniel Patrick Moynihan. Hochbrueckner said, "We won't let it fall in the ocean….We can make a strong case….based on the fact that this is the second public works project that George Washington authorized. And it's important as a navigation aid and cultural and tourist site." He thought the federal government would cover 70-percent of the funding needed, with the balance coming from New York State and private sources.[395]

The seawall was designed to be 770-feet long, its base containing 9-ton boulders set at least 25-feet above the low tide line. Smaller stones weighing about a ½-ton apiece would be set in place above the boulders. The 320-foot revetment built by the Coast Guard would be rebuilt using larger stones. In addition the corps planned to rebuild a rock wall installed by the Montauk Historical Society in 1990. Four to five years was estimated to complete the project.

Dick White supported the recommendation: "The work that was done with the cooperation of the Army Corps and the Coast Guard withstood the December 11 storm and the blizzard. We didn't lose anything." He added that the society received a $300,000 grant from the state to reinforce 150-feet of the shoreline north of the Point with large rocks. However, an equal amount had to be raised for the grant's matching funds. The society hoped to raise this money, in part, from a "Back at the Ranch" concert in August 1993 on Montauk.[396]

Greg Donohue called the nor'easter "the worst storm in 30 years on the site… [but] no damage was done. I think we're able to perch that lighthouse there for another hundred years."[397] During the storm, waves 15 to 18-feet high, along with a 6½-foot tidal surge pounded the bluffs for two days. According to an article by Donohue in the 1993 edition of *The Beacon*, "the wave run-up, often reaching twenty feet above average sea level continually engulfed the seawall. While the unprotected bluffs in the region were severely eroded, the erosion control project at Montauk Point passed the test with flying colors. A post-storm inspection revealed no loss of land and no shifting of stone or damage to the seawall."[398]

The next test came a few months later when a heavy blizzard blasted the area in March 1993 with winds exceeding 80-mph and 15 to 20-foot waves on top of a 4-foot tidal surge. Fortunately, the storm hit at low tide and the protected bluffs again endured.

During 1993 work began to secure some 250-feet of bluff on the south side of the lighthouse property and into Turtle Cove. In the winter of 1994-1995, Keith Grimes, a local contractor, installed 250-feet of the revetment—a little more than a third of the total footage. The project was completed in 1998. The key to the stabilization of the revetment at Montauk Point was the installation of acrylic fiber cloth, a material effective in preventing loss of sediment. Also important were the armor stones, each carefully selected and set in place. Approximately 28,000-tons of stone were delivered 30-tons at a time in special "bath tub" tractor trailers.[399]

On June 2, 1996 New York Governor George Pataki called for federal intervention to help in the battle against coastal erosion at Montauk: "We must act aggressively to protect Montauk Point and to preserve this invaluable landmark so that it can be enjoyed by our children and our grandchildren."[400] Congress agreed to fund half of the $800,000 needed to conduct a study of how best to protect the lighthouse property from additional erosion. The study was expected to take several years to complete, but first the government had to commit to funding 65-percent of the construction phase, expected cost approximately $7 million.[401]

Dick White was pleased with the governor's announcement: "On the eve of the 200th anniversary of the lighthouse, we are delighted Governor Pataki is taking strong action to support this much-needed erosion control project. Completion of this project will help ensure that we celebrate many more anniversaries at this historic place."[402]

A short time after the Montauk Historical Society took ownership of the lighthouse property in 1996, interest in continuing the feasibility study at Montauk Point was sparked by the Army Corps of Engineers and the New York State Department of Environmental Conservation. Congress and the New York State Legislature approved a 50/50 cost share for the feasibility study. It addressed, among other things, the long-term needs of the erosion control project.

In the meantime, new upgraded protection kept the bluff stabilized against the effects of severe weather. On January 5, 1998 the final 250-feet of erosion control stabilization began and by April 16 the Erosion Control Project was complete. Under the guidance of the Montauk Historical Society and the direction of Greg Donohue, the project was to be maintained on a yearly basis.

The same camera angle thirty years later shows a stabilized toe and bluff face. The cooperative efforts of the U.S.A.C.O.E., the U.S.C.G. the N.Y.S.D.E.C., the Long Island Office of Parks, Recreation and Historic Preservation and the Montauk Historical Society have improved the erosion control protection at Montauk Point.
(c 1995 Peter Paul Muller Jr.)

About 1995, the Erosion Control Project had stabilized the toe and bluff face. (Photo by Peter Paul Muller Jr. Courtesy of Greg Donohue)

On September 7, 2000 the U.S. Senate approved $250,000 for an Army Corps of Engineers coastal erosion study. Three stages were indicated. First, the toe of the Point had to be protected with a stone wall around the cliff that would act as barrier against wave attack. Second, once the stone wall was in place, terrace construction would be done followed by planting with a "combination of indigenous wind and water-resistant plants, grasses like Rosa rugosa, blue stem, and Cape American that adapt well to sandy soil…all have strong and well-developed root systems." The final step was the test of time. Greg Donohue expressed everyone's hope when he said, "I fully expect this to last for at least the next few generations."[403]

A second federal appropriation in 2000 paved the way for the Army Corps of Engineers to conduct a more extensive $900,000 feasibility study to find a long term solution to the erosion problem. The one-year study determined the best method for maintaining or supplementing the 1400-foot stone revetment completed in 1998. The primary finding was an urgent need to re-point cracked sandstone blocks and repair water intrusion. The study estimated the repair cost at $1.48 million.

On October 30, 2000 Sen. Charles Schumer announced an appropriation of $287,000 for 2001, which when added to previous federal and state appropriations fully funded the study. It was scheduled to begin immediately. Schumer said: "The Montauk Lighthouse has stood atop Montauk Point as Long Island's most recognizable and cherished landmark for more than 200 years. This funding will allow the Army Corps to determine the best way to ensure that it remains standing for another 200." Museum director Tom Ambrosio added: "The rocks stabilized it. They didn't permanently fix it. We're looking for a long term permanent fix."

After the revetment's completion, Ambrosio noted: "We haven't experienced any major erosion, but we haven't been hit by a hurricane. In 1985 [Hurricane] Gloria came in at low tide, but what if we had a hurricane that hit at high tide? We want to prevent high tide wave action against the bluff that could destabilize it."[404]

On October 31, 2005 Greg Donohue went to Washington, D.C. to meet with members of the Army Corps of Engineers' Civilian Review Board to evaluate the feasibility study and to determine whether the government would continue to participate in the Storm Reduction Planning for the Montauk Point Lighthouse. The Board's vote was 5-0 in favor of continuation. This cleared the way for engineering and design of the revetment upgrade. Donohue was confident that the additional funding for the engineering would be forthcoming.

In early September 2006 the government approved $12 million for an 840-foot stone revetment around the bluffs at Montauk Point, which would be constructed by the New York District of the Army Corps of Engineers starting in 2009 or 2010. Donohue commented: "The reason this $12 million in funding is so important is that there has never been an engineered plan to correctly stabilize these bluffs…We've always done this piecemeal, so it's exciting that we now have a specific plan to stabilize these bluffs to withstand even the most powerful storms and hurricanes."[405]

The project actually will cost $14 million. The additional $2 million will be raised by the State Department of Environmental Conservation and the Montauk Historical Society. According to Donohue, the project will elevate the stone revetment high enough to prevent storm waves from washing over the top, and it also will be sunk deeper into the ground.[406]

Betsy White, president of the Montauk Historical Society said, "We're very happy that we can finally secure this area and save this historic site."

The promise of a bright future for the lighthouse was quickly tarnished by the East End chapter of the Surfrider Foundation. In November 2006, the group stated that the new construction would affect the quality of surfing at Montauk Point, as well as neighboring beaches. Their recommendation was to move the lighthouse some 800-feet inland and they cited examples of relocations, such as Cape Hatteras Lighthouse in North Carolina, Highland Light on Cape Cod, and Block Island Southeast Lighthouse.

The effects of severe weather created a snowy work of art in the cliffs at Camp Hero just west of the Montauk Point Lighthouse in December 2005. (Author Photo)

The Army Corps of Engineers looked into the feasibility of moving the lighthouse. The procedure, an extremely delicate and technical operation, would cost $27 million and would, according to *Newsday* reporter Bill Bleyer, "ruin the historic nature of the site and possibly cause the structure to crumble."[407] The Army Corps' project engineer, Frank Verga, pointed out that the lighthouse was situated on a bluff (Turtle Hill), which complicated the proposed move: "They talk about other lighthouses that have been moved. But those were more on flat terrain and more easily maneuverable. Here there are a lot of question marks about whether it would survive a move."[408]

An angry Greg Donohue said of the Surfriders, "Suddenly, they come along and think they know better…They have no scientific knowledge, they just say, 'We're for saving the beach'…If they had hard scientific information on how our work is going to destroy their wave, we would look at it. Instead, they're just beating a drum and playing the politics of beach erosion. They are spreading propaganda and innuendo and false information to politicians."[409] He further stated that the Army Corps' plan was the first one based on full engineering studies through the use of a wave tank at the University of Delaware. It showed no adverse impact on beaches or surf.

The late Giorgina Reid, the leader in the fight against erosion at Montauk Point, would have been ecstatic to hear of plans for the new revetment and probably up to the task of fighting the claims of surfers too. Greg Donohue, who got his start at the lighthouse as an erosion control volunteer with Reid, recalled her tenacity: "Down she would go, sometimes with volunteers, sometimes alone, always moving the project forward. The daily assignment was to dig like a mole and climb like a goat."[410]

Unfortunately, the tireless and determined Reid died before the battle to save the lighthouse was won. On her gravestone in Calverton National Cemetery are inscribed the words: "Keeper of the Light." Her friends believe, however, that the true monument to her stands on the windy, weathered bluff at Montauk Point.

CHAPTER 8
Weather at Montauk Point

Weather has been a decisive factor in Montauk Point Light's long history. The actions of the sea and weather, most notably severe storms and hurricanes, continually reshape the Montauk shores and cause periodic damage to structures on the lighthouse property. Heavy surf and rains constantly erode the bluffs, snow and ice sculpt the soil and wear down the exteriors of buildings, and wind—pleasantly persistent but occasionally damaging—is an ever-present element.

In the 1940s the U.S. Weather Bureau listed Montauk Point as the "windiest spot on the Atlantic Coast...[it receives] twice as much wind as the center of the island, and averages one hundred and nine separate winds a year whose velocity is over fifty miles an hour."[411]

Jutting more than 100-miles into the Atlantic Ocean from the mainland, Montauk Point often snags storms whirling northward along the coast. One of the earliest storms on record was the gale of December 8, 1796. It broke several panes of glass in the lantern of the new lighthouse and delayed the lighting of the beacon for several months. (see Chapter 1). On April 2, 1799 a "terrible tornado…accompanied with a violent wind and heavy storm of large hail" again broke most of the glass in the lantern. Keeper Jacob Hand was tending the light at the time and was cut on his face and hands.[412]

The so-called "Christmas Storm" of December 24, 1811 struck with severe winds and freezing temperatures and drove numerous boats ashore along the length of Long Island. Even worse was the hurricane of September 21, 1815, which did significant damage not only to the lighthouse but to the shoreline as well. Henry Packer Dering reported that the lighthouse "…had received considerable damage and that the Lantern was so much injured a light could not possibly be kept…I found nearly all the Glass broken and blown out of the sashes in the lantern the copper and sheathing from the deck or platform ripped up by the violence of the wind and the windows of the Light house and keepers house much broken—By exerting ourselves we got the light reestablished on the 23rd."[413] Dering brought glass and a glazier to repair the lighthouse.

Record books are rife with storm damage—A letter dated May 15, 1820 from Dering to William H. Crawford, Secretary of the Treasury, noted the damage from a windstorm on December 30, 1819: "…[the] vane that turns the head on the top of the dome and thro which the smoke from the lamps passes had been carried away by a violent gale of winds on the 30th of Dec. last."[414]

On March 19, 1866 keeper Jonathan A. Miller reported the "…entire fence around the Lt House property [was] destroyed by the recent heavy gales, and the materials of which the fence was built are entirely rotten and unfit for the use in rebuilding the fence."[415] Miller recommended building a new fence of "…chestnut posts and pine boards" at a cost of $665 total.[416] Repairs were authorized a month later.

On September 23, 1869 the Third District engineer reported that a hurricane had destroyed the barn built by Josiah Hand in 1806 and that all four chimneys on the keeper's dwelling were blown down, along with damage to the roof and numerous windows. The front stoop and steps were demolished. Even the privy was destroyed. The keeper's horse suffered injuries, the wagon was damaged, and crops were ruined. The district engineer gave orders concerning "a two story brick building…at this station which was formally used as a keeper's dwelling, and is still in tolerable good condition….to convert this building into a barn and stable, by putting it in good repair."[417]

On January 9, 1886, when Captain James G. Scott was keeper at the lighthouse, a strong snowstorm and heavy winds toppled the kitchen chimney and destroyed the well house. Two winters later, in the now-famous Blizzard of 1888, Captain Scott described the events of March 12th to 15th:

> *Rain and Snow, gale of wind S.E. to N.N.E. at 4 P.M. commenced to snow. Barometer 29 degrees, then 28 at 5 P.M. Started trumpet. Worst storm this winter. March 13, Gale wind and snow, wind N.N.E. by E. at 6 A.M. Stopped trumpet 7 A.M. Started trumpet 2:30 P.M. stopped it, end of snow. Very low barometer, going from 29 to 18. During the night 2 chimneys broke on account of the snow. March 14, Cloud to snow. Strong S.S.E. to N.E. winds at 8 A.M. Barometer 29.78 then 28. Trumpet started 1 P.M. and stopped 2 P.M. March 15, Clear fresh N.W. winds 8 A.M.*[418]

A snowstorm described as the worst since the Blizzard of 1888 struck the south shore of Long Island on February 12, 1894. Its intensity limited the visibility of the Montauk

Lighthouse to less than a mile and a half. Members of the life saving station, known as beach-pounders for their regular patrols of the shoreline, were blinded by a combination of windblown sand and snow and were forced to double up when they went on shore patrols.[419]

On December 9, 1917 keeper John E. Miller wrote to the Third District Inspector that a gale out of the southeast had destroyed scaffolding and a chimney under construction on the northeast side of the keeper's dwelling and also broke a window.[420] Another "heavy S.E. gale" struck Montauk Point at about 2:20 a.m. on the morning of January 25, 1928, destroying the two west chimneys on the keeper's dwelling and wrecking a portion of the front porch roof.[421]

More horrific than any previous storm on record was the great Hurricane of September 21, 1938. Considered the twentieth century's only major hurricane to hit the north Atlantic coast, it came ashore at high tide and damaged much of Long Island and Southern New England. The old fishing village at Fort Pond Bay was ruined. Twenty-nine fishing boats were blown on shore at Lake Montauk. People who were stranded spent the night at the Montauk Manor.

Carolyn Kennedy Tyson of Second House was 33-years-old at the time and in East Hampton. She recalled: "I was at the hairdresser on Newtown Lane and all hell broke loose. Just as I was about to put the car in the garage there, the roof blew off. That meant we had to stay on the street, which was full of falling trees…We wanted to drive home to Montauk. We didn't know what happened to my daughter. We had left her in the Montauk school…and we had no way to get in touch with her. We couldn't get back because the water cut us off."[422] (The high storm surge came ashore at Napeague.)

The next day, Tyson, her husband, and her father made

it through the water to Second House where they found "...the front door had blown off and a lot of the dormer windows were gone, and the waves had come up to the gate across the highway...anyway it didn't blow away."[423]

It took nearly two weeks for Montauk Highway to be fully cleared through Napeague to allow emergency vehicles to reach Montauk. In the village the water rose to a height of 12-feet when the ocean broke over the dunes in the vicinity of today's IGA store at the corner of Montauk Highway and South Elder Street.

Montauk resident Peg Winski recorded the memories of several hearty Montauk citizens who lived through the ordeal of the great hurricane. The current oldest living native born Montauk resident, Mary Smith Fullerton (born 1915), recalled riding out the storm at the family's Wyandanee Inn, located just west of the lighthouse on the Old Montauk Highway. A few gazebos on the property were blown around by the wind; one was "picked up and blown off the cliffs." The inn itself survived and provided shelter for many.[424]

Gene Beckwith, Jr. recalled being held at the Montauk School as the storm raged outside. He looked out the school windows and saw the "fishing village was gone...[and] nothing but water and floating telephone poles could be seen." The school children were sheltered in homes in Shepherd Neck while some of their parents were secure at the Montauk Manor and other parents were working away from the Montauk area. Beckwith claimed that the fishing village wasn't totally destroyed by the storm and that "quite a number of families returned to the village, picked up the pieces, rebuilt their homes, and went on with their lives."[425]

Elizabeth Job remembered her father working at his dock at Lake Montauk during the hurricane: "As the water rose, the fishermen cut the lines of their boats to keep them from crashing into the dock. A tremendous wave washed the boats to the east side of the lake. All the men crawled off the dock and just as they reached the parking lot a thunderous noise was heard. They looked back to see everything blown apart. The dock and the building were in shambles."[426]

Paul Cook's family home was moved off its foundation by the high waves, as was the post office where Ted Cook, Paul Cook's father, worked. When the hurricane struck, Ted Cook looked out a window and "...noticed telephone poles passing by. He realized he was not in a boat and that the post office was torn from its meager foundation and floating away." He managed to grab the registered mail before he escaped from the building. He took refuge with his family at Montauk Manor.[427]

Gene McGovern, a local fisherman, was at the Montauk Post Office getting his mail as the storm made landfall. Wind slammed the walls and the water rose inside the Post Office so quickly McGovern barely had time to leap out a rear window. Seconds later, the building was carried away by the storm surge.

In the aftermath of the storm, the Montauk community was virtually isolated for a time. Ed Ecker, Sr., who was only 9-years-old at the time, said the railroad was not passable for three days. There was great loss of property almost everywhere on Montauk, but people worked together in the face of the great tragedy: "No looting occurred and strangers were not allowed in town for probably three or four weeks."[428]

About 150 fishermen were left homeless, and many fishing boats were destroyed. The hurricane nearly wiped out Montauk's year-round fishing industry.[429] Some one-hundred homes were damaged, and six homes were washed into Fort Pond Bay. There was no electricity, no working water lines or telephones, and the railroad tracks were mangled. Perry Duryea, East Hampton's Town Supervisor, and owner of the commercial fishing depot at Montauk, sent a radio message to federal authorities and the Red Cross asking for assistance. His message summed up the situation: "Montauk fishing village practically destroyed, number of boats lost, residences destroyed, several lives lost and missing. No water, light or phone connections, fishing industry wiped out. Immediate aid necessary."[430]

The ocean had raged unimpeded over the low lying beaches of eastern Long Island, carrying with it various forms of sea life. Dr. William T. Helmuth of East Hampton noted: "Only at Montauk Point itself, where steep bluffs largely prevented oceanic matter from being washed ashore far inland did the truly marine flotsam accumulate upon the shore itself, but its quantity was incalculable and one could wade knee-deep in stranded mussels, moon shells, surf clams, crabs and lobsters without ever setting foot upon the underlying shingle."[431]

Days after the storm, some of those who died were recovered along the beaches. The body of Sam Edwards washed ashore at East Hampton. He was one of a party of four Montauk residents who had the misfortune of being at sea when the storm struck. The other three—Gill Edwards, Vivian Smith and Herbert Fields—were missing. Deputy Sheriff Robert Fisher "...credited the small loss of life in the village [of Montauk]—only three dead—to the fact that the 125 to 150 children all were in school when the storm struck. The teachers kept them there for several hours. Adults were able to find refuge on higher ground before the waves swept their homes off the foundations."[432]

A summary of damages sustained at the Montauk Point Lighthouse following the hurricane of 1938 were recorded in the lighthouse journal (commas added by the author):

> *...part of front porch, one chimney, three chimney tops and shingles on roof and one door was carried away...and several windows and sash broken out on main dwelling...several windows were broken and the shingles and part of ridge roll on roof of signal house was carried away causing considerable damage to engine room. Range light window was blown in, the toilet blown over, the doors and part of the ridge roll and some of the shingle on roof of garage and pump house door was carried away by the wind, storm door of office blown off.*[433]

Following the hurricane, the roofs of all structures at the Montauk Point Light Station were renewed with red, slate-surfaced asphalt shingles. The Shagwong Reef range light, severely damaged in the hurricane was relocated to the interior of the lantern in April 1939 to protect it from future storms.[434]

The Great Hurricane of 1938 went down in the record books with a barometric pressure reading below 28.00-millibars (27.94 at the Bellport Coast Guard Station)—the lowest recorded pressure of any storm on Long Island. It also set records for wind velocity and tidal surge. Historians and meteorologists, alike, consider it one of the country's great natural disasters.

Other hurricanes followed but paled by comparison. On September 15, 1944 the category three "Great Atlantic Hurricane" hit eastern Long Island with driving rain and high winds. Commercial fishermen at Montauk lost much of their equipment. The navy's torpedo base sustained heavy damage, as did homes along the shore of Fort Pond Bay. No damage was mentioned at Montauk Point Lighthouse.

Hurricane Carol struck Long Island on August 31, 1954 and washed away the home of Tom Joyce, pushing it into Tuthill Pond. The house was salvaged and still exists today. (Peg Winski)

A decade later, on August 31, 1954, Hurricane Carol struck the region with a storm surge similar to the Great Hurricane of 1938. The eye of the storm passed over the East Hampton/Montauk area at about noon and brought heavy winds and high seas, including an 8-foot tidal surge over Montauk Highway and the railroad tracks at Napeague, isolating Montauk from about 10:30 a.m. to 6:00 p.m. The water was 4-feet deep and a mile wide. The railroad tracks and ties were "twisted grotesquely and in places thrust into the air." Some of the radar equipment was swept away at Camp Hero, where winds of 110-mph were recorded. [435] Nearly thirty boats were lost, twenty-five cottages and motels lost their roofs, and about forty cabanas blew down at the Montauk Surf Club.[436]

The ocean also surged across Montauk Highway at

Second House and into Fort Pond, isolating Shepherd's Neck for a time. A Mackay Overseas Radio tower at Napeague was knocked across the railroad tracks. The home of Montauk resident Tom Joyce ended up in Tuthill's Pond. He climbed to the attic of the house for safety and later was rescued unharmed by the Coast Guard.[437]

The U.S. Army evacuated campers from Hither Hills and from the summer colony at Ditch Plains. Viking Dock and Gosman's Dock sustained damage. An observer noted that the ocean "…looked like a gigantic caldron whipped up by an immense egg beater, waves 20 and 30 feet high twisting and whirling in all directions."[438]

Hurricane Carol, the second most destructive storm to hit Long Island in the twentieth century, made landfall at mid-island, with winds west of Fire Island reaching only 40-mph. The eastern side of the cyclone, unhindered by land, hit Montauk Point full-force. Gusts at the lighthouse were clocked at 120-mph—that is, until the measuring equipment blew away!

Not two weeks later, on September 11, 1954, Hurricane Edna skirted Long Island. The storm track was farther east than Hurricane Carol's path, but still caused heavy rain and flooding. The Old Montauk Highway was closed for two days, since low lying spots were under water and parts of Montauk Highway at Napeague were covered for several hours. Once again, Montauk Manor was pressed into service to provide shelter for forty evacuees in advance of Edna's arrival. On September 12, 1960 Hurricane Donna slammed Montauk. Moving northeast at a speedy 40-mph, the category 3 storm carried sustained winds of 100-mph over the East End. Stronger gusts were recorded at the Montauk Point Lighthouse.

On August 31, 1954, flood waters from Hurricane Carol washed out the Old Montauk Highway where it merged with Montauk Point State Parkway at Hither Hills State Park. Note the sign directing military vehicles, presumably, to Camp Hero. (Montauk Library)

About 4½-inches of rain fell in an 18-hour period. Communications, being much improved since 1938, allowed Montauk residents ample time to head for higher ground as the storm approached. Some 350 people were evacuated from homes and motels by Air Force personnel and sheltered inside the old gun emplacement bunkers at Camp Hero. The Montauk Air Force Base tracked the eye of the storm over Riverhead as it traveled toward Connecticut and Rhode Island. Ocean tides were 10-feet above normal and for several hours flooded a mile wide swath of Montauk Highway at Napeague to a depth of 2-feet.[439] The ocean breached the land into Fort Pond Bay and caused minor damage to motels on Montauk. With regard to the bunkers used as shelters, Alan Rattiner, head of Montauk's Red Cross, said, they "could house everybody in the Town if needed."[440]

Hurricane Esther swept by eastern Long Island on September 21, 1961. Montauk Highway again was awash at Napeague for several hours, with 2 to 4-feet of water covering the road for 6-miles. The Montauk Air Station at Camp Hero recorded winds of 92-mph. The gun emplacement bunkers provided shelter for a few hundred citizens. The eye of the storm passed about 40-miles east of the lighthouse and the Montauk Lifeboat Station reported winds of 65-mph, with stronger gusts.[441]

A nor'easter that was nearly as powerful as a summer hurricane hit the region during March 6-7, 1962. (A nor'easter is named for the winds that blow from the northeast and drive it along the warm waters of the Gulf Stream.) Though winds were measured between 65 and 70-mph at the lighthouse, the storm came close but did not isolate Montauk from the rest of Long Island.[442]

What was described by the *East Hampton Star* as a "freak gale" swept across Montauk on November 29-30, 1963 during a full moon, causing astronomical high tides. Average winds were clocked at 40-mph at the lighthouse. Surprisingly, the wind velocity was higher at East Hampton—70-mph.[443] Another nor'easter struck the Montauk Peninsula on January 13, 1964 causing heavy drifting of snow in certain spots. A few bulkheads and homes were destroyed in East Hampton, and the Montauk Point Lighthouse measured winds at 60 to 65-mph.[444] When Hurricane

Belle came by on August 9, 1976, Montauk Point took only a glancing blow. The worst damage occurred at a gas station in town where plywood was torn off the windows.[445]

Hurricane Gloria struck on September 27, 1985. Forecast as the "Storm of the Century," it failed to measure up, losing much of its punch before reaching Long Island and rated only as a tropical storm when it arrived. It still brought 65-mph winds and heavy rain. Damage to structures on the East End indicated winds in excess of 110-mph. At the lighthouse, Petty Officer Gene Hughes estimated wind gusts up to 100-mph. Though the storm brought little rain, Hughes said the wind "blew out 12 storm windows here, a skylight in the shop, and blew out the front porch supports."[446] About 100,000 trees were destroyed in East Hampton Town, and Gurney's Inn and the Snug Harbor Motel in Montauk lost portions of their roofs.

Hurricane Bob, a category two storm, sideswiped Long Island on August 17, 1991. The eye passed just east of Montauk Point at about 1:30 p.m. The Coast Guard station at Montauk estimated the storm surge at 10-feet above normal. A dock was destroyed at the Gone Fishing Marina, waves broke into the Kahuna Café, and a dock was smashed at the Rough Riders condominiums. In addition, extensive damage occurred at Duryea's Ice House and Lobster House at Fort Pond Bay.[447] At the lighthouse, about 50-feet of restorative work on the erosion problem on the southeast face of the bluff was washed out. Repairs were made. (See Chapter 7.) A weather observer at the lighthouse recorded a wind speed of 88-mph, the highest on Long Island during the storm. Lighthouse erosion control expert Greg Donohue reported 6-inches of rainfall. More trees were lost in the Town of East Hampton in Hurricane Bob than were lost during Hurricane Gloria. The erosion control work at the lighthouse withstood the storm's fury with no loss of land.[448]

On October 30, 1991 the infamous Halloween storm descended on Montauk Point. It crumbled large chunks of the bluffs with near-record high tides. The worst damage occurred along Dune Road in Westhampton Beach where twenty-five homes were destroyed by the tide.[449] At Montauk Point Lighthouse, a section of bluff "suffered 30 years' worth of erosion in three days." The intense waves and tides broke down the steep bluff face behind the barrier of boulders and gabions. Greg Donohue said the south side bluffs held up well, and if it weren't for the terracing work done there in 1990, "the whole hill would have been lost." The force of the waves was so great at the lighthouse, Donahue said, that when they struck the south bluffs they actually "broke over them, leaving a pond on top to run off and dissipate by the time of the next swell."[450] If there was a bright side during the storm, it was that it resulted in improving beach access for equipment being used to stabilize the bluffs around the lighthouse.[451]

The last storm of note, Hurricane Floyd, came on September 16, 1999 and was predicted to be another "Storm of the Century." It also fizzled out before it reached Long Island. However, it did collapse 10 to 15-feet of bluffs at Ditch Plains. Ocean swells were as high as 11-feet, among the highest seen in the region. Wind gusts peaked at 64-mph.[452]

Today, no one is in a better position to observe weather at the Montauk Point Lighthouse than caretaker Marge Winski, who has lived in an apartment in the keeper's dwelling since 1987. Her observations of recent storms are excellent first-hand accounts—She reflected on the fury of a December 1992 nor'easter at the station: "The world seemed to shrink as the weather deteriorated to near white-out conditions…I felt as if the lighthouse was adrift on a sea of snow, slowly slipping out of sight of land..." Through hurricanes, nor'easters, lightning, and squalls, "I often have thoughts of the former keepers who tended the light in similar circumstances. It is almost incomprehensible to think of the earliest keepers who lived in what is now the garage at the base of the hill. How did they struggle up the hill in the midst of gale force winds and subzero temperatures? I picture them tied to a lifeline as they navigated their way up to the tower."[453]

During the Halloween storm of 1991, Winski stood on the bluff just below the lighthouse to film the chaotic scene, noting that the "cliff vibrated with each break of the waves [and] when the surf finally splashed over the top of the bluff I realized what a dangerous location it was. One misstep and I could have tumbled into the churning white water and been swept out to sea."[454]

During this terrible winter snowstorm, Winski recalled: "Every part of the house shook, from the pictures on the walls, dinner plates on the table, to the bed…At one point I was so convinced that the house could not withstand any further battering, I packed my bags and prepared to spend the night at the base of the lighthouse tower." Once the storm passed, she went out to assess the damage and found very little. Even the newly installed rocks around the Point held fast and not a trace of land had been lost.

After the Halloween storm, Winski easily summed up the lighthouse's entire career when she said: "The Montauk Lighthouse had weathered another blast and stood, resolute, waiting the next challenge."[455]

Ominous skies seen from the top of Montauk Point Lighthouse, looking southwest over Turtle Cove, on November 13, 2004 portended a storm. The weather at Montauk is a marvel of nature. (Author Photo)

CHAPTER 9

Reflections, Observations, and Accounts of Visits to Montauk

Since the Montauk Point Lighthouse Museum opened in 1987, it has welcomed visitors not just from Long Island and all corners of the United States, but from numerous countries around the world. Visitors from foreign lands are especially fascinated by the exhibits, the tower, and the beautiful views from atop Turtle Hill. They are quick to express their appreciation and write comments in the museum guest register. But these people were not the first to express their feelings about Montauk Point Lighthouse.

One of the earliest visitors to Montauk Point was Timothy Dwight (1752-1817), President of Yale College. He described the lighthouse in May 1804 as "…a landmark of the first importance. Perhaps no building of this useful kind was ever erected on this side of the Atlantic in a spot where it was more necessary for the preservation of man."[456]

Theodore N. Porter and John B. King of New York noted in 1838 that keeper Patrick Gould had treated them to "…a ramble on the beach, a visit to the top of the lighthouse and more than all, a most admirable supper, rendered thrice as welcome by the dreary region through which we had wended our way hither." The meal included wild goose, broiled chicken, and oysters fried and raw.[457]

Of course not all opinions about Montauk were favorable. In 1839 Joseph P. Osborne, Superintendent of the Sag Harbor lighthouse district, wrote to Stephen Pleasonton, head of the U.S. Lighthouse Establishment, comparing a trip to New York as being easier, cheaper and seemingly more pleasant than going to Montauk Point:

> *My visits to Montauk Point have always been made by land as no one here thinks of going by water it is attended with more expense and more hazard there being no harbor or any good landing place except in very good weather. The stable price for horses and carriage is from 10 to 12 dollars – I have generally taken my own horses and carriage and charged $12 which covered all expenses of horse keeping and board two days and one night from 2 to 3 Dollars I am aware that this is a great price for the distance of 30 miles but I can get to New York or Boston with as much ease and as little expense as to Montauk Point there is no public stage running within 20 miles nor is there any settlement within 15 miles of the Light House.*[458]

New York State Senator David Gardiner (1784-1844) wrote in 1840 of the magnificent view from the lighthouse: "From the gallery on the top of the tower and outside of the lantern, the prospect is grand and majestic. In the west, the island, the main and sound are seen, and in the east and south is presented to the eye the illimitable ocean without a mark, without a bound."[459]

Gardiner extolled the virtues of a visit to the Point and the fine hospitality of lighthouse keeper Patrick Gould: "The air around differs but little from that felt at sea upon the deck of a vessel, and the valetudinarian may derive from a salt and invigorating atmosphere, a renewal of health and an increased appetite, which the well supplied table of the keeper of the light will pleasurably satisfy."[460]

Another 1840 visitor said a trip to Montauk Point was a potential cure for insomnia. After hiking 10-miles to the lighthouse from First House, he suggested one:

> *...call for supper and ascend to the top of the lighthouse, remain there until the joyful sound of supper rings in your ears. Descend, place yourself at the nicest looking table you ever saw, bountifully spread with the good things of this life, to say nothing of mackerel fresh from the sea, and chickens from the barnyard, drink five cups of tea, eat two mackerel and a whole chicken, with their concomitants, four slices of bread and butter lengthways of the loaf, then proceed to the top of the lighthouse for the second time. When you are cool, descend and put on a nightcap- this is furnished by the host- go to bed, and if the eternal roar of the old ocean does not put you to sleep in three minutes then you must be sorely troubled in mind, body and estate.*[461]

Connecticut-born engraver/history writer, John W. Barber (1798-1855), praised Montauk's rugged isolation in 1842: "There is a sublimity and wildness, as well as solitariness here, which leave a powerful impression on the heart. In a storm, the scene which the ocean presents is awfully grand and terrific."[462] In the same time period, Long Island historian, Nathaniel S. Prime (1785-1856), wrote of Montauk's suitability for rearing livestock: "...its wonderful supply of fresh water from the springs, swamps and vast ponds...its luxurious pastures—the refreshing sea breezes, and the entire absence of flies and mosquitoes...render it one of the most delightful retreats for domestic animals; where, in the course of a few weeks, they become fat and healthy."[463]

Lydia Howard Sigourney (1791-1865), one of America's first women writers, described a trip to Montauk in 1845. For her, the place was "…most solitary and peculiar. No track or furrow from a previous wheel directs your course. The traveler depends wholly on his guide, the driver of one of those large, strong-bodied Long-Island vehicles, which are adapted to that precipitous region."[464] Of the lighthouse, Sigourney penned, "The light-house upon this point is a structure of the highest importance. Perhaps no land-mark in our country is more conspicuous, more valuable in a commercial point of view, or more necessary for the preservation of human life. Who can tell how many hearts have leaped at the sight of this beacon light? – how many storm-tossed mariners it has guided homeward…"[465]

Episcopal clergyman Morgan Dix (1827-1908), who was a Columbia University student in 1846, described his family's experience dining at the lighthouse: "Arriving at the lighthouse in mid afternoon, too late for 'Dinner' served at noon and too early for supper served at 9 pm they were treated to an admirable meal of bass, chicken, black duck, all 'capital' edibles served with Indian pancakes. The cooks were Indian women who lived in wigwams and shacks on the fringe of the keeper's house."[466]

Dix found Montauk to be "…a remarkable place…no road is visible but a few marks of wagon wheels upon the greensward…before and behind extend a narrow strip of land; on either side grumble the deep-sounding billows of the Atlantic. Here at length you may imagine yourself to have reached the very limit of creation."[467]

Probably Long Island's most famous historian, Benjamin F. Thompson (1784-1849), described Montauk Point

Lighthouse in 1843 as "…built in the most durable manner, and would seem almost to defy the effects of time, and the elements. The view from the top is very extensive and beautiful, and although its dome is about two hundred feet above the sea, yet persons will find themselves well rewarded for the labor of ascending to it".[468]

Simply reaching Montauk Point in those days was a lesson in perseverance. Poet Jared Augustus Ayres, who made the journey during the summers of 1846 and 1847, recorded the travail. He began with the Napeague stretch where: "…the surf breaks so heavily in storms as sometimes to mingle its waters with those of the bay along the northern shore. In the well known September gale [presumably September 21, 1815] channels were cut in this way from the ocean to the bay, so deep that a horse could scarcely cross them without swimming."[469]

Ayres continued at length:

> *The only access to Montauk is by way of Neapeague, and the ride across it is always tedious in the extremes. The depth of the sand renders the progress necessarily slow, and an hour to an hour and a half after you leave the upland, finds you dragging wearily along the beach. Nothing breaks the monotony of the scene, but the loud whistle of the Tell tale or the harsh scream of the Tern, and almost without cessation your attention is claimed by a sad annoyance…It seems the very father-land of the insatiate mosquito, and unless a favoring wind has swept them away…they literally fill the atmosphere…[However] before you had ridden a quarter of a mile upon Montauk they have left you entirely.*[470]

He described the lighthouse as being properly maintained and offered his thoughts on the region's potential:

Were it not for the difficulty of access, Montauk would no doubt become a place of fashionable resort...but so long as a tedious ride of eighteen to twenty-five miles, across Neapeague and its own rough surface, lies between it and the nearest villages, it must remain what it is now, one of the most perfectly delightful places for a summer sojourn, that our coast can furnish. There is nothing to recall the busy and anxious scenes of life, and even the grave and sedate man is apt to feel and act like a boy.[471]

Ayres believed a person had to approach Montauk with a proper state of mind in order to reap the maximum benefit of the visit: "...sadly deficient in his own resources must a man be, who finds himself at a loss in what manner to occupy his time, or who cannot pass at least a few days here most pleasantly."[472]

An artist named Hubbard Fordham (1794-1872) visited the lighthouse in the 1850s and rendered a painting of it on a piece of wood found along the beach. The work may have been given to keeper Patrick Gould as payment for a meal Fordham had at the dwelling. After being passed down in the Gould family for generations, it is now in the possession of the lighthouse museum.

An article in the *Brooklyn Daily Eagle* in 1859 gave a travel warning to those who dared to venture beyond Amagansett:

...we passed the last farm-house on Long Island...and thence pressed forward into the desert of Napeague. Five miles of dry sand! Dry! Dry! Dry!...[Napeague should] be swept entirely away as soon as old Neptune can make the job convenient; for it seems to be the very father-land and brooding place of the Mosquito--

prince of bandits...Hour after hour passed away, and still left us fighting mosquitoes...until just as the sun went down, we bade final adieu to our tormentors, and ascended the green hills of Montauk. As we mounted the first eminence, the mosquitoes began to drop off from our backs, and in five minutes not one of the little singers was to be seen...[We reached First House where] the very moment Mrs. Osborn's kindly face beamed upon us we felt really at home. I am indebted to her for the best two meals and the soundest sleep I ever enjoyed in my life.[473]

Despite the pleasures First House afforded, the *Brooklyn Daily Eagle* writer realized its occupants, living so close to the ocean, had more serious duties to perform than entertaining visitors: "...shipwrecked vessels have been dashed almost to the dooryard; and many a time have the family been roused on a stormy night to receive the survivors of a castaway crew. Often too a sadder duty falls upon them: that of burying the unclaimed bodies that are washed ashore. I do not envy them their lonely post."[474]

Upon finally reaching the Montauk Point Lighthouse the writer proclaimed:

He who loves ocean scenery in its grandest effects, should pay at least one visit to Montauk Point. I would dwell upon the peculiar advantages of this place, but I know that the best description is insipid to him who has seen the roll of breakers, and incomprehensible to him who has not. The sentiments of the sea can be felt only on the seashore...It has been our good fortune to get a room at the "Fourth House". This is occupied...by Mr. Gardiner, the keeper of the lighthouse. Our sojourn with him and his amiable lady has been inexpressibly pleasant. Mr. Gardiner has a hearty way of receiving visitors, which would of itself pay any one for the journey to his house; and as to Mrs. Gardiner, I shall long remember her as a model hostess.[475]

The beloved Long Island-born poet, Walt Whitman (1819-1892), wrote in 1861 of an adventure on Montauk:

Montauk Point! how few Americans there are who have heard of thee-- although there are equally few who have seen thee with their bodily eyes, or trodden on thy greensward...Montauk is fertile and verdant. The soil is rich, the grass is green and plentiful...The point where the lighthouse stands—and it is the extreme point-- is quite a high hill...The light-house here is a very substantial one of an old-fashioned sort, built in 1795; the lights are two hundred feet above the level of the sea. Sheltered in a little vale near by is the dwelling of the keeper and his family, the only comfortable residence for many miles. It is a tolerably roomy cottage—a sort of public house; and some inveterate sportsmen and lovers of nature in her wild aspects come here during the summer and fall, and board awhile and have fun...there were innumerable wonders and beauties all along the shore, and edges of the cliffs. There were earths of all colors, and stones of every conceivable shape, hue, and destiny, with shells, large boulders of a pure white substance, and layers of those smooth round pebbles called "milk stones" by the country children...We rambled up the hills to the top of the highest, we ran races down, we scampered along the shore, jumping from rock to rock...we threw our hats in the air, aimed stones at the shrieking sea-gulls, mocked the wind, and imitated the cries of various animals in a style that beat nature all out![476]

After Whitman and his friends finished exploring the beach, they returned to the lighthouse keeper's dwelling. Whitman continued:

Our master of the revels had utterly failed to negotiate a dinner for us at the cottage! Three several [separate?] parties had been in advance of ours, that day, and had eaten up the last crumb in the house! Wasn't this enough to make Rome howl?...Something must be done, and quickly...We luckily spied a flock of well-grown chickens feeding near the cottage door...We proceeded in solid phalanx to the landlady—the Mrs. Lighthouse Keeper—and with an air showed we were not going to stand on trifles, gave voice to our ultimatum. The landlady attempted to demur, but the major domo loudly proposed that if all else failed, we should eat the landlady herself; and this motion being passed by acclamation, the good woman gave in. Six fat pullets had their heads off in as many minutes, and shortly afterwards we made a solemn procession down to the water, each man carrying a part of the provender, in its raw state. For we determined to cook our meal on board the sloop, and owe no thanks to those inhospitable shores...All worked to charm. Amid laughter, glee, and much good sport...we cooked that dinner...We pulled up stakes, and put for home [Greenport].[477]

A correspondent for the *Brooklyn Times* described the Montauk Point Lighthouse in 1868:

Montauk Light is one of the finest beacons of which our land can boast...Three keepers are constantly in atten-

dance, the delicate character of the machinery (which is of French invention) demanding the most assiduous care. Uncle Sam has lodged them most comfortably, and they are at all times well prepared to accommodate such visitors as have the enterprise and taste to venture a peep at this "Ultima Thule" of our "sea girt" shore. The scenery is wild and beautiful in the extreme. In a violent storm it must be truly sublime. From the heaving ocean the eye turns to equally heaving land, covered only by a short grass, on which vast herds of cattle find their sustenance. No sign of human life breaks the strange monotony of the landscape. The notes of the sea bird or the plover alone relieve the sullen boom of the restless waves.[478]

An 1873 guest at nearby Third House described Montauk in the guest book: "Montauk grand glorious Montauk! Ask me to name its equal in romantic scenery, & I will tell you of the far off Pacific coast you will not find it there, & away beyond in the isles of the Sea still you find it not. No, it is not to be found, only here. There is but one Montauk."[479]

A trip from New York City to the lighthouse by lithographer Charles Parsons (1821-1899) and some friends was recorded in *Harper's New Monthly Magazine* in 1871. It gives a sense of the complexity of reaching Montauk Point in the nineteenth century. The travelers first took a boat up the East River, then went the length of Long Island Sound, and spent the night at Sag Harbor. From there they boarded a stage for East Hampton where they drew sketches of local scenery before staying the night in the village. The next morning they started early and reached Amagansett around 8:00 a.m. The trip across Napeague Beach was arduous and the group was grateful to reach First House and have refreshments. They continued to Second House, home of the Osborn family, where they spent the night. The following morning they walked along the beach, noting debris from numerous shipwrecks. By noon they reached Third House where they saw a large herd of cattle grazing on the hills around Great Pond. In the distance they caught their first glimpse of the Montauk Point Lighthouse. They sketched more scenery, and, after dinner, continued toward the lighthouse.[480]

(Today, the same trip from New York City to the lighthouse takes only a few hours by automobile.)

The account of the group's visit to the lighthouse follows:

> *We reached Montauk Light, and the end of our second days' tramp, a little after dark. Later in the evening we accompanied the keeper (Mr. Ripley) on a tour of inspection. Going through a passageway we found ourselves in the oil room, neatly paved with colored tiles, the oil being stored in large tanks on one side of the room. The ascent is by 137 steps, winding around the central shaft and the walls are of enormous thickness, the tower, erected in 1796, was some years since strengthened by building a solid brick lining inside the original structure. Immediately below the lamp is the keeper's room and the apparatus which keeps the revolving "flash" in operation. Here through the weary watches of the night, one hundred and eight feet above the sea, exposed to the full force of the wild Atlantic storms, these faithful sentinels keep vigil. On their fidelity and constant watchfulness depends the safety of the many thousands of vessels that annually traverse*

this highway of sea.

A few steps higher and we are in the lantern, containing a "Fresnel" flash light [lens] of the first order made by Henry LePaute. It is a miracle of ingenuity in the scientific concentration of the lenses. We step inside the lenses as the "flash" slowly revolves, and the next moment are enclosed in light which is visible for thirty-six miles seaward. The flash throws a flood of brilliant light around the entire circle, disappearing and reappearing every two minutes.

Mr. Ripley explains to us that the lamp has two reservoirs-- an upper and a lower; the former being five feet above and directly over the lower one. They are connected by two pipes. The lower reservoir contains a pump, by which the oil is forced through one of the pipes into the upper reservoir. The feed pipe with the lamp has a chamber which contains a small float, by which the flow of oil is regulated, allowing 120 drops per minute. The oil that is not consumed passes down into a receiver under the lamp, to which a small tube is attached, conveying it into the lower reservoir, to again be pumped up. During the long winter nights the lamp will consume two and one-half gallons of refined lard-oil, and the oil will flow four hours without pumping. The upper reservoir will contain nine gallons. The flash is propelled by clock-work, which, when wound up, will run three hours. The lenses are twelve feet in height and six feet in diameter. The lamp is placed inside of the lenses, having four wicks, the largest being three and a half inches in diameter. During the day the lenses are covered with linen curtains to prevent the rays of the sun from striking the lamp and unsoldering the brass-work. The height of the lantern is nine feet, the frame of solid iron. No wood of any kind is used in the tower.

Much trouble is experienced in keeping oil from congealing during the cold winter nights, owing to the want of stoves in the oil room. Attention to this matter by the Light-House Board would add much to the comfort of the keepers and the efficiency of the light...

Stepping out on the balcony that surrounds the tower, the glorious panorama of the moonlit sea lay all around us, and at that moment two ships were crossing the glinting light of the moon. The raw, chilly night air soon drove us below to the comfortable fireside of the keeper's family, where we sat listening to stories of storms from the southeast, during which the whole weight of the Atlantic is thrown directly upon Montauk head. The light-house is built of granite, and, founded on rock, stands on the bluff sixty feet above the beach. The sea is silently eating its way toward the tower, and this will soon compel a removal to the higher ground west.[481]

Prominent Long Island resident, William Cullen Bryant (1794-1878), poet and longtime editor of the *Evening Post*, gave his eloquent impressions of Montauk in 1872: "...a summer jaunt along the cliffs of Montauk Point has a charm difficult to match. The hills are like the open downs of England, and their rich grasses afford such excellent grazing that great numbers of cattle and sheep are every year driven there for pasturage. The peaceful herds upon the grassy slopes of the hills; the broken, sea-washed cliffs; the beach, with the ever-tumbling surf; the crisp, delicious air from the sea; the long, superb stretch of blue waters- all these make up a picture that is full both of exhilaration and of repose."[482]

Bryant described Montauk Point as a "...bold, solitary point of land, composed of sand, bowlders, and pebbles, with far stretches of sea on three of its sides. The storms here are grand, the wide Atlantic rolling in with unbroken force upon the shores. On the extreme point stands a tall, white light-house, erected in 1795, and one of the best-known lights of the coast."[483]

Historian Richard M. Bayles (1846-1930) of Middle Island described Montauk in 1873 as a place with a "...cool and refreshing sea breeze...and the entire absence of annoying insects; and we find this spot peculiarly favored for the purpose to which it has been appropriated for more than two hundred years."[484]

Montauk Point, Bayles continued, was a place of adventure and of vulnerability to the open sea:

> *"...the shore in the neighborhood of the Point is rocky, and the bottom of the ocean for a long distance eastward is strewn with huge boulders...The ceaseless action of the surf upon this point, directly exposed as it is to the angry beating of the Atlantic, is slowly but surely wearing it away. It has been estimated that altogether about two acres of the surface of this peninsula is by this means torn down and washed away every year. The point presents a bold cliff, rising abruptly sixty feet or more above the water, and against its base the everlasting surges of the ocean are almost continually dashing with irresistible fury. During a storm, when the waves, driven landward, are breaking among the rocks and thundering upon the shore, the scene presented here is terrific and impressively sublime."*[485]

He described the lighthouse as being "…eighty-five feet high, built of stone, the walls of which were afterward lined with brick. The height of the lantern above the sea level is one hundred and sixty feet [with the light being] visible twenty nautical miles distant, and under favorable circumstances several miles further."[486]

More than anything else, Bayles was grateful that Montauk remained unblemished:

> *Wrapt in a halo of solitude, Montauk sleeps peacefully amid its wild surroundings, and dreams of its unwritten tragedies, its un-told legends, its forgotten history of unknown ages past…The hand of civilization came and spangled the neighboring wilderness with cities, towns, and villages…but this spot, situated for two hundred years in the very midst of these transformation scenes…has remained to the present time with scarcely a mark of improvement upon its former condition. [The]…busy hand [of development] has scarcely turned a stone, or drawn a line, or left a finger mark upon this wildly beautiful peninsula.*[487]

Time and again, writers voiced their amazement at the solitude and wildness of Montauk Point, which seemed a world away from other places on Long Island. During the winter of 1879, Elizabeth Cartwright of East Hampton rode to Montauk Point in a covered carriage in snow so deep that "they [the driver and team] drove over the rail fence at the entrance to Montauk. One woman, at the Point with three keepers, said she had not seen a woman's face before in six weeks."[488]

Charles Lanman (1819-1895), an author, government official, artist, librarian, and explorer, included Montauk in an 1881 publication of his travels to various parts of the world. Montauk Point Lighthouse, Lanman said, "...stands within a few hundred paces of the extreme eastern point of Long Island—a spot called by the Indians Wampono-mon...For fifty-three years it performed its office, after the fashion of the olden times, during which period it was surmounted by the effigy of an Indian's head; but in 1849 the Government thought proper to dress it up with modern improvements at a cost of eleven thousand dollars, so that the prospects have been much brightened."[489]

An image of Montauk Point Lighthouse, ca. 1880s, probably was used as a souvenir postcard. (National Archives)

Lanman noted that the keeper's salary at the time was $700 per year. The beauty of Montauk struck him: "A better place to study the phases of the ocean, the beauties of the sky, the powers of the wind, or the fantastic performances of the fog, cannot be found on the Atlantic coast; and any lover of nature who may be privileged to spend a week or a month on this spot will have freighted his mind with emotions and thoughts that will be cherished to the end of his days."[490] Delving into the Point's past, Lanman said that Montauk had once been:

> *...completely covered with luxuriant forests, but in 1815 and 1823 it was visited by two hurricanes, which leveled all the towering vegetation, and the trees having rotted away or been used as fuel, the hills having only in later years put on their beautiful vesture of green.*
>
> *At various localities on the Montauk coast there have been established a number of Relief Houses, where at all times may be found a supply of fuel and food and clothing, as well as signal guns, appropriate cordage and life-boats, which, during the rigour of winter, have been found of the greatest benefit to the unfortunate mariners.*
>
> *To be there [at Montauk Point] in a heavy fog, when the alarm bell is sounding forth its dismal warnings; or when the trampling surf and the booming thunder, all in the glare of sheeted lightning, are striving to excel each other in their tumultuous roarings, would be to have experiences never to be forgotten. But if a thing of beauty is indeed a joy forever, it only requires a brief sojourn at the Point, for a man to store away in his memory an ever-varying collection of pictures, marvellous for their loveliness.*
>
> *[From the top of the lighthouse he looked down]...upon a fleet of more than a hundred mackerel fishermen, with a whale rolling along in the offing, and sporting defiance to the toilers of the sea.*[491]

A year after Lanman's visit to Montauk Point, historian William S. Pelletreau (1840-1917) of Southampton arrived. He was equally impressed with the natural splendor. The land, Pelletreau said, "...remains in primeval grandeur, as unsubdued by the toil of man as when the Indian roamed over it with undisputed sway. A small portion is covered with woods, but the greater part is clear and has probably always been so. The land is broken and hilly, and from the summits of the highlands may be seen a magnificent prospect of bay and ocean. The view from the extremity of the point is exceedingly grand."[492]

A trip by foot or wagon was not the only route to Montauk Point, but it may have been the least tumultuous. In August 1886 a man from Brooklyn journeyed to the lighthouse aboard the *C. P. Daly* from Sag Harbor:

> *...ocean waves have been high and fierce, but the Daly is securely anchored in the bay in front of the Montauk Point Lighthouse. The mate takes me ashore in a small boat...[then I headed for] the lighthouse, where I find a cordial welcome and a fish dinner fit for a king. The point is exposed to the blasts from every direction and the winds whistle through the house, as in a Winter's storm. Captain Scott, the lighthouse keeper, has not experienced such a day this Summer. A climb to the lighthouse observatory and a grand view is spread before the vision...The ocean was dotted with white sails, and in the bay below were a dozen fishing smacks anchored to escape the storm...From this broad plateau is one of the grandest views imaginable. There is no obstruction to the gaze. On one side the ocean comes dashing upon the rocks, bearing often the wreck of some ill fated vessel, while on the side to the north, the waters are more peaceful.*[493]

If such a location was within fifty miles of New York and near a railroad the land would be worth $100 a foot. It is difficult to imagine a more delightful location. There is no other place by which to make a comparison. From which ever way the breezes come these Montauk people are sure to have the benefit of them.[494]

Another Brooklynite, apparently in good physical shape, decided to walk to Montauk Point from East Hampton in the summer of 1887. When others heard of his plans, they warned of numerous dangers he might face, so many that he said, "I felt as if I were leaving for Africa." Though he never reached the lighthouse, some of the outlandish advice he received is evidence of the exaggerated and misleading information available at the time:

Look out for the snakes when you go through the Amagansett woods...Mind you don't lose yourself. If you go astray in those jungles beyond Easthampton you'll wander around in them for a month before you strike the road again...You must carry your dinner and a tank of ice water, for there's nothing to eat or drink for nearly twenty miles...If those green flies don't eat the whole face off from you, then I lose my guess...There's no undertow worth talking about, but the shore is just lined with sharks... Did you know that the sea serpent was seen going out of the shrub oaks this side of Montauk? He mowed down bushes and left a trail three feet wide. Better take a gun.[495]

Two years later a group of four men, including an 11-year-old-boy, set out to hike all the way from Brooklyn to Montauk Point. They reached Amagansett, where they were informed of the difficult terrain that lay ahead. They decided to "drive to Montauk Point for the sake of familiarizing ourselves with the road and country."

The lightkeepers, a child, and the station dog were photographed in 1884 by the fog signal building. Note the fog trumpet protruding from the exterior wall. The dwelling was in the rear at left. (National Archives)

When they reached the hills of Montauk, they reflected on their journey across the Napeague stretch: "We can hardly believe we are on Long Island when we think that there is a place within one hundred miles of Brooklyn which had the power of possessing us with feelings of such utter loneliness and at times almost fear at the thought of missing what was almost a blind track. All agreed that we could hardly feel further away from home were we in the center of Africa."[496]

The group passed First House and Second House, and then stopped to rest at Third House. They arrived at the lighthouse at about 4:00 pm:

> *...which gave us an opportunity to take in this extremely eastern point of Long Island; not that it offers many opportunities for sight seeing other than gazing upon the Atlantic, which was upon three sides of us, and so great in appearance as to seem possessed of the world except the few miles directly in back of us. Paid our respects to Old Ocean by taking a hand bath. By that time supper was announced. Apropos, we had wondered how we were going to fare for eating, as there were no apparent signs of cultivation. But our fears were groundless, as our two meals at this place proved. Didn't suppose such an isolated place could produce such meals, but nature, aided by the able hands of the light house keeper's wife, made a regal meal. The keeper himself, as well as an assistant, proved most agreeable persons.*[497]

A tour of the light station confirmed the fastidious habits of the lighthouse keepers: "...we could not but notice the marked neatness of everything, which order prevails in their dwelling houses." The visitors spent the night in the keeper's dwelling in "most inviting and comfortable beds."[498]

Before they departed the next day, the group thanked their gracious hosts and eagerly returned to Amagansett,

"…which had seemed to us before leaving it a very insignificant place", [but now resembled]…a great metropolis and alive to every improvement of this advanced age." They agreed that nothing could lure them back to Montauk Point. As for the lighthouse's occupants, the visitors had "…every sympathy for this lonely family, who are almost twenty miles away from any church, schools, society or amusements…It seems only just that the Government should put every means possible within the power of these persons to enable them to get some comfort and pleasure out of their forced insulation from the world at large."[499]

An unusual accomplishment was a bicycle ride from Rockville Centre, Long Island to Montauk Point in August 1890 by a man named Wheeler. He left home on a Tuesday evening and arrived at the lighthouse Wednesday night. It was a first.[500] A decade later, it was suggested a cycle path be built from Amagansett to the Point: "If the honorable commissioners will build it and levy a toll of say a dime on each wheelman using it, I will promise them that it will pay for itself in a single season…The ride would be worth coming from the uttermost parts to take."[501]

A group from upstate New York, who journeyed to Montauk Point Lighthouse in 1892, described the trip from East Hampton to the lighthouse:

> *…after riding nearly twenty miles, the lofty white tower of the Montauk Light House at last broke our view. Soon we were there, at the land's end, but it seemed on alighting as if we would be blown into the water…We were glad to get into the Keeper's house, and through it into the Light House, with which there is an inside connection. His daughter, a pleasant young lady, let us in, and the Keeper himself, Mr. James G Scott, gave us a friendly welcome, and treated us with the utmost kind-*

ness. First he took us into the ante room to the tower, where are kept all the extra lamps and accessory apparatus ready at any moment for a possible accident to the light shining up on top. It was interesting to see what precautions had been taken to repair any damage or to prevent any delay in rekindling the light, if it should be extinguished...At length we reached the top and came to the great lantern nine feet high set in a frame of solid iron...The keeper told us that it is intended to change the "flash light" so that instead of appearing every two minutes it will appear at only half minute intervals. As the lamp consumes two quarts of oil every hour, it would require, of course, when the days and nights are equal, six gallons of oil from sun set to sun rise. Punctually at set of sun the light is always burning, and just as punctually as sun rise it is always put out...There is an iron railing or balcony around the top of the tower with a window looking out to sea. Stepping upon it, but holding fast by the window frame, for the wind was blowing too furiously to be entirely comfortable, and the idea of being blown off from that height...was not at all attractive. The truth is, one did not care to stand there very long, for the wind was so strong that it made even the solid tower vibrate and tremble under our feet. And yet the faithful keeper and his assistant here keep watch through the long tempestuous winter nights, and guard with unceasing vigilance the light to which so many eyes are turned, and upon whose brightness depend the lives of so many hundreds of the brave and hardy toilers of the sea.[502]

East Hampton historian Jeannette Edwards Rattray (1893-1974) recalled a family trip to Montauk from East Hampton in 1899 when she was 6-years old. Her experience is noteworthy, since it mentions the repeated complaint of all travelers taking this route. Starting out at about 4:00 a.m., the family made their way across Napeague where they "...smelled fearfully from a liberal dousing with oil of citronella to prevent the mosquitoes...from lifting us bodily out of the carriage."[503]

As late as the beginning of the twentieth century, the journey was arduous. Rattray recalled the road through Hither Hills being a "mere wagon track up hill and down dale, but hard and dry..." The trip was rough once more after passing Ditch Plain and the two life saving stations where "...the hills began again and the horses were given a breathing spell at Third House...Finally we passed Money Pond of Captain Kidd legends, and reached the Point, along towards noon. After going up in the Light, and looking at Captain Scott's Indian arrowhead collection, we would picnic on the side of the hill overlooking Turtle Bay and the striped-bass fishing stands jutting out into the surf; finishing off our lunch with wild strawberries picked on the spot, fragrant and warm with the sun."[504]

The lure of photographing Montauk Point was noted in a diary kept by an enterprising Reverend Loren A. Rowley of the East Marion Baptist Church, who visited on September 4, 1900. He took five pictures of the lighthouse and spent the night there. Later he would sell these photos to keeper James G. Scott's wife for 25-cents each. She in turn sold them to horse and buggy tourists for 35-cents each.[505]

One of the last recorded visitors to the Montauk Point Lighthouse while Captain Scott was keeper was Eleanor Ferguson, who came to the station shortly before 1910:

An 1897 picture depicted the solitude and loneliness of Montauk. The desolate bluffs near Ditch Plains trailed away toward Montauk Point Lighthouse in the distance. (Courtesy of Suffolk County Historical Society.)

[A] wild diversion was riding out to the lighthouse. This must have been at least five miles from the village...We rode in a surrey-- complete with fringe-- and fought mosquitoes all the way...Captain Scott was the Keeper. He was not a young man but was still able to climb up and down the narrow spiral stairs and tend the big kerosene lamps that send their magnified light through the revolving prisms in their assigned code of flashes. The heavy glass that surrounded this tower room was pitted and pockmarked by the beaks of birds that had hit it, dazzled by the light, and had gone to their deaths below. We climbed the light more than

once and left our names in the visitors' book in the nautically immaculate room below.[506]

New York photographer and historian, Eugene L. Armbruster (1865-1943), described a 1923 trip to the Point from Third House along the very hilly Old Montauk Highway (now a dead end road):

...the upper part of the lighthouse comes into view but is soon lost again; then a larger portion of the structure can be seen; another hill affords a still more extended view, and eventually Montauk Point lies before your eyes, a truly beautiful sight.

The original [lighthouse] structure was built up to and including the red painted part. The upper white portion was added soon after 1860. Before the end of the road is reached at the lighthouse, you pass the Wyandank, a hospitable place kept by Mrs. Smith, where you can get lunch.[507]

From the tower, Armbruster noted a lack of greenery: "Turtle Hill and the entire Point seem to be an immense sand pile, packed so tight that it is equal to a giant rock." He also referred to the fisherman's dock that stood off the Point in those years: "Little bridges running out from the rocky shore are built for the use of the fishermen. They have to be rebuilt every year, as the winter storms destroy them."[508]

Fannie August Allis wrote fondly in a 1933 newspaper article of her first look at Montauk Point:

We could have set for hours and gazed upon the scene spread out before us, never tiring of watching the steady, ceaseless rolling of the surf with its white foam topping the giant waves as they rushed on, and then broke on the line of rocks so near the pebbly, moss-strewn beach. Not only was the coloring of the waves perfect with all their varying tints of ocean-blue, but that wide-open expanse of the ocean itself, as it finally merged into the far-reaching horizon, gave one a sense of both majesty and solemnity, making one feel as never before the littleness of man before the omnipotence of God.[509]

Montauk Point Light attracted tourists throughout its career. A group was shown visiting the station on July 27, 1934. (Courtesy Suffolk County Historical Society)

Two years later, *East Hampton Star* reporter, Guy Duval, recalled a visit to the lighthouse as a young man, when he spent the night in the keeper's dwelling and awakened to "the delicious flavor of the fish brought from the water but an hour before it was served at the breakfast table."[510]

With the arrival of automobiles and the development of a highway system on Long Island, the ordeal of a long trip to such a remote and lonely destination as Montauk came to an end. Montauk Point State Parkway now whisks the traveler to the lighthouse with ease. The once 6-hour trip by horse and wagon from East Hampton can be accomplished in an automobile in about 30-minutes.

Regardless of the route, the time involved, or the mode of transportation, Montauk Point remains a truly beautiful and historic place to visit.

The fishing pier (lower left) was visible in this July 27, 1934 image of Montauk Point Lighthouse. (Courtesy of Suffolk County Historical Society)

CHAPTER 10
Montauk Point Lighthouse Museum

On October 11, 1948, the Commandant of the U.S. Coast Guard received the following letter from the Commander of the Third Coast Guard District:

> *An exhibit is maintained at...[Montauk] light station which is open to the public for visit and inspection. This exhibit consists of photographs of various phases of Coast Guard operations and models of some types of standard equipment and apparatus. Visitors are permitted to inspect the light station as a part of the exhibit.*
>
> *To assist in the accommodation of the some 400 visitors per day during the period 1 June to 15 September, three additional men were assigned to the light station during that period for temporary duty to act as guides.*
>
> *The signature register at the exhibit indicates that people from many countries of the world were among the visitors who showed a seemingly genuine interest in the display.*

It is believed that continuance of the exhibit is desirable as an aid to good public relations.[511]

The same letter could be written today. Just as in 1948, Montauk Point Lighthouse offers guided tours of the station, displays of its history, and a guest register listing names of visitors from around the world. The Museum, like the Coast Guard occupants of the station's past, is a dedicated "aid to public relations." Its docents perpetuate not only the history and lore of the station, but also its reputation as a place to visit and learn.

Montauk Point Lighthouse has always been a bit of a showoff! From its earliest days, the light's keepers relished giving tours, sharing their hobbies and collections, and occasionally hosting visitors overnight. Poets and painters flocked to the Point and left their impressions on paper and canvas; newspaper reporters penned beguiling descriptions of the Point's sequestered tranquility. The Coast Guard—no less enamored of Montauk Point than any of its previous tenants—expressed its pride in the station with a formal exhibit in 1948 and another larger one in 1981.

Today, the Montauk Historical Society continues the museum tradition at Montauk Point Lighthouse, greeting thousands of visitors each year. The society was chartered on January 25, 1962 and among its many accomplishments over the years are historical records for area cemeteries, the development of Second House Museum, fundraising events such as craft fairs, and contributions to a variety of historic and environmental projects and organizations. But getting to this point took time, effort, and talent.

In April 1986 representatives of the Montauk Historical Society met with Coast Guard officials at Governor's Island in New York City to discuss a 20-year lease for the lighthouse property. The Montauk Chamber of Commerce, led by Al Holden, pledged support for the project. It was decided that a small museum previously operated by the Coast Guard at the lighthouse would be reopened and expanded. By July, an agreement was reached to convert the Montauk Point Lighthouse to a museum.

The tower's 3½-order bivalve Fresnel lens had served for 83-years and was still in place in the lantern.[512] Montauk Point also was the only remaining light station in New York State still manned by Coast Guard personnel. However, the light was slated to be automated. Chief Warrant Officer Barrie Kline of the Shinnecock station said automation was "...more cost-effective because there are no salaries and housing of staff to pay for. Montauk's time had to come." He added that the tower was slated to be "hardened," meaning it would be sealed off after the light was automated to prevent vandalism.

Once this plan was made public, the Montauk Historical Society stepped in to keep the lighthouse open for public access. "People out here have an affection for the lighthouse and didn't want to see it closed up and abandoned," said Chairman of the Lighthouse Committee Dick White in 1986.[513] White still serves in several capacities at the museum, but his roots in Montauk go back many generations. His grandfather established White's Drug Store in the village in 1928. White is a civic activist and has held numerous important positions in his career, including East Hampton Town Councilman, Town budget director, Commissioner of the Montauk Fire Department, and member of the East Hampton Town Planning Board. He also found time to operate White's Liquor Store in Montauk for many years. When the Montauk Historical Society began efforts to acquire the lighthouse for museum purposes, White was selected as chairman of the newly formed Lighthouse Committee. Considering his passion for local history and his lifelong devotion to the interests of Montauk, there was no better choice.

On Friday, September 12, 1986 the Montauk Historical Society took control of the lighthouse in an official ceremony attended by the Coast Guard, military personnel, and several prominent citizens. The last keeper, Petty Officer W. Gene Hughes, officially "disestablished" the light station and turned it over to the Society. Coast Guard Captain Allen Taylor made the following comments in the Record of Inspection book: "Ceremony a historic event in the continuing history of Montauk Lighthouse. A touching and well attended ceremony that marks the end of an era and the beginning of a new one. My best wished to O in C [officer in charge] Hughes and crew and the Montauk Historical Society."[514]

More than 300 Montauk residents attended the ceremony and listened as Lieutenant David Pekoske, chief of the Shinnecock Group of lighthouses on eastern Long Island, spoke of Hughes and his predecessors' dedication to maintaining the Montauk Point Light Station: "[They] not only kept the light faithfully, they also helped perform search-and-rescue missions, located lost mariners and helped with thousands and thousands of tourists who have come to the lighthouse."

Peg Joyce, President of the Montauk Historical Society, vowed to develop a museum inside the keeper's dwelling that would keep alive the spirit of the lighthouse keepers.[515] Dick White announced plans for the creation of the museum, including a display of the beautiful 3½-order bivalve Fresnel lens and other important artifacts. Originally, the plans called for two apartments to be occupied by a patrolman from the Long Island State Parkway Police and the museum's curator.

Top—A December 26, 1986 photo of Montauk Point Light, shortly before automation, was taken from Camp Hero. (Author Photo)

Bottom— A rare 3½ order bivalve Fresnel lens, weighing 5,000-pounds and manufactured by Henry LePaute of Paris, was installed in the Montauk Point Lighthouse on June 15, 1903. (It replaced a 1st-order Fresnel lens that weighed twice as much) Originally 86,000 candle-power, it emitted a single flash every 10-seconds. The brilliance was increased to 2,500,000 candlepower with a 5-second flash in 1961. The classical lens was removed on February 3, 1987 when the light was automated. It is now a featured exhibit in the museum. Photo taken in 2005.(Author Photo)

On February 3, 1987 automation work began. The Fresnel lens was removed from the lantern and replaced with twin 24-inch rotating spotlights. The priceless 3½-order lens was carefully moved to the base of the tower in sections and reassembled in the oil room as an exhibit in the soon-to-be-museum. The fog signal was connected to a strobe that could detect fog conditions and start the signal automatically.

On March 3, 1987 the U.S. Coast Guard officially leased the lighthouse property to the Montauk Historical Society for a period of thirty years "to restore, preserve and operate a historic site to be used with educational, historic, recreational, and cultural programs open to and for the benefit of the general public. Theme displays, museum, gift shop, and open exhibits are authorized. Appropriate portions of the existing improvements may be utilized as living quarters if desirable for security purposes."

The Disestablishment Ceremony of Light Station Montauk Point took place on April 1, 1987 when the Montauk Historical Society leased the lighthouse from the Coast Guard for a 30-year period. The museum's site manager, Laura King, and her husband had already moved into an upstairs apartment as a security presence. Robert Hefner, museum director, began working with Dick White to catalog furniture and other items left behind by the Coast Guard.[516] As part of the ceremony, the Coast Guard ensign was lowered from the flagpole and replaced with the flag of the Montauk Historical Society.

The Montauk Point Lighthouse Museum officially opened to the public on May 23, 1987. A newly constructed ticket booth, designed to resemble an old oil storage house, stood by the fence ready to receive visitors. Admission was $1.50 for adults and $0.75 for children. According to Dick White, an estimated $12,000 was spent preparing the lighthouse grounds for opening day.

Photos dating back to 1897 and diagrams of the construction of the lighthouse and its 1860 renovation adorned the former head keeper's living room. The room housing the 5000-pound, 3½-order bivalve Fresnel lens contained additional lenses loaned to the museum by the Mystic Seaport Museum in Connecticut.

The front parlor of Montauk Point Lighthouse Museum was once the living room of the head keeper. Its exhibits include the authorization to build the lighthouse (over the mantel), a model of the slave ship *Amistad* (right), and items donated by the family of keeper James G. Scott (left). Presentations on the history of the lighthouse are given in this room. Photo taken in 2005. (Author Photo)

In September 1987 the museum received a letter from R. G. Kuerner of Little Rock, Arkansas stating he had located the ship's bell from the USS *Montauk* in a scrap yard and wanted to donate it to the village of Montauk or a local organization. The ship saw service in WWII carrying troops and cargo in the Pacific from 1944-45. On April 1, 1945 it was attacked by *kamikaze* off Okinawa. In December 1945 it was transferred to the Atlantic fleet and based at Charleston, South Carolina. The ship was decommissioned in 1947 and stricken from the register on September 1, 1961. By the winter of 1987, the 250-pound bell had a new home on the lighthouse grounds at the base of the flagpole in front of the museum building.

At the conclusion of the 1987 season, the society announced that over 75,000 visitors had come to the Lighthouse Museum from May 23 through November 29. A few months later, Dana Brancato was hired as the site manager for the museum.

In 1990 the museum acquired an original document dated October 24, 1791 authorizing George Washington to set aside funds for the building of the Montauk Point Lighthouse. Judith Lowry, owner of a rare book store in Manhattan, sold the document to the Montauk Historical Society. A $9,000 grant from Mr. and Mrs. E. Virgil Conway helped pay for the artifact.[517] It went on public display the following year.

The *Day Mark*, a pamphlet about museum activities, began publication in 1990. Also that year, Barbara Strong and her family—descendants of lighthouse keeper James G. Scott—restored and donated for display an original copy of the *Brooklyn Daily Eagle* dated October 10, 1910. It pro filed Scott's life. During Lighthouse Weekend in 1990, the 1838 dwelling was opened to the public with an exhibit of photographs by Neil Schoil. In May 1991 the Indian arrowhead collection owned by Irene Graham, great-daughter of keeper Captain James G. Scott, was donated to the museum.

The Erosion Room at Montauk Point Lighthouse Museum was formerly the bedroom of the head keeper. Today the room is devoted to the work of Giorgina Reid and her erosion control method called "Reed Trench Terracing". Exhibits show how erosion has shaped Montauk Point over the centuries and how Reid's efforts helped to control it and save the lighthouse from destruction. Photo taken in 2005. (Author Photo)

Beginning in 1992 the video, *The Montauk Lighthouse: Sentinel of Long Island* began showing in the museum. Narrated by well-known talk show host, Dick Cavett, it was written, produced, and directed by Sharon Ames of East Hampton. Help with research was provided by Dorothy King of the Long Island Collection in the East Hampton Library, local historian Robert Hefner, and former Lighthouse Committee member Joseph Burgess.

The museum continued to grow, but there was another equally important aspect of the society's mission that required attention. The tower and other buildings on the property had to be maintained. In 1992 the keeper's dwelling underwent a $125,000 renovation, restoring the house to its 1938 appearance. Dick White recalled: "If we had done [the restorative work] to 1860, there would be no electricity, no plumbing, no insulation, no gas. You would have an 1860 house. Nineteen thirty-eight was the period of least disturbance...Prior, there were outdoor privies, it was lit by oil lamps, heated by fireplaces and coal stoves."[518]

In December 1992 work began on a new gift shop. The former kitchen and rooms of members of the Coast Guard were stripped bare, original flooring was restored, and windows were repositioned in their 1860 configuration. The shop opened at the beginning of the 1993 tourist season.[519]

In 1994 the Lighthouse Museum Committee commissioned Lester Associates of Nyack, New York to build four models depicting the changes that have occurred at Montauk Point Lighthouse in its 200-year history.

The highlights of each include:

- 1796: Newly constructed tower and original keeper's dwelling at the foot of Turtle Hill.
- 1860: Tower renovation and new keeper's dwelling, along with the 1838 addition to the old keeper's dwelling, plus a large garden
- 1903: Marconi wireless station, rescue of wrecked ship *Cuba*, wrecked at the Point December 18, 1903, eight rescued, ship lost.
- 1943: Camouflaged submarine spotting tower, army barracks, Coast Guard colors on buildings, fishing pier built and rebuilt by fishermen over the years, army pillbox on Turtle Hill (today lying along the shore).

Collectively, all four scenes show the dramatic effects of erosion at the Point. The display is located in the museum's Erosion Room, which formerly was the bedroom of the head keeper.

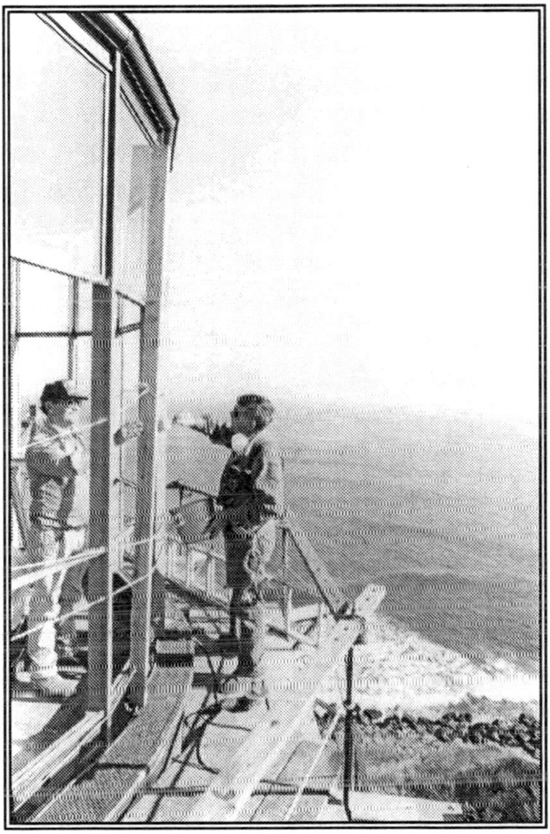

An image from the mid-1990s caught workers preparing the lantern for the Lighthouse Bicentennial in 1996. (Montauk Point Lighthouse Museum)

In 1995 Tricia Wood, who had been a tour guide at the

lighthouse since its first season, became assistant site manager to Dana Brancato. Two years later, she was promoted to site manager, a position she still maintained in 2007 when this book was completed.

International Chimney Corporation of Buffalo, New York re-glazed the lantern window curtain walls in time for the lighthouse bicentennial celebration on June 1, 1996. The glass was "eaten away" according to Tricia Wood, "and since the light is still in use, kept going by the Coast Guard, we had to do something to eliminate leakage and preserve the room." The $155,000 price tag was raised by the Montauk Historical Society.[520]

The bicentennial was celebrated with a grand ceremony at the site on June 1, 1996. Master of ceremonies, celebrity Dick Cavett, proclaimed, "The sea does not want the lighthouse. It has spoiled its best-laid plans. By some miracle, we come and go. It stays here. Let's hope it outlives us."

Father Raymond Nugent of St. Therese of Lisieux of Montauk, a descendant of surveyor Ezra L'Hommedieu, gave the invocation. Giorginia Reid, then 88, was honored by Dick White for her successful efforts to halt the erosion at Montauk Point: "Twenty-six years ago she said it could be done. It's done." Others present at the ceremony included Margaret Buckridge Bock, daughter of keeper Thomas Buckridge, Irene Graham, great-granddaughter of keeper James Scott, and former keeper Charles Schumacher. Suffolk County Executive, Robert Gaffney, called the East End the "soul of Suffolk County" with the lighthouse as its symbol.

A notable special guest was Admiral Robert E. Kramek (1939-), Commandant of the Coast Guard from 1994 to 1998, who with his wife enjoyed a three-day stay at the lighthouse. He noted in his speech on bicentennial day that in his entire Coast Guard career he had not seen a station as well maintained as Montauk Point.

In 1996 the work of Giorgina and Donald Reid was honored with the dedication of the Erosion Room at the museum. Displays depicted the causes and effects of the erosion problem and the Reids' efforts to combat it. Also in 1996 the lighthouse diorama in the central hallway was opened, displaying twenty-eight lighthouses around Long Island. The museum welcomed its one-millionth visitor during 1996.

Since January 30, 1996 the light station has been a Coast Guard Differential Global Positioning System site (DGPS), a high-tech satellite navigation method accurate to within 10-meters (32.8-feet). GPS standard positioning accuracy is 100-meters (328-feet).

On September 30, 1996 President Bill Clinton signed legislation transferring the lighthouse property from the U.S. Coast Guard to the Montauk Historical Society. The effort was spearheaded by Republican Representative, Michael Forbes, of Shirley. A ceremony celebrating the transfer of the deed took place on May 29, 1997. Five days prior, the Bicentennial Illumination Celebration had commemorated the first lighting of Montauk Point Lighthouse's original thirteen whale oil lamps by keeper Jacob Hand in April 1797.

Tom Ambrosio became assistant site manager in 1997 and moved into the position of museum director in 1999. One of his first major projects was to make foreign visitors feel more welcome. In the summer of 1998, the museum began printing brochures in five languages. It was the first attraction in Nassau or Suffolk County to do so.

"We wanted to do this so that those visitors can have a more meaningful visit and really comprehend what the history of the lighthouse is all about," said Ambrosio. He had advised the society that about 15-percent of visitors either did not speak English or spoke it as a second language. The new brochures were printed in Spanish, German, Japanese, French, as well as English. The brochures quickly became popular souvenirs. In addition, a home page on the Internet was created: www.montauklighthouse.com. [521]

In 1998 a weekend celebration was held to honor Theodore Roosevelt and his Rough Riders, 100-years after the date of his visit to the lighthouse on September 6, 1898. Colonel Roosevelt, portrayed by Jim Foote, and President and Mrs. William McKinley, portrayed by E. Virgil Conway and his wife Elaine, took part in the ceremony. Upon arrival they were greeted by lighthouse keeper Captain James G. Scott, portrayed by Bruce Beyer. The enactment was presented so convincingly that Marge Winski, lighthouse caretaker, wrote: "If you closed your eyes you really felt as if you were transported back into history…it was indeed 1898."

In early spring of 1997 an inspection of the tower revealed bulges in the brickwork, water runoff off the brickwork, and several bricks that were loose. In addition, severe corrosion was discovered under the parapet at the top of the tower. From March 16, 1998 to April 14, 1999 the exterior of the lighthouse underwent a restoration by the International Chimney Corp. (The corporation has moved four lighthouses and gained nationwide attention in July 1999 when they relocated the Cape Hatteras Lighthouse inland on North Carolina's Outer Banks).

Loose mortar joints, cracks in the sandstone, and the metalwork were repaired. A lime-rich mortar was used, allowing for greater flexibility. The old paint was stripped from the tower and new paint was applied. The special paint, resistant to temperatures as low as 20°F, sets rapidly in humid weather. It was applied with a urethane finish. The Montauk Point Lighthouse Restoration Project was completed on March 31, 1999.

The Lost at Sea Memorial opened to the public in 1999. The names of 117 commercial fishermen are carved into its granite face, memorializing those who lost their lives in the waters off Montauk Point. The memorial features an 8-foot tall statue of a shirtless fisherman standing in a dory and symbolically facing seaward. The name, age, and date of loss for each fisherman are engraved in the pedestal. The total weight of the sculpture is 2,600-pounds and it rests on a pedestal weighing 10½-tons. It was designed by Malcolm Frazier at a cost of $225,000 and was dedicated in October 1999.

Newsday reporter, Bill Bleyer, said of the memorial: "For those whose loved ones are lost at sea, there is no face in repose to look at one last time, no casket to touch, no body to bury. The person who has died has simply disappeared into the darkness and silence of the sea. [Perhaps] the Lost at Sea Memorial will ease some of the pain felt by those left behind."[522]

On August 27, 1999 the museum welcomed former Israeli Prime Minister Benjamin Netanyahu, his family, and other personnel in his entourage. When told the group could enter as special guests of the museum, Netanyahu insisted on paying admission. His group was impressed with the museum's displays and artifacts. Another dignitary to visit the museum was New York Governor George Pataki who came to the lighthouse on January 14, 2000 to film a television commercial for the Long Island Power Authority (LIPA).

For the 2000 season, a number of new exhibits were created and more work was done on the lighthouse. Twelve original documents of Ezra L'Hommedieu, valued at approximately $5000, were donated to the museum by actress/model Cheryl Tiegs. She arranged for the artifacts to be purchased at an auction by a private agent. However, when the time came to transfer the documents to the museum they could not be found. After several years of searching the artifacts were located. Two were put on exhibit at the Museums at Stony Brook (now the Long Island Museum) from May to October 1999. The two papers, along with the other ten documents, were transferred to the Lighthouse Museum for display in 2000.

A display documenting the slave ship *Amistad*, which ran aground on Montauk in 1839, also went on exhibit in 2000. In May 2000 a model of the Montauk Lighthouse, constructed by Farmingdale High School carpentry students under the guidance of teacher Jim Lawlor, was presented to Lighthouse Committee members. In October work began on the refurbishing of the deck and tower.

In 2001 the keeper's exhibit was opened to the public. It featured a desk owned by second keeper Jared Hand, son of first keeper Jacob Hand. Seated at the desk in the Windsor armchair is a mannequin of keeper James G. Scott, keeper from 1885-1910, wearing a period uniform. The mannequin was created by Dorfman Museum Figures; the $10,000 funding for it was donated by fashion designer, Ralph Lauren. There also are displays of documents and photos about lightkeepers and Coast Guard personnel stationed at Montauk, including several items donated by the family of Captain James Scott.

The room was used as an office from 1888 to 1942 by civilian lightkeepers and also housed radio beacon equipment for the station from 1940 to 1982. Records refer to it as the "radio room." It was used by the Coast Guard as the O.I.C.'s (officer in charge) office from 1982-1987.[523]

The cistern display in the Passageway of the museum opened in time for the 2001 tourist season. A cistern for water collection and storage was a standard part of an

1860-type "Double Dwelling for Keepers of First Order Lights" and was built at locations where obtaining well water was difficult. Gutters and leaders on the buildings' roofs conducted the rainwater to the cistern. A pipe led from the cistern to the kitchen, which at Montauk Point Light Station was located in the south basement where there was a pump and metal sink.

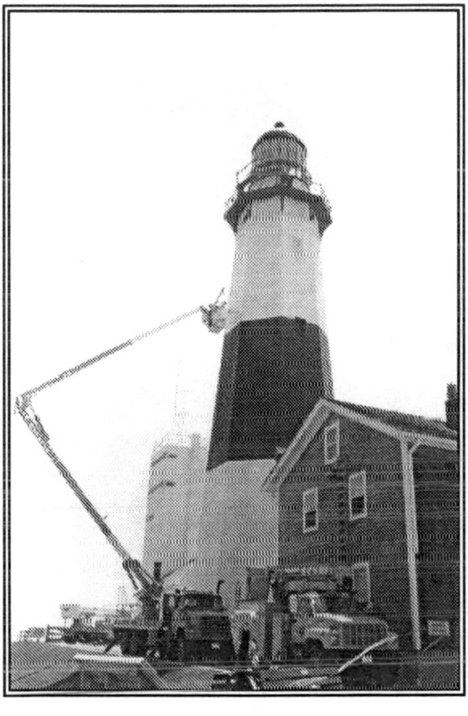

A fresh coat of paint was applied to the tower in preparation for the Lighthouse Bicentennial in 1996. Modern-day painters used a lift and cherry-picker, conveniences not available to the light keepers of old. (Montauk Point Lighthouse Museum)

The dramatic Lost at Sea Memorial was dedicated in 1999. It remembers commercial fishermen who lost their lives off the shores of Montauk. (Author Photo)

The 12-foot deep, 8-foot-wide cistern was constructed of brick with cement plaster on the inner surface to make it watertight. It was emptied and cleaned once a year. A pure chalk powder known as "whiting" was mixed into the water periodically to remove impurities. In 1909, keeper

James Scott ordered 15-pounds of "French Whiting for Cistern Water." The cistern was used until 1938 when electricity reached the lighthouse property and a motorized pump was installed over the well at the foot of Turtle Hill.[524]

In the fall of 2000, First Lady Hillary Rodham Clinton toured the Lighthouse Museum, escorted by Dick White. She came to Montauk to meet with local fishermen regarding their concerns about fisheries regulations. Clinton is one of several celebrities who have visited or donated to the museum. A bronze wall plaque of donors to the Montauk Historical Society includes Steven Spielberg, Billy Joel, Paul Simon and Ralph Lauren.

On July 24, 2001 the DCB-224 airport beacon was removed from the lantern room and replaced with a Vega VRB-25 DC low voltage marine rotating beacon. Manufactured in New Zealand, it was a 12-volt system powered by a 35-watt bulb. Five other bulbs were available on an automatic changer, each able to rotate into position and activate if the previous bulb failed. A battery pack served as backup if the power failed. The system was equipped with an electric eye (similar to those on streetlights) that enabled the light to turn on and off as needed. The 5-second flash of 293,700-candlepower was visible between 15 and 22-nautical miles depending on weather conditions. The fog signal was converted to a 12-volt system with an audible range of one-mile, a third of its original range.

Following the upgrade of the light in 2001, which reduced visibility of the beacon and range of the fog signal, locals complained. Safety, history, and aesthetics were the concerns. In response, in 2002, the Coast Guard increased the visible range of the light with 50-watt bulbs and added four foghorns to boost the audible range to 2-miles. These improvements, according to Lieutenant Marc Sennick of the Coast Guard, were the maximum changes possible with the existing infrastructure.[525]

A New Zealand-manufactured Vega VRB-25 DC marine rotating beacon was installed in the lantern at Montauk Point in July 2001. Weighing only 57-pounds, its light is powered by a 50-watt bulb and is visible approximately 19-miles at sea. (Author Photo)

Alterations to the light were not well received by many Montaukers. Janis Hewitt of the *East Hampton Star* spoke for many when she described the light as a:

> *...pitiful beam...Many of us locals...are upset with this monumental change, which was deemed to be penny-wise by the United States Coast Guard, the entity that manages the Light, as part of its coastal austerity program. In place of the sweeping light that shined and rotated 24 hours a day and flashed a shadowy beam a*

mile away into my dining room window every five seconds at night is a Vega RB-25, which in comparison throws a beam of light resembling a weakened flashlight. The glass dome at the tip of the tower looks barren, like an empty womb...Many in the hamlet of Montauk miss the Light dearly, Lighthouse officials say...The official report states that the light was downgraded to save money. But isn't something as historical as the Montauk Point Lighthouse worth a few extra pennies a day? After all, I'm sure it's our tax dollars footing the electric bill. Is it too late to restore it? I hope not. I do hope, however, that Coast Guard officials realize that sometimes the best idea isn't always the brightest.[526]

On February 23, 2002, while on vacation out of the country, Montauk Historical Society president, Peg Joyce, died. During her years as president from 1980-2002 the society accomplished many things, including securing the deed to the lighthouse property and establishing the museum. Dick White described Joyce as "a Montauk institution." The vacant seat of president was filled by long-time society member Betsy White.

Following the departure of museum director Tom Ambrosio in the fall of 2002, Ann Shengold took over, starting work in March 2003. Under her leadership and guidance, the planning and construction of two major projects began in 2004: the E. Virgil and Elaine Wingate Conway Visitor Center and a series of new, interactive, and permanent exhibits entitled "Where Land Meets Sea and Sky: Exploring Montauk History through the Richard T. Gilmartin Galleries."

The Conway Visitor Center opened to the public in March 2005 and featured a new and larger gift shop and an open-air patio. The official ribbon-cutting ceremony took place on June 25 with remarks from Mr. and Mrs. Conway, Lighthouse Committee Chairman, Dick White, Montauk Historical Society President, Betsy White, and others.

Meanwhile, the four rooms formerly used for the gift shop in the museum building were renovated to house the aforementioned "Gilmartin Galleries." The galleries' exhibits were designed to be interactive and focus on four subjects: "First People: the Montauketts", "Gifts of the Sea: Commercial and Sport Fishing", "Taken from the Sea: Shipwrecks," and "Fish Boards and Lollipop Boxes: Land Use." The project was named in memory of the late Richard T. Gilmartin (1904-1964), who was elected first president of the Montauk Historical Society in 1963. The idea for the galleries came from the Gilmartin family.

Ann Shengold was responsible for the steady progress and ultimate completion of the project. On December 3, 2005 members of the Montauk Historical Society, museum employees, and invited guests were treated to a sneak preview of the Gilmartin exhibits, with the first public viewing in February 2006.

Many visitors to the Montauk Lighthouse wonder if there are ghosts in the keeper's dwelling. When asked this question in 2000 building caretaker, Marge Winski, said, "I won't go into the cellar at night." Former museum director, Tom Ambrosio, said he didn't "like the attic on winter afternoons when the sun is low in the sky." He sometimes heard doors slam and said framed pictures fell from the walls at night. There was also an incident in the parlor room of the museum where a captain's chair was moved across the room to a window and positioned to appear as though someone had been sitting in it gazing outside.

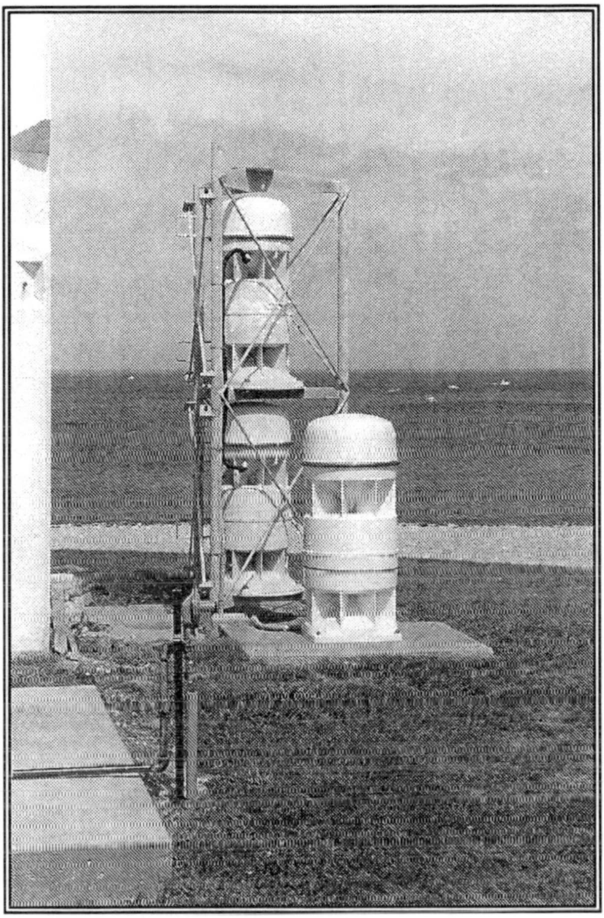

Piggyback dual foghorns from 2001, augmented by a third horn in 2002, send audible signals over the ocean at a range of two miles. Visitors are reminded to stay clear of the signal during foggy conditions when it emits a deafening blast every 15 seconds. (Author Photo)

A spectacular view in any era, Montauk Point Lighthouse was photographed from the bluffs at Camp Hero in December 2005. (Author Photo)

Ambrosio thought any ghosts in the dwelling were the spirits of the three children of keeper James G. Scott, all of whom died young—a daughter from scarlet fever, a son from a burst appendix when the doctor lost his way to the lighthouse, and another son from drowning in Money Pond. Ambrosio said the children's wakes and funerals undoubtedly were held in the keeper's dwelling and that "the victim of premature death keeps coming back."[527]

Marge Winski has called the lighthouse home since she moved in on April 1, 1987. Her family came to Montauk in 1968, but in the nearly 20 years that followed she never went to the lighthouse. Winski lived in Maine for a number of years and acquired a taste for lighthouses. After returning to Montauk and taking a job at the local post office, she began exploring ways she could assist the Montauk Lighthouse and the museum. The job of caretaker was a perfect fit.

When asked what living in a lighthouse is like, Winski replied, "Food for the soul. I just love being out here surrounded by nature…to walk…[and] being here to watch the seasons."[528]

The Museum in 2007

- **Parlor**: It houses lighthouse drawings and photographs from 1791 to 1939.
- **Bedroom**: It served as the head keeper's bedroom from 1860-1947. It now displays four models of the Montauk Point Lighthouse and its terrain. The models depict the structural changes that occurred in 1796, 1860, 1903, and 1943. They also show the effects of coastal erosion over the years. The room is dedicated in honor of Giorgina Reid who initiated the Erosion Control Project.
- **South Basement**: It served as a central kitchen and dining area for keepers and their families. An additional kitchen was built in 1892 in the north basement for the assistant keepers. The head keeper used the south basement kitchen until it became a recreation room in 1943. Today the video, *The Montauk Point Lighthouse, Sentinel of Long Island* is shown here.
- **Central Hallway**: It connects the keepers dwelling to the oil room and tower. The exhibit, *Lighthouses Surrounding Long Island*, opened here in March 1996. The hallway is 15-feet long and 4-feet wide,

and depicts 28 lighthouses in and around Long Island.

- **Radio Room**: This was the communication center where weather and radio beacon signals were transmitted, emergency distress calls were received, and rescue units were notified. It now houses exhibits devoted to lighthouse keepers.
- **Second Assistant Keeper's Quarters**: This room houses *Where Land Meets Sea and Sky: Exploring History Through the Richard T Gilmartin Galleries*
- **Oil Room**: Once the storage area for oil and supplies for the lighthouse, it now provides the only access to the tower. It houses several Fresnel lenses, including the original 3½-order bivalve lens which served the lighthouse from 1903 until February 3, 1987.
- **Gilmartin Galleries**: Described above.
- **Fresnel Lenses** (The museum is home to the largest collection of Fresnel lenses on Long Island.)

1) 3½-order bivalve: manufactured by Barbier, Benard & Turenne in France in 1900 and located at Montauk Point from 1903-1987.
2) 4th-order flashing six panel: manufacturer, year and original location unknown. It includes the windup clockworks mechanism.
3) 4th-order flashing four panel, manufactured by American Gas Accumulator, Elizabeth, NJ in 1933. Its original location is unknown. Only two panels are displayed.
4) 5th-order fixed four panel classical with reflector plate, manufactured by Henri LePaute of France, year unknown, original location unknown. It included a 5th-order lamp.

5) 375mm lens: manufacturer, year, original location unknown.
6) Incandescent Oil Vapor Lamp, manufacturer unknown; possibly made in the early 1900's; original location unknown

Other Major Structures

- **1838 Building**: Built as an addition to the original 1796 keeper's dwelling, it now serves as a garage.
- **Lost at Sea Memorial**: Dedicated in 1999, it remembers commercial fishermen who lost their lives at sea off Montauk.
- **Oil House**: Built 1904, it was used to store lamp fuel.
- **Fog Signal Building**: It housed equipment pertaining to fog signals, but now is used for storage.
- **Fire Control Tower**: Built in 1942 as a submarine watch tower to survey ocean waters for German submarines during WW II, it is no longer active.
- **Sentry Booth**: Built during WW II as a lookout post, it was deactivated after the war.

The annex to original keeper's dwelling was built in 1838. It was converted into a garage in the late 1930s. Currently, it serves as a garage/storage facility for the Montauk Point Lighthouse Museum. (Author Photo)

EPILOGUE

Reflections on Montauk

The Montauk of today is two-thirds public park land, but the journey to its present pristine status was hard-earned—a perpetual battle between land hungry developers and private citizens who wanted a small parcel of eastern Long Island to remain unspoiled.

As the previous chapters show, a continual parade of pioneers, speculators, and entrepreneurs marched out to Montauk, hoping to secure their fortunes. Some were content to fish and run cattle; others had higher aspirations. Men such as Arthur Benson, Austin Corbin, and Carl Fisher came to Montauk primarily as developers rather than environmentalists and conservationists. Though their grand schemes fell short of expectations, reminders of their presence are scattered about the Montauk countryside—Benson's Montauk Association homes, Corbin's Long Island Railroad, and the numerous structures of the Fisher era such as the Montauk Manor, the Yacht Club, buildings in the "downtown" area, not to mention miles of roads and dredging in Lake Montauk.

In later years individuals, businesses, and civic groups began to recognize and respect the natural beauty and historic significance of the Montauk Peninsula and try to preserve it. One of the earliest visionaries was Robert Moses, who acquired nearly 2,000-acres in the 1920s to create Montauk Point State Park and Hither Hills State Park. Giorgina Reid left her signature on the bluffs of Montauk, along with hundreds of nameless volunteers whose only desire for Montauk was to preserve its sweeping ocean vistas and venerable old lighthouse.

In the early 1960s, the Montauk Historical Society formed to preserve the Point's history. For over forty years, society members have preserved and made public the photos, documents, and memorabilia that tell Montauk's story. Among the society's responsibilities are the maintenance of museums at Second House and at Long Island's oldest and most notable landmark, the Montauk Point Lighthouse. The establishment of the E. Virgil and Elaine Wingate Conway Visitor Center in 2005 and the opening of the Richard T. Gilmartin galleries depicting the many facets of Montauk history in 2006 enhance the enjoyment of the visitor experience and foster an appreciation of Montauk's wild, colorful, and unique history.

Other organizations have contributed to the Montauk of today. In 1970 developers wanted to build 1,400 homes in the vicinity of Big Reed Pond. The Concerned Citizens of Montauk (CCOM) was created to block this plan and urge Suffolk County to purchase 1,100-acres for parkland. The result was the establishment of Theodore Roosevelt County Park, formerly Montauk County Park.

Over the years the CCOM has been instrumental in preventing overdevelopment of Montauk, preserving open land, and demonstrating concern for the environment. In 1984 the group helped avert the auctioning of Camp Hero to developers. In 1986 they donated funds to support the Erosion Control Project at the Montauk Point Lighthouse, and in 1988 and 1991 they pushed for Suffolk County to purchase over 1,300-acres to establish the Hither Woods Preserve. The CCOM fought to prevent ocean dumping off Montauk Point, developed plans to clean up Lake Montauk in 1988, and opposed high speed ferries from Connecticut to Montauk in the late 1990s. They are one of the most effective citizens' groups on Long Island's East End.

Another organization, the Montauk Anti Pollution Coalition, was formed in 2003 to fight noise pollution created by idling Long Island Railroad diesel trains at the Montauk train station. The CCOM and other groups, such as the Montauk Citizens Advisory Committee, the Concerned Citizens Group, and the management of the Montauk Manor, joined in the effort to preserve the quiet of Montauk.

Other parklands on Montauk include state parks at Montauk Downs and Shadmoor, plus the Leo Koppleman Nature Preserve and the Andy Warhol Preserve. The newest land acquisition was announced by New York Governor George Pataki in July 2005 with the purchase of 122-acres known as Amsterdam Beach. Nearly half of the parcel is sensitive wetlands and maritime grasslands populated with various plants and animals critical to its health.

The work of concerned individuals and groups has successfully preserved most of Montauk for future generations to enjoy. Despite plans that might have opened Montauk to intense development and erased its quiet seaside character, it remains largely untouched. The Montauk of today is "...savored by thousands, rather than by millions; and is all the sweeter for that." When East Hampton Town historian, Jeannette Rattray made this prophetic statement in 1938, she probably had no idea it would hold true seventy years later. Montauk continues to thrive as a charming summer community with hundreds of acres of parklands and picturesque bays, ponds, and cliffs.

The centerpiece of this beautiful landscape is the cherished and well-maintained Montauk Point Lighthouse, now in its third century of service to mariners and a destination for thousands of visitors annually. Like poet Walt Whitman, today's visitors still may "stand as on some mighty eagle's beak" to appreciate the wondrous tableau of sea, sky, and rolling hills…interrupted only by the ancient lighthouse perched on high battered bluffs.

A paved road and sidewalk welcomes visitors to Montauk Point Lighthouse. The old sentinel has much to celebrate these days: Erosion is under control, trees have returned to the landscape, the tower has been renewed with critical repairs and paint, and visitors flock to the museum. (Author Photo)

APPENDIX A

Civilian Head Keepers at Montauk Point Light-house: Dates of Appointment and Annual Salary

Jacob Hand	November 4, 1796	$266.33
Jared Hand	January 28, 1812	
Henry Baker	February 24, 1814	$333.33
Patrick Gould	May 9, 1832	
John Hobart	October 29, 1849	
Silas P. Loper	August 17, 1850	$350.00
Jason M. Terbell	November 25, 1850	$350.00
Jonathan Payne (temp)	April 30, 1857	
William Gardiner	June 12, 1857	$350.00
Joseph Stanton	May 20, 1861	$550.00
Jonathan A. Miller	January 1, 1865	$700.00
Thomas P. Ripley	May 13, 1869	$700.00
Jonathan A. Miller	December 3, 1872	$700.00
Jared Wade	October 15, 1875	$700.00
Henry A. Babcock	March 2, 1876	$700.00
James G. Scott	September 26, 1885	$700.00
John F. Anderson	October 1, 1910	$720.00
John E. Miller	May 16, 1912	
Thomas Buckridge	January 1, 1930	

APPENDIX B

Coast Guard Headkeepers at Montauk Point Lighthouse and Dates of Appointment

BMC Archie Jones	August 1946
BMC Charlie Shoemaker	September 1954
BMC Ira Lewis	January 1959
BMC William B. Harvey	August 1959
BMC Charles Nehibars	October 1963
BMC John A. Mason	December 1963
BMC Kenneth P. Borrego	October 1966
BMC George E. Newman	October 1967
BMC Ralph W. Conant	June 1971
BMC Frank B. Abel	May 1975
BM2 Kevin T. Reed	July 1976
BM1 Earl E. Wilson Jr.	October 1976
BM1 Paul R. Driscoll	September 1979
BM1 W. Gene Hughes	July 1983

BMC, BM1: Boatswain's Mate First Class
BM2: Boatswain's Mate Second Class

A "boatswain" (pronounced "bosun") is a ship's petty officer in charge of the deck crew and equipment.

APPENDIX C

Some Assistant Civilian Keepers: Dates of Appointment / Arrival/Departure and Some Annual Salaries

William Gardiner		1857	
Josiah Lee	1st asst	September 21, 1857 -	$300
		May 1861- October 18, 1864-	$300
Samuel G. Bailey	2nd asst	September 21, 1857 -	$300
J. Webber	1st asst	February 1, 1859	$300
William Reeves	2nd asst	March 23, 1859 -	$300
Stephen B. Bennett		March 17, 1863 - April 1, 1864	$300
	1st asst	November 15, 1872- May 7, 1873	$400
Jonathan A. Miller		October 13, 1864 – December 12, 1865	$300
Elbert Edwards		January 3, 1866– July 21, 1866	$300
Daniel Loper Jr.		June 7, 1867 - August 29, 1868	$300
Elias Wales		August 12, 1869 - January 27, 1870	$400
Henry P. Fields		October 12, 1869 -	
Charles H. Payne		January 27, 1870 - March 31, 1871	$400
Lewis L. Bennett		August 29, 1868 - October 18, 1869	$400
		September 21, 1870 - November 15, 1872	$400
	2nd asst	May 6, 1873 -	$400
		February 19, 1874 - September 3, 1875	$450

HENRY OSMERS

William H. Lugar		March 10, 1871 - April 30, 1872	$400
	2nd asst	March 2, 1876 - May 3, 1876	$400
	1st asst	May 3, 1876 - March 16, 1881	$450
Albert W. Bennett		April 30, 1872 - November 15, 1872	$400
John Donnelly	1st asst	December 31, 1875 - February 1876	$450
Stephen Topping	2nd asst	May 24, 1876 -	$400
Charles Miller	2nd asst	May 1, 1877- March 16, 1881	$400
	1st asst	March 16, 1881- July 1, 1881	$450
Joseph De Castro	2nd asst	March 21, 1881- July 1, 1881	$400
	1st asst	July 1, 1881- October 1, 1881	$450
David G. Mulford	2nd asst	July 5, 1881- March 16, 1882	$400
James L. Edwards	1st asst	October 1, 1881 - December 5, 1885	$450
Cornelius H. Payne	2nd asst	March 16, 1882 - September 28, 1882	$400
David P. Osborn	2nd asst	September 28, 1882 - December 14, 1885	$400
Charles Z. Miller	1st asst	December 5, 1885 - September 1, 1888	$450
Clarence Miller	2nd asst	December 14, 1885 - February 10, 1886	$400
Eugene Mulligan	2nd asst	February 10, 1886 - September 25, 1890	$400*
David E. Davis	2nd asst	September 15, 1888 - April 1, 1889	$400**
Thomas Gurnett	2nd asst	April 1, 1889 - October 3, 1889	$450
William Alonzo Baker	2nd asst	October 14, 1889 – September 25, 1890	$450
	1st asst	September 25, 1890 - April 4, 1891	$500
Freeman Douglas	2nd asst	April 6, 1891 - June 10, 1892	$450
David E. Johnson	2nd asst	October 23, 1890 - March 26, 1891	$450
David G. Morrison	1st asst	April 7, 1891 - September 28, 1892	$500
Everett King	2nd asst	July 6, 1892 - September 19, 1892	$450

	1st asst	September 19, 1892-	$500
Charles L. Mulford	2nd asst	September 14, 1892 - April 1, 1897	$450
Harry Scott	2nd asst	March 31, 1897 - January 19, 1899	$450
John Miller	1st asst	November 26, 1903-	
John Price	1st asst	May 1, 1904-	$500
John F. Anderson	2nd asst	November 1, 1906 - January 5, 1908	$450
John F. Anderson	1st asst	January 5, 1908 - October 1, 1910	$500
Raymond O'Neill	2nd asst	May 1, 1904-	$450
Freeman Douglas	2nd asst	September 1, 1904-	$450
Stephen Hall	2nd asst	November 1, 1904-	$450
George E. Hansen	2nd asst	January 16, 1908-	$450
John William Smith	2nd asst	January 1, 1908-	$450
William L. Baker	2nd asst	April 1, 1908-	$450
Evard Janson	1st asst	1910	
William Follett	2nd asst	February 2, 1912 – March 29, 1912	
	1st asst	March 29, 1912 – September 29, 1917	
Carl Anderson	2nd asst	October 20, 1917-	
John Miller	1st asst	November 1, 1917-	
Harold N. Kierstead	2nd asst	April 23, 1919-	
Phillips A. Channell	2nd asst	October 1, 1920 - April 13, 1921	
Harry Bell	2nd asst	May 12, 1921 - October 29, 1923	
Charles E. Morgan	2nd asst	November 5, 1923-	
James Kirkwood	2nd asst	January 2, 1924 - November 24, 1928	
George W. Warrington	2nd asst	December 26, 1928 – January 28, 1942	
Jonathan (Jack) A. Miller	1st asst	1930's – January 30, 1942	

*Eugene Mulligan's salary raised to $500 November 1, 1888
**David E, Davis' salary raised to $500 November 1, 1888

APPENDIX D

Montauk Point Lighthouse Chronology

April 12, 1792: George Washington authorizes a lighthouse to be built at Montauk Point

March 2, 1793: Congress sanctions $20,000 for construction of the lighthouse

Aug. 24, 1795: John McComb, Jr. signs contract to build the lighthouse

June 7, 1796: Laying of the lighthouse cornerstone

Sept. 22, 1796: Construction of keeper's dwelling completed

Nov. 5, 1796: After just 5 months, construction of the tower completed

April 1797: First lighting of Montauk Point Lighthouse

1806: Josiah Hand develops the "spider lamp", containing a single reservoir for fuel and 32 spouts

Nov. 1812: Argand lamp installed by Winslow Lewis

Jan. 1826: Montauk Point Lighthouse considered the "best in the United States"

June 1838: New keeper's dwelling completed

1849: New lantern and chandelier with 15 brass oil lamps installed

April 1854: An inspection reveals numerous structural problems in the tower and keeper's dwelling, more of which would be noted in the next few years

Jan. 1, 1858: New first order Fresnel lens is first lit at Montauk Point Lighthouse. It became a flashing signal (every two minutes)

Feb. 20, 1858: The *John Milton* wrecks on the rocks near Montauk Point; its captain, Ephraim Harding, mistakes the steady beam of the newly lit Shinnecock Lighthouse for the Montauk Point Lighthouse

June 1860: Work begins at Montauk Point to enable the station to meet the standards of a First-Order Light Station. Tower renovated, new keeper's dwelling constructed.

Sept. 26, 1860: Renovations completed.

May 1873: Fog signal installed

1884: Kerosene becomes the source of fuel for the lighthouse, replacing the already scarce whale oil used from the beginning

1897: Fog signal house built

Sept. 6, 1898: Colonel Theodore Roosevelt visits the lighthouse while at Camp Wikoff with the Rough Riders

May 1899: Daymark painted on the tower

Dec. 13, 1899: First telephone installed. It reaches Amagansett

June 15, 1903: New 3 ½ order bivalve Fresnel lens installed in the lantern. Signal becomes a flashing white light every 10 seconds

Dec. 3, 1907: Incandescent vapor lamp installed in the lens

1912: Keeper's dwelling extended fourteen feet to the north for additional living space for assistant keeper's families

1938: Keeper's dwelling receives electric power

July 1, 1940: The lighthouse is electrified

1942: Montauk Lighthouse becomes part of the Eastern Coastal Defense Shield during WW II. Fire Control Tower built.

1946: U.S. Coast Guard begins occupation of the lighthouse

April 1, 1987: Lighthouse is automated. Buildings leased to Montauk Historical Society.

May 23, 1987: Montauk Point Lighthouse Museum opens to the public

Sept. 30, 1996: President Bill Clinton signs into law the transfer of the lighthouse property to the Montauk Historical Society Lighthouse Museum Committee

May 29, 1997: Montauk Point Lighthouse Transfer of Deed Ceremony

Mar. 16, 1998: Tower undergoes year-long restoration project

1999: Lost at Sea Memorial first displayed to the public

July 24, 2001: Vega VRB-25 beacon installed in the lantern.

June 25, 2005: E. Virgil and Elaine Wingate Conway Visitors Center ribbon cutting ceremony

Feb. 2006: First public viewing of new exhibit: *Where Land Meets Sea and Sky: Exploring Montauk History through the Richard T. Gilmartin Galleries*

APPENDIX E

Excerpts from U.S. Coast Guard Record of Inspection Forms at Montauk Point Lighthouse 1960-1987

Inspections at Montauk Point Lighthouse were taken seriously by the Coast Guard. Attention to every detail is evident in the subjects brought to light when "white glove" type inspections were conducted. Deficiencies were noted, along with exemplary conditions and conduct. The station had increasingly good reports from the late 1960s until automation, as the following selected items illustrate. In some cases the response from the Officer in Charge (OIC) is shown, indicating immediate attention to problems in a relatively short period of time.

References to the erosion problem at Montauk Point were noted in several reports. These are mentioned in chapter nine.

Records of Inspection courtesy of Montauk Point Lighthouse Museum (spelling and punctuation standardized)

May 6, 1960: Routine monthly inspection

Main tower in need of painting. Bricks in garage in need of pointing. Put file letters on report jackets as per filing manual.

December 2, 1960: Monthly inspection

Showed safety film on safe driving. T-12815 (vehicle) should be replaced. Odometer reading over 70508 miles. Body shows rusted spots in many places.

Response from OIC: *16 December 1960 New truck requested.*

February 3, 1961: Clothing inspection

[One officer] did not have the following items: 1 cap, blue working; no identification on service dress blue cap; needed 1 white hat. Needs 1 jacket blue working. Needs 2 pair black socks. [Another officer] needs 1 pair drawers and 1 pair dress gloves.

Response from OIC: *Men were instructed to procure missing items of clothing, and to properly mark same. 15 February 1961.*

July 10, 1961: Routine district financial inspection

Files in excellent condition, commissary records very good, as are supply records. Galley exceptionally clean for station of this type. Material condition of station and grounds very good, storerooms spaces adequately free of clutter.

September 5, 1961: Routine monthly inspection

Lookout: New waste basket needed. Put cover plate over electrical junction box. Remove stumble hazard on platform.

Garage: Obtain bid for replacing window frames (old frames beyond repair due to rot).

Response from OIC: *New waste basket will be ordered next ordering date. Cover plate lens installed 9/5/61. Stumbling hazard on platform were removed 9/8/61. Garage: bids are being obtained and will be submitted.*

May 4, 1962: Monthly inspection

The station is being remodeled. The family quarters occupied by Wall, James D. BM3 and family is presently torn up. It is recommended that the family move out for the time being so the job can be finished more rapidly. Lookout tower needs seasonal painting also the main tower on the outside. Soda acid fire extinguisher last dated 1-15-61.

Response by OIC: *The lookout tower and light tower will be painted after 1 June 1962, estimated completion date 1 September 1962. Soda acid fire extinguisher recharged 4 May 1962.*

August 3, 1962: Monthly inspection, fire drill, personnel inspection

A fence is being installed around the property for safety and to

prevent visitors from trespassing from all directions. Held fire drill, unsatisfactory. Personnel inspection. Personnel need haircuts (2) and vaccine inoculation for immunization.

Response from OIC: *Holding fire drills more often to improve efficiency, crew have proper hair cuts and shots have been given. 5 September 1962.*

May 1, 1963:

Fog signal giving only one blast in 30 seconds on radiobeacon timer. Electronic technicians working to correct this trouble.

Response from OIC: *Fog horn timing corrected this date. 3 May 1962.*

May 21, 1963:

Recommendation- Light tower to be drilled at base to allow water from condensation to be drained out in order to dry out the masonry structure. Exterior tower to be prepared for waterproofing, keeping same characteristic of color scheme. Lantern area (inside and out) to be repaired and recaulked

May 21, 1964:

The old lawn mower will need replacing in the near future.

January 7, 1965:

No drills held due to extensive work in office in charge quarters. Renovation of galley by C&R Detachment, St George Base. The deck and lens in lens room is dusty and should be kept clean after contractors sweep up when they complete their work. Generator building is dusty.

February 5, 1965: Annual clothing inspection

One man needed a haircut. All personnel should be inspected by the officer in charge beforehand and minor deficiencies corrected before group or area inspection is held. Held quarterly safety inspection with the following noted: Ice on driveway on hillside should have rock salt scattered on trails to melt the ice and eliminate fall hazard.

January 12, 1967:

Unit to initiate procurement of face shield to protect personnel servicing main light against possibility of lamp shattering. State park-

ing lot in front of station being expanded. This affects access road to station.

Response from OIC: *Lamp was replaced 1/12/67, new face shield was obtained 1/20/67.*

March 20, 1967: Informal inspection
Station is well maintained—neat and clean—shows definite sign of a well led and interested crew. No discrepancies.

August 2, 1967:
A very well run station. Attitude of personnel and general appearance of buildings and grounds were excellent, but light tower will soon require painting if it is not to become an eyesore.

August 21, 1968: Staff inspection.
Unit shows above average effort by the officer-in-charge and all assigned personnel. The unit is a credit to the Coast Guard.

October 30, 1975:
Conducted Group Commander quarterly inspection. Conducted personnel, material and operation inspection, conducted request and complaint mast. Condition and appearance of station very good. OIC and crew are commended on aggressive and effective manner in which they are managing and operating the unit. A pleasure to inspect!

October 28, 1976: Familiarization inspection.
Station personnel are to be commended for their diligence in maintaining this unit as a show place. Maintenance is being done, housekeeping is outstanding. Recommended that shade be procured for the lantern room to reduce reflected sunlight damage.

May 12, 1977: Familiarization visit.
Neat, clean station that is obviously being maintained by personnel who are interested in keeping a good Coast Guard image at this important historic site that has served mariners well for a long time.

Response by OIC: *All comments were noted and appreciated.*

BIBLIOGRAPHY

Notes on sources

Record Group 26 in the collection of the National Archives was a virtual treasure-trove of information, with numerous documents and letters shedding light on the events leading up to construction of Montauk Point Lighthouse, the everyday lives of its keepers, and the various responsibilities keepers had at the station.

The writings of Jeannette Edwards Rattray were a joy to read, particularly *Montauk: Three Centuries of Romance, Sport and Adventure, East Hampton History*, and *Ship Ashore!* All three works portray vivid adventures of Montauk and the challenges of land and sea. In addition, her numerous articles in the *East Hampton Star* were particularly helpful, with details on a local level.

Various logbooks, letters and photographs available at the Montauk Point Lighthouse Museum gave a personal look at lighthouse life in the nineteenth and twentieth centuries.

The most valuable information came from the Morton Pennypacker Collection of the East Hampton Free Library. The collection's numerous newspaper clippings and documents proved extremely fruitful.

Books and Articles

Allen, Everett S. *A Wind to Shake the World; the Story of the 1938 Hurricane*. Boston: Little, Brown & Co. 1976.

Armbruster, Eugene L. *Montauk*. New York: 1923.

Ayres, Jared Augustus. *The Legends of Montauk*. Hartford: Edwin Hunt. 1849.

Bailey, Paul. *Long Island: A History of Two Great Counties; Nassau and Suffolk*. New York: Lewis Publishing Co., Inc., 1949.

Bachand, Robert G. *Northeast Lights*. Norwalk, CT: Sea Sports Publications. 1989.

Barber, John W. "Historical Collections of the State of New York." *Exploring the Past: Writings from 1798 to 1896 Relating to the History of the Town of East Hampton*. ed. Tom Twomey, pp. 227-232. New York: Newmarket Press, 2000.

Bayles, Richard M. *Historical and Descriptive Sketches of Suffolk County*. New York: Port Jefferson, 1874.

Bryant, William Cullen. "Picturesque America." *Exploring the Past: Writings from 1798 to1896 Relating to the History of the Town of East Hampton*. ed. Tom Twomey, pp. 301-306. New York: Newmarket Press, 2000.

Christman, Henry M. ed. *Walt Whitman's New York: From Manhattan to Montauk*. New York: MacMillan & Co., 1963.

Clavin, Tom. *Dark Noon: The Final Voyage of the Fishing Boat "Penguin"*. New York: International Marine/McGraw Hill, 2005.

Crompton, Samuel and Michael J. Rhein. *The Ultimate Book of Lighthouses*. San Diego: Thunder Bay Press, 2001.

DeWire, Elinor. *Lighthouses of the Mid-Atlantic Coast*. Stillwater, MN: Voyageur Press, 2002.

Dwight, Timothy. "Journey to Long Island, 1804." *Journeys on Old Long Island*, ed. Natalie A. Naylor. Interlaken, NY: Hofstra University/Empire State Books, 2002.

Epstein, Jason and Elizabeth Barlow. *East Hampton: A History and Guide*. New York: Random House, 1985.

Ferguson, Eleanor F. *My Long Island*, ed. Anne Nauman. Las Vegas, NV: Scrub Oak Press. 1993

Flint, Martha Bockee. *Early Long Island: A Colonial Study*. New York: G. P. Putnam's Sons. 1896.

Gardiner, David. "Chronicles of the Town of Easthampton." *Exploring the Past: Writings from 1798 to 1896 Relating to the History of the Town of East Hampton*, ed. Tom Twomey, pp. 105-226. New York: Newmarket Press, 2000.

Geus, Averill Dayton. *From Sea to Sea: 350 Years of East Hampton History*. West Kennebunk, ME: Phoenix Publishing, 1999.

Gish, Noel. "Pirates." *Awakening the Past: The East Hampton 350th Anniversary Lecture Series 1998*, ed. Tom Twomey, pp. 249-267. New York: Newmarket Press. 1999.

Heatley, Jeff, editor. *Bully! Colonel Theodore Roosevelt, The Rough Riders and Camp*. Montauk Historical Society, Pushcart Press. 1998

Hefner, Robert J. "Montauk Point Lighthouse: A History of New York's First Seamark." *Long Island Historical Journal* 3 (Spring 1991): 205-16.

Holden, Albert R. *A Pictorial History of Montauk*, 2nd ed. Montauk: Holden's Publications, 1983.

Holland Jr., Francis Ross. *America's Lighthouses: An Illustrated History*. New York: Dover Publications, 1981.

Hummel, Charles F. *With Hammer in Hand: The Dominy Craftsmen of East Hampton, New York*. Charlottesville, VA: University Press of Virginia, 1968.

Journal of the Trustees of the Freeholders and Commonalty of East Hampton Town 1772-1807, 1845-1870, 1870-1897. Compiled by H. D. Sleight. East Hampton, 1927.

Keatts, Henry and George Farr. *The Bell Tolls: Shipwrecks and Lighthouses of Eastern Long Island*. Eastport, NY: Fathom Press, 2002.

Lanman, Charles. *Recollections of Curious Characters and Pleasant Places*. Edinburgh: David Douglas 1881.

List of Light-Houses, Beacons and Floating Lights of the United States. Washington DC: C Alexander, 1848.

Lists of Lights and Fog Signals on the Atlantic and Gulf Coasts of the United States, 1902. Washington DC: Government Printing Office, 1902.

Miller, Mary Esther Mulford. *An East Hampton Childhood*. East Hampton: Star Press, 1938.

"Montauk Point, Long Island." *Harpers New Monthly Magazine*, vol. 43, no. 256, September 1871.

Műller, Robert. "History of the Montauk Point Light Station." *The Long Island Light Keeper*. January/February 2002. Published by the Long Island Chapter of the U.S. Lighthouse Society.

______, _____. *Long Island's Lighthouses Past and Present*. Interlaken, NY: Heart of the Lakes Publishing, for the Long Island Chapter of the US Lighthouse Society, 2004.

Pelletreau, William S. "History of Suffolk County." *Exploring the Past: Writings from 1798 to 1896 Relating to the History of the Town of East Hampton*, ed. Tom Twomey, pp. 324-412. New York: Newmarket Press, 2000.

Peters, George H. "The Flora of Long Island." *Long Island: A History of Two Great Counties, Nassau and Suffolk,* ed. Paul Bailey. New York: Lewis Historical Publishing, 1949.

Prime, Nathaniel S. *History of Long Island: From its First Settlement by Europeans to the Year 1845*. New York: Robert Carter, 1845.

Rathbun, Capt. Benjamin F. *Capsule Histories of Some Local Islands and Light Houses in the Eastern Part of L.I. Sound*. New London: Quality Printers, Inc., 2001

Rattray, Everett T. *The South Fork: The Land and the People of East-*

ern Long Island. Wainscott: Pushcart Press, 1989.

Rattray, Jeannette Edwards. *East Hampton History Including Genealogies of Early Families*. Garden City: Country Life Press, 1953.

_____ ____*Montauk: Three Centuries of Romance, Sport and Adventure*. East Hampton: The Star Press, 1938.

____ _____*Ship Ashore*! New York: Coward-McCann Inc, 1955.

____ _____*The Story of Second House, Montauk*, 1969. (Pamphlet)

Rowley, Marion A. "Versatile Reverend." *Long Island Forum*. September 1975.

Sigourney, Lydia Howard. *Scenes in My Native Land*. Boston: James Munroe & Co., 1845.

Specifications for a First Order Lighthouse. Washington DC: Government Printing Office, 1861. Library of Congress.

Stoff, Joshua. *From Canoes to Cruisers: the Maritime Heritage of Long Island.*. Interlaken, NY: Empire State Books. 1994.

Thompson, Benjamin F. *History of Long Island: From its Discovery and Settlement to the Present Time*. 3rd ed. 2. New York: Robert H. Dodd. 1918.

Tooker, William. *Indian Place Names on Long Island*, 1911. Reprint; Port Washington, NY: Ira J. Friedman, 1962.

Towne, Charles Hanson. *Loafing Down Long Island*. New York: The Century Co. 1921.

Twomey, Tom ed. *Awakening the Past: The East Hampton 350th Anniversary Lecture Series, 1998.* New York: Newmarket Press, 1999.

_____ ______. *Exploring the Past: Writings from 1798 to 1896 Relating to the History of the Town of East Hampton.* New York: Newmarket Press, 2000.

Winski, Peg. *Montauk: An Anecdotal History*. Montauk Historical Society, 1997.

Woodward, Nancy Hyden. *East Hampton: A Town and its People, 1648-1994*. East Hampton: Fireplace Press, 1995.

Newsletters

Beacon. Montauk Historical Society. 1987-2005.

Daymark. Montauk Point Lighthouse Museum.

Documents, Letters, and Miscellaneous Sources

"Civil War Letters and Journal of Elbert Parker Edwards." ed. Averill Dayton Geus. 1978. Long Island Collection, East Hampton Free Library. Typescript.

Congressional Document #24. 25th Congress. 3nd Session, House. December 12, 1838.

Congressional Document #138. 25th Congress. 2nd Session, Senate. January 26, 1838.

Guest Register May 9, 1897 – August 20, 1908. Captain J. G. Scott. East Hampton Free Library.

Hefner, Robert J. "Montauk Point Light Station: Tower, Oil House and Passage, a Historic Structures Project." Manuscript prepared for the Montauk Historical Society. 1989.

Hefner, Robert J. "Montauk Point Light Station: 1838 Keeper's Dwelling, a Historic Structures Report." Manuscript prepared for the Montauk Historical Society. 1994.

Letter from Phillips Channell to Arthur Channell, November 16, 1920. Montauk Point Lighthouse Museum.

Letter from Sandra Clunies to Ann Shengold, Montauk Point Lighthouse Museum, November 1, 2004.

Letter from Commander, 3rd Coast Guard District to the Commandant, October 11, 1948. Treasury Department.

Letter from Tench Coxe to John McComb Jr. Bricklayer, New York. August 18, 1795. Long Island Collection, East Hampton Free Library.

Letter from Lighthouse Engineer O. C. Luther to the Lighthouse Service, March 5, 1928. Montauk Point Lighthouse Museum.

Letter from James G. Scott to Samuel H. Miller, April 5, 1886. Montauk Point Lighthouse Museum.

Letter from Captain G. H. Weller, US Coast Guard to Giorgina Reid, October 7, 1969. Robert Muller, LI Chapter, US Lighthouse Society.

"Lights and Shadows of Montuuk" 1832-1857. Manuscript in the collection of Montauk Point Lighthouse Museum..

Margaret Buckridge Bock. Scrapbook 1930-1943. Montauk Point Lighthouse Museum.

Montauk Point Light Station, Record of Inspections, 1965 to 1986. Montauk Point Lighthouse Museum.

National Archives, Record Group 26.

"Report of the Officers Constituting the Lighthouse Board." Washington D.C.: U.S. Congress, 1852.

U.S. Coast Guard website, www.uscg.mil.

Visitors Logbook. Montauk Point Lighthouse Museum.

INDEX

ENDNOTES

[1] William Wallace Tooker, *Indian Place Names on Long Island*, 1911. Reprint; Port Washington: Ira J. Friedman, 1962, p. 142.
[2] Ibid. p. 271.
[3] Jeannette Edwards Rattray, *The Story of Second House, Montauk*, 1969, pamphlet, p. 10.
[4] Ibid. p. 8.
[5] "Montauk Point." *Brooklyn Daily Eagle*. July 14, 1901.
[6] William S. Pelletreau, "History of Suffolk County, New York, with Illustrations, Portraits and Sketches of Prominent Families and Individuals." 1882. *Exploring the Past: Writings from 1798 to 1896 Relating to the History of the Town of East Hampton*, Tom Twomey (ed). (New York: Newmarket Press. 2000). p. 370.
[7] Albert R. Holden, *A Pictorial History of Montauk* (Montauk: Holden's Publications, 1983), pp. 141,143.
[8] Jeannette Edwards Rattray, *Ship Ashore*! (New York: Coward, McCann Co. 1955), p. 12-13.
[9] Ibid. pp. 16-17.
[10] Debbie Tuma, "Light Shed on Precious Document." *Newsday*. September 8, 1990.
[11] David Gelston to New York Chamber of Commerce, November 19, 1792 in *Journal of the Trustees of the Freeholders and Commonalty of East Hampton Town 1772-1807*. Compiled by H. D. Sleight. (East Hampton, 1927). p. 334-336.

[12] Joseph Anthony to Tench Coxe, January 8, 1793. Letters to the Bureau of Lighthouses 1789-1804, Book C, p. 49. National Archives Record Group 26. (National Archives Record Group 26 hereafter referred to as NARG 26)
[13] C. Miller to Tench Coxe, January 14, 1793. Letters to the Bureau of Lighthouses 1789-1804, Book C. p. 53. NARG 26.
[14] William Allibone to Tench Coxe, March 18, 1795. Letters to the Bureau of Lighthouses 1789-1804, Volume A, p. 236. NARG 26.
[15] Ezra L'Hommedieu to New York Chamber of Commerce, November 19, 1792 in *Journal of the Trustees of the Freeholders and Commonalty of East Hampton Town, 1772-1807*, p. 334-336.
[16] Abraham Miller to Tench Coxe, July 6, 1795. Letters to the Bureau of Light Houses, 1789-1804, Book C, p. 197, NARG 26.
[17] Tench Coxe to George Washington, August 11, 1795. Correspondence of the Light-House Establishment 1785-1852. Letter Book 1, 1792-1798. NARG 26.
[18] Tench Coxe to John McComb Jr. August 18, 1795. Long Island Collection, East Hampton Free Library.
[19] Henry P. Dering to Tench Coxe, April 23, 1796. Letters to the Bureau of Light Houses 1789-1804. Book C. p. 253. NARG 26.
[20] Henry P. Dering to Tench Coxe, August 30, 1795. Letters to the Bureau of Light Houses 1789-1804. Book C, p. 215. NARG 26.
[21] Records of the Light-House Service. Site File, New York No. 71, Montauk Point. NARG 26.
[22] Contract between Tench Coxe and John McComb Jr, August 24, 1795. Records of the Light-House Establishment 1785-1852. Contract Volume A. NARG 26.
[23] Henry P. Dering to Tench Coxe, April 23, 1796. Letters to the Bureau of Lighthouses 1789-1804. Book C, p. 253. NARG 26.
[24] Robert J. Hefner, "Montauk Point Lighthouse: A History of New York's First Seamark." *LI Historical Journal*, vol. 3, no. 2, p. 208.
[25] *Journal of the Trustees of the Freeholders and Commonalty of East Hampton Town 1772-1807*, p. 139.
[26] Henry P. Dering to Tench Coxe, June 20, 1796. Letters to the Bureau of Light Houses 1789-1804. Book C. p. 261. NARG 26.
[27] Henry P. Dering to Tench Coxe. August 29, 1796. Letters to the Bureau of Light Houses 1789-1804. Book C, p. 275. NARG 26.

[28] Tench Coxe to Thomas Randall, New York. September 16, 1796. Correspondence of the Light-House Establishment, 1785-1852. Letter Book 1, 1792-1798, p. 325. NARG 26.
[29] Henry P. Dering to Tench Coxe. October 10, 1796. Letters to the Bureau of Light Houses, 1789-1804. Book C, p. 283. NARG 26.
[30] William Heyer to Tench Coxe. September 20, 1796. Letters to the Bureau of Light Houses, 1789-1804. Book C, p. 277. NARG 26.
[31] Tench Coxe to Secretary of the Treasury. October 14, 1796. Correspondence of the Light-House Establishment, 1785-1852. Letter Book 1, 1792-1798, p. 329. NARG 26.
[32] Henry P. Dering to Tench Coxe. November 18, 1796. Letters to the Bureau of Light Houses 1789-1804. Book C, p. 293. NARG 26.
[33] Hefner, "Montauk Point Lighthouse: A History of New York's First Seamark." p. 208.
[34] *Journal of the Trustees of the Freeholders and Commonalty of East Hampton Town 1772-1807*, pp. 86-178.
[35] Contract between Tench Coxe and John McComb Jr. August 24, 1795. Records of the Light-House Establishment 1785-1852. Contract Volume A. NARG 26.
[36] Tench Coxe to Thomas Randall. November 26, 1796. Correspondence of the Light-House Establishment, 1785-1852. Letter Book 1, 1792-1798, p. 344. NARG 26.
[37] Henry P. Dering to Tench Coxe, December 10, 1796. Letters to the Bureau of Light Houses 1789-1804. Book C, p. 301. NARG 26.
[38] Debbie Tuma, "Lighthouse Illuminates History," *New York Daily News*. May 26, 1996.
[39] Henry P. Dering to Tench Coxe, March 8, 1797. Letters to the Bureau of Light Houses 1789-1804. Book C, p. 319. NARG 26.
[40] Henry P. Dering to Tench Coxe, October 1, 1797. Letters to the Bureau of Light Houses 1789-1804. Book C, p. 359. NARG 26.
[41] Henry P. Dering to Tench Coxe, April 5, 1799. Letters to the Bureau of Light Houses 1789-1804. Book C, p. 413. NARG 26.
[42] Henry P. Dering to Tench Coxe, April 23, 1796. "Letters to the Bureau of Light Houses 1789-1804." Book C, p. 253. NARG 26.
[43] Henry P. Dering to Tench Coxe, August 29, 1796. "Letters to the Bureau of Light Houses 1789-1804." Book C, p. 275. NARG 26.
[44] Ibid.

[45] Ezra Waite to Tench Coxe, January 7, 1796. "Letters to the Bureau of Light Houses 1789-1804." Book C. p. 289. NARG 26.
[46] William Heyer to Tench Coxe, September 20, 1796. Letters to the Bureau of Light Houses 1789-1804. Book C, p. 277. NARG 26.
[47] John Seward to Tench Coxe, December 5, 1796. Letters to the Bureau of Light Houses 1789-1804. Book C. p. 299. NARG 26.
[48] D. Sweeny, Treasury Department to Henry P. Dering, November 4, 1796. Correspondence of the Light-House Establishment, 1785-1852. Letter Book 1, 1792-1798, p. 336. NARG 26.
[49] Robert J. Hefner, "Montauk Point Light Station. A Historic Structures Report," 1989. Montauk Point Lighthouse Museum. p. 65.
[50] Henry P. Dering to Tench Coxe, November 27, 1797. Letters to the Bureau of Light Houses 1789-1804. Book C, p. 370. NARG 26.
[51] Henry P. Dering to --, October 10, 1799. Letters to the Bureau of Light Houses 1789-1804. Book C. p. 431. NARG 26.
[52] Henry P. Dering to William Miller, Commissioner of Revenue. July 1, 1801. Letters to the Bureau of Light Houses 1789-1804. Book C. p. 491. NARG 26.
[53] Henry P. Dering to Albert Gallatin, July 7, 1806. Correspondence of the Lighthouse Establishment, 1785-1852. Letter Book G, p. 109. NARG 26.
[54] Henry P. Dering to Albert Gallatin, April 6, 1807. Correspondence of the Lighthouse Establishment, 1785-1852. Letter Book G. p. 128. NARG 26.
[55] Henry P. Dering to Albert Gallatin, July 3, 1809. Correspondence of the Lighthouse Establishment, 1785-1852. Letter Book G, p. 179. NARG 26.
[56] Henry P. Dering to Albert Gallatin, January 14, 1812. Correspondence of the Lighthouse Establishment, 1785-1852. Letter Book G. NARG 26.
[57] Henry P. Dering to Albert Gallatin, November 1, 1809. Correspondence of the Lighthouse Establishment, 1785-1852. Letter Book G. p. 185. NARG 26.
[58] Francis Ross Holland Jr., *America's Lighthouses: An Illustrated History* (New York: Dover Publications, 1981), pp. 26-27.
[59] Henry T. Dering to Stephen Pleasonton. November 27, 1822. Correspondence of the Lighthouse Establishment, 1785-1852. NARG 26.

[60] Henry T. Dering to Stephen Pleasonton, January 3, 1826. Correspondence of the Lighthouse Establishment, 1785-1852. NARG 26.
[61] John P. Osborn to Stephen Pleasonton May 18, 1838. Correspondence of the Lighthouse Establishment, 1785-1852. NARG 26.
[62] John P. Osborn to Stephen Pleasonton, July 21, 1840. Correspondence of the Lighthouse Establishment, 1785-1852. NARG 26.
[63] Congressional Document #138, 25th Congress, 2nd Session, Senate. January 26, 1838.
[64] Ibid.
[65] Ibid.
[66] Stephen Pleasonton to Secretary of the Treasury. December 27, 1838. Correspondence of the Lighthouse Establishment, 1785-1852. Volume 14, p. 107. NARG 26.
[67] Report of Lt. George Bache, US Navy. Congressional Document #24, 25th Congress, 3rd Session, House. December 12, 1838.
[68] Stephen Pleasonton to Winslow Lewis, April 20, 1846. Correspondence of the Lighthouse Establishment, 1785-1852. Letter Book 21, 1845-1846, p. 490. NARG 26.
[69] Stephen Pleasonton to Winslow Lewis, March 24, 1849. Correspondence of the Lighthouse Establishment, 1785-1852. Letter Book 27, 1848-1849, p. 219. NARG 26.
[70] John P. Osborn to Stephen Pleasonton, January 21, 1837. Correspondence of the Lighthouse Establishment, 1785-1852. NARG 26.
[71] Contract Volume F. Records of the Lighthouse Establishment, 1785-1852. NARG 26.
[72] Ibid.
[73] Robert J. Hefner, "Montauk Point Light Station: 1838 Keepers Dwelling, a Historic Structures Report." Prepared for the Montauk Historical Society, 1994. p. 32.
[74] Henry Thomas Dering to Stephen Pleasonton. August 7, 1843. Correspondence of the Lighthouse Establishment, 1785-1852. Superintendent's Correspondence, Sag Harbor. Volume 1812-1849. NARG 26.
[75] *List of Lighthouses, Beacons and Floating Lights of the United States*. Washington: C. Alexander, 1848. p. 15.
[76] Robert Muller, "History of the Montauk Point Light Station." *The Long Island Light Keeper*. Vol.2, Issue 1. Long Island Chapter of the U.S. Lighthouse Society.
[77] Holland Jr., *America's Lighthouses*, pp. 32-33.

[78] Ibid. p. 34-35.
[79] "Report of the Officers Constituting the Light-House Board." Washington DC: US Congress, 1852, p. 134.
[80] Annual Report of the Light-House Board for 1856. NARG 26.
[81] A. Ludlow Case to Thornton Jenkins, August 19, 1853. Letters to the Light-House Board from the Inspector 1853-1862. Volume 1853-1855, p. 119. NARG 26.
[82] A. Ludlow Case to Thornton Jenkins, April 17, 1854. Letters to the Light-House Board from the Inspector, 1853-1862. Volume 1853-1855, p. 411. NARG 26.
[83] Ibid.
[84] Ibid.
[85] Lt. J. C. Duane to W. B. Franklin. April 8, 1857. Correspondence Received by the Light-House Board 1853-1900. Letter Book 51, p. 54. NARG 26.
[86] Lt. J. St. C. Morton to W. B. Franklin, April 26, 1859. Field Records of the Light-House Board and Bureau, Third District. Miscellaneous Letters Sent by the Engineer, 186-1871. Volume April 26, 1859 to January 17, 1865, pp. 1-4. NARG 26.
[87] Annual Report of the Light-House Board 1857. NARG 26.
[88] Rattray, *Montauk: Three Centuries of Romance, Sport and Adventure.* (East Hampton: The Star Press, 1938) p. 34.
[89] Lt. James St. C. Morton to William B. Franklin. April 26, 1859. Miscellaneous Letters Sent by the Engineer, 1865-1871. Volume April 26, 1859 to January 17, 1865, pp. 1-4. NARG 26.
[90] Rattray, *Ship Ashore*! p. 67.
[91] Ibid. p.
[92] Mary Esther Mulford Miller, *An East Hampton Childhood* (East Hampton: Star Press, 1938), p. 39.
[93] Ibid. p. 39.
[94] Capt. Benjamin F. Rathbun, *Capsule Histories of Some Local Islands and Light Houses in the Eastern Part of L.I. Sound* (New London: Quality Printers, Inc., 2001), p. 29.
[95] Noel Gish, "Pirates", in *Awakening the Past: The East Hampton 350th Anniversary Lecture Series 1998*. Tom Twomey (ed). (New York: Newmarket Press, 2000), p. 262.
[96] Rattray, *Ship Ashore*! p. 67.

[97] Jeannette Edwards Rattray, *East Hampton History and Genealogies of Early Families* (Garden City: Country Life Press, 1953), p. 141.
[98] A. M. Pennock to -----. May 23, 1860. Letters to the Light-House Board from the Engineer, 1860-1893. NARG 26.
[99] *Sag Harbor Corrector*. Sag Harbor, New York. June 16, 1860. Vol. 39, No. 4; in Long Island Collection, East Hampton Free Library.
[100] "Long Island Items". *Brooklyn Daily Eagle*. June 15, 1860.
[101] John Oct to A. Pennock. August 15, 1860. Miscellaneous Letters Received by the Inspector 1853-1861. Volume August 1858 to July 1862, p. 87. NARG 26.
[102] Ibid. August 27, 1860. p. 96.
[103] A. M. Pennock to the Light-House Board. September 26, 1860. Letters to the Light- House Board from the Engineer, 1860-1893. NARG 26.
[104] "Specifications for a First-Order Lighthouse." Washington DC: Government Printing Office, 1861. Library of Congress.
[105] Ira Winn to A. Pennock. July 3, 1860. Miscellaneous Letters Received by the Inspector, 1853-1861. Volume August 1858 to July 1862. p. 78. NARG 26.
[106] J. P. Morris & Co, Philadelphia to Light-House Board. July 6, 1860. Index to Letters Received, 1792-1811, 1852-1899. Records of the Lighthouse Service. NARG 26.
[107] "Civil War Letters and Journal of Elbert Parker Edwards." Averill Dayton Geus, typescript 1978.
[108] "Montauk Light Ready for Long Winter." *New York Daily News*. October 5, 1939.
[109] Rathbun, *Capsule Histories of Some Local Islands and Light Houses*, p. 28.
[110] Letters to the Light-House Board from the Engineer 1860-1893. Volume May 30, 1863 to April 26, 1866. p. 670. NARG 26.
[111] A smaller version of the garden exists today in the same area of the lighthouse property.
[112] Field Records of the Light-House Board and Bureau, Third District. Miscellaneous Letters Sent by the Engineer, 1865-1871. Volume March 30, 1871 to October 26, 1871, p. 335. NARG 26.
[113] Annual Report of the Light-House Board, 1894. NARG 26.
[114] Thomas Tag. Email correspondence. December 14, 2006.
[115] Holland, Jr. *America's Lighthouses*, p.23.

[116] Annual Report of the Light-House Board 1876. NARG 26.
[117] Monthly Report for June 1872 from John Bailey, Supt. of Construction to J. G. Woodruff, Engineer, p. 473. Annual and Monthly Reports of the Engineer 1868-1910. NARG 26
[118] Annual Reports of the Light-House Board, 1875,1877,1878,1891,1900. Annual Reports to the Light-House Board from the Engineer, 1876,1901,1903,1905. NARG 26.
[119] Journal of Light-house Station at Montauk Point, January 11, 1875. NARG 26.
[120] Annual Report of the Light-House Board, 1897. NARG 26.
[121] Monthly Report for October 1897 from Major David Heap Engineer to Light-House Board, p. 10. NARG 26.
[122] Annual Report of the Light-House Board, 1898. NARG 26.
[123] Jeannette Edwards Rattray. "Lighthouse Log Reveals Old Days at Montauk Pt," *East Hampton Star.* May 5, 1938.
[124] Jeannette Edwards Rattray, "Lighthouse Log Reveals Old Days at Montauk Pt," *East Hampton Star*. May 5, 1938.
[125] "Light Keepers as Signal Men," *Brooklyn Daily Eagle*. June 18, 1898.
[126] Jeff Heatley, editor. *Bully! Colonel Theodore Roosevelt, The Rough Riders and Camp Wikoff* (Montauk Historical Society. Pushcart Press. 1998), p. 286.
[127] Guest Register May 9, 1897 – Aug. 20, 1908. Captain J.G.Scott. Long Island Collection, East Hampton Free Library.
[128] Ibid.
[129] Monthly Report for September 1904 from Major William Russell, Engineer to Light-House Board, p. 429. NARG 26.
[130] Annual Report for year ending June 30, 1899 from Major David Heap, Engineer. p. 299. NARG 26.
[131] Monthly Report for April 1899 from Major David Heap to Light-House Board, p. 239. NARG 26.
[132] Major William Russell to the Light-House Board, December 5, 1901. Correspondence Files 1901-1939. 626 Aids to Navigation and 601 Operations. NARG 26.
[133] Major William Russell to the Lighthouse Board, December 16, 1901. Correspondence Files 1901-1939. 626 Aids to Navigation and 601 Operations. NARG 26.

[134] Light-House Board to Major William Russell, January 14, 1902. Correspondence Files 1901-1939. 626 Aids to Navigation and 601 Operations. NARG 26.
[135] Holland Jr, *America's Lighthouses*, p. 38.
[136] Notice to Mariners April 30, 1903. Correspondence Files 1901-1939. 626 Aids to Navigation and 601 Operations. NARG 26.
[137] "Lists of Lights and Fog Signals on the Atlantic and Gulf Coasts of the United States, 1902". Washington: Government Printing Office, 1902. pp. 80, 81.
[138] Monthly Report for December 1907 from Major William Porter, Engineer to the Light-House Board, p. 172. NARG 26.
[139] "Description of Montauk Point Light Station", August 10, 1911. "Correspondence Files 1901-1939. 626 Aids to Navigation and 601 Operations". Box 50. NARG 26.
[140] Commander Officer, U.S.S. Shubrick to Commissioner of Lighthouses, October 9, 1919. Correspondence of the Bureau of Light-Houses 1911-1939. Box 1004, E50, File 1546E. NARG 26.
[141] John E. Miller to Commissioner of Lighthouses, November 15, 1919. Correspondence of the Bureau of Lighthouses 1911-1939. Box 1004, E50, File 1546E. NARG 26.
[142] List of light stations to be observed from the Bartlett Reef Light Vessel, January 1922. Field Records of the Light-House Board and Bureau, Third District. Correspondence Files 1901-1939. 626 Aids to Navigation and 601 Operations, Box 133. NARG 26.
[143] Repairs to Montauk Point Light Station, August 14, 1923. Correspondence of the Bureau of Lighthouses, 1911-1939. Box 1004, E 50, File 1546. NARG 26.
[144] "Kerosene Still Lights Montauk Pt Beacon," *East Hampton Star*. May 1933.
[145] Meier Steinbrink to Commissioner, Bureau of Lighthouses, November 23, 1937. Correspondence of the Bureau of Lighthouses, 1911-1939. Box 1004, E 50, File 1546E. NARG 26.
[146] H. D. King, Commissioner of Lighthouses, to Meier Steinbrink, December 2, 1937. Correspondence of the Bureau of Lighthouses 1911-1939. Box 1004, E 50, File 1546E. NARG 26.
[147] Department of Health to Bureau of Lighthouses, November 20, 1935. Correspondence of the Bureau of Lighthouses, 1911-1939. Box 1004 E 50, File 1546. NARG 26.

[148] Recommendation as to Aids to Navigation, February 12, 1934. Correspondence of the Bureau of Lighthouses 1911-1939. Box 1004 E 50, File 1546. NARG 26.
[149] Superintendent Dillon to J. T. Yates, July 1930. Margaret Buckridge Bock Scrapbook 1930-1943. Montauk Point Lighthouse Museum.
[150] J. T. Yates to Superintendent Dillon, July 22, 1930. Margaret Buckridge Bock Scrapbook 1930-1943. Montauk Point Lighthouse Museum.
[151] Edward Adolphe, "Montauk Light is Polishing Up To Greet the Summer's Visitors," *New York Herald Tribune*, May 9, 1937.
[152] "Montauk Light Ready For the Long Winter," *New York Daily News*. October 5, 1939.
[153] District Superintendent to Commissioner of Lighthouses, April 2, 1937. Correspondence of the Bureau of Lighthouses, 1911-1939. Box 1004 E 50, File 1546E. NARG 26.
[154] Deputy Commissioner of Bureau of Lighthouse to Superintendent of Lighthouses, Third District, April 26, 1937. Correspondence of the Bureau of Lighthouses, 1911-1939. Box 1004, E 50, File 1546E. NARG 26.
[155] O. C. Luther, Assistant Superintendent to Supt of Lighthouses, Third District, April 29, 1925. Correspondence of the Bureau of Lighthouses. Box 1004, E 50, File 1546E. NARG 26.
[156] "Over 10,000 Visitors Climb Historic Montauk Lighthouse," *East Hampton Star*. August 24, 1939.
[157] "Washington Does Not Plan Closing Montauk Light," *East Hampton Star*. June 3, 1937.
[158] Recommendation as to Aids to Navigation, October 14, 1938. Correspondence of the Bureau of Lighthouses 1911-1939. Box 1004, E50, File 1546. NARG 26.
[159] Journal of Light Station at Montauk Point. March 1, 1936 to August 31, 1940. Lighthouse Station Logs, 1897-1946, Box 107. NARG 26.
[160] T. L. Bludworth to H. D. King, May 13, 1937.Correspondence of the Bureau of Lighthouses, 1911-1939. Box 1004, E50, File 1546B. NARG 26.
[161] J. T. Yates to H. D. King, May 19, 1937. Correspondence of the Bureau of Lighthouses, 1911-1939. Box 1004, E50, File 1546B. NARG 26.
[162] Department of Commerce, June 18, 1937. Correspondence of the Bureau of Lighthouses, 1911-1939. Box 1004, File 1546B. NARG 26.

[163] Journal of Light Station at Montauk Point. September 1, 1940 to April 30, 1943 Lighthouse Station Logs, 1897-1946, Box 107. NARG 26.
[164] USCG Log Books, 1943, Box 928. NA, Suitland.
[165] USCG Log Books, 1944, Box 1244. NA, Suitland.
[166] USCG Log Books, 1945. Box 614. NA, Suitland.
[167] USCG Log Books, 1945, Box 614. NA, Suitland.
[168] Jeannette Edwards Rattray, "Montauk's Old Mill Moves Again," *New York Times*, August 16, 1942.
[169] Russell Drumm, "All Clear at Camp Hero," *East Hampton Star*. May 31, 2001.
[170] Kurt Kahofer, "Fire Control Station," *Beacon*, Montauk Historical Society. 1991.
[171] Joshua Stoff, *From Canoes to Cruisers: The Maritime Heritage of Long Island* (Interlaken: Empire State Books, 1994), p. 91.
[172] Everett T. Rattray, *The South Fork: the Land and People of Eastern Long Island*. (Wainscott: Pushcart Press, 1989), p. 119.
[173] Averill Dayton Geus, *From Sea to Sea: 350 Years of East Hampton History* (West Kennebunk, ME: Phoenix Publishing, 1999), p.107.
[174] Stoff, *From Canoes to Cruisers: The Maritime Heritage of Long Island*, p.87.
[175] "'Vox Pop' Broadcast From Lighthouse," *East Hampton Star*, January 8, 1948.
[176] Patrick Fenton, "The Keepers of the Light," *Newsday*, June 2, 1996.
[177] Tom Clavin, *Dark Noon: The Final Voyage of the Fishing Boat "Pelican"* (New York: International Marine/McGraw-Hill, 2005), p. 213.
[178] Henry Keatts and George Farr, *The Bell Tolls: Shipwrecks and Lighthouses of Eastern Long Island* (Eastport: Fathom Press, 2002), p. 121.
[179] "Light at Montauk Gets Brighter Glow," *New York Times*, December 8, 1960.
[180] John G. Rogers, "Montauk Light's in News With $5.50 Bulb," *New York Herald Tribune*, April 2, 1961.
[181] Arthur Roth, "The Keeper of the Montauk Light," *East Hampton Star*, February 9, 1967.
[182] Ibid.
[183] Ibid.

[184] Ibid.
[185] Ibid.
[186] Ibid.
[187] Ibid.
[188] "Montauk to Get Automated Light," *Newsday*, December 24, 1968.
[189] "Montauk Point Light Station. Record of Inspections, November 9, 1965 to August 21, 1968. November 8, 1966. November 21, 1966. Montauk Point Lighthouse Museum.
[190] Record of Inspection. May 12, 1977. Montauk Point Lighthouse Museum.
[191] Record of Inspection. June 17, 1963. Montauk Point Lighthouse Museum.
[192] Record of Inspection. August 17, 1968. Montauk Point Lighthouse Museum.
[193] Bruce Poli, "Montauk Light Dimming?" *New York Times*, October 9, 1983.
[194] "The Pre-Automation Light," *East Hampton Star*, February 20, 1986.
[195] Ibid.
[196] Patrick Fenton, "The Keepers of the Light," *Newsday*, June 2, 1996.
[197] Joanne Ramey, "A Beacon Beckons With Love," *New York Times*, June 21, 1981.
[198] Record of Inspection. April 23, 1980. Montauk Point Lighthouse Museum.
[199] Samuel Crompton and Michael J Rhein, *The Ultimate Book of Lighthouses* (San Diego: Thunder Bay Press. 2001), p. 32.
[200] Elinor DeWire, *Lighthouses of the Mid-Atlantic Coast* (Stillwater MN: Voyageur Press. 2002), p. 96.
[201] Holland, *America's Lighthouses*, p. 43.
[202] DeWire, *Lighthouses of the Mid-Atlantic Coast*, p. 102.
[203] Journal of Light-House Station at Montauk Point, July 1, 1890 to June 30, 1900. Lighthouse Station Logs 1897-1946, Box 107. NARG 26.
[204] "Lights and Shadows of Montauk 1832-1857". Montauk Point Lighthouse Museum.
[205] DeWire, *Lighthouses of the Mid-Atlantic Coast*, p. 113.
[206] Holland, *America's Lighthouses*, p. 45.
[207] Ibid. p.54.

[208] Rattray, *East Hampton History Including Genealogies of Early Families*, p. 357.
[209] Henry P. Dering to ----. October 6, 1800. Letters to the Bureau of Light Houses, 1789-1804. Book C, p. 463. NARG 26.
[210] Henry P. Dering to Albert Gallatin. April 30, 1804. Correspondence of the Light-House Establishment, 1785-1852. Letter Book G, p. 20. NARG 26.
[211] Henry P. Dering to Albert Gallatin. July 7, 1806. Correspondence of the Light-House Establishment, 1785-1852. Book G. p. 110. NARG 26.
[212] Ibid.
[213] Montauk Proprietors to Albert Gallatin. July 3, 1806. Correspondence of the Light-House Establishment, 1785-1852. Book G. NARG 26.
[214] Rattray, *East Hampton History Including Genealogies of Early Families*, p. 357.
[215] Jacob Hand to Albert Gallatin, May 26, 1808. Letters Received by the Treasury Department, 1785-1812. Entry 17A. NARG 26.
[216] Montauk Proprietors to Albert Gallatin, May 30, 1808. Letters Received by the Treasury Department 1785 1812. NARG 26.
[217] Henry Packer Dering to Albert Gallatin. June 1, 1808. Correspondence of the Light-House Establishment 1785-1852. Letter Book 3, 1802-1809. NARG 26.
[218] Ibid.
[219] Albert Gallatin to Henry P. Dering. June 27, 1808. Correspondence of the Light-House Establishment 1785-1852. Letter Book 3, 1802-1809, p. 453. NARG 26.
[220] Albert Gallatin to Henry P. Dering. January 28, 1812. Correspondence of the Light-House Establishment 1785-1852. Letter Book 4, 1809-1817. p. 154. NARG 26.
[221] Henry P. Dering to Secretary of the Treasury. January 3, 1814. Correspondence of the Light-House Establishment, 1785-1852. Superintendent's Correspondence, Sag Harbor. NARG 26.
[222] Anne C. Fullam, "Renovations Upgrade the Keeper's Dwelling in Montauk Lighthouse". *New York Times*. July 5, 1992.
[223] Henry P. Dering to Secretary of the Treasury. March 2, 1815. Correspondence of the Light-House Establishment, 1785-1852. Superintendent's Correspondence, Sag Harbor. NARG 26.

[224] Rattray, *East Hampton History Including Genealogies of Early Families*, p. 213.
[225] John P. Osborn to Stephen Pleasonton. April 21, 1832. Correspondence of the Light-House Establishment, 1785-1852. Superintendent's Correspondence, Sag Harbor. NARG 26.
[226] Charles F. Hummel, *With Hammer in Hand: The Dominy Craftsmen of East Hampton, New York* (Charlottesville, VA: The University Press of Virginia, 1968), p. 239.
[227] Ibid. p. 232.
[228] Jericho was located just to the west of the present village of East Hampton.
[229] www.uscg.mil
[230] Stephen D. Gould, "The Light at the End of the Island", *Beacon 2001,* Montauk Historical Society.
[231] Visitors Log. Courtesy of Montauk Point Lighthouse Museum.
[232] John P. Osborn to Stephen Pleasonton, January 21, 1837. Correspondence of the Light-House Establishment 1785-1852. Superintendent's Correspondence, Sag Harbor. NARG 26.
[233] John P. Osborn to Stephen Pleasonton, July 21, 1840. Correspondence of the Light-House Establishment 1785-1852. Superintendent's Correspondence, Sag Harbor. NARG 26.
[234] Nancy Hyden Woodward, *East Hampton: A Town and its People, 1648-1994* (East Hampton: Fireplace Press, 1995), p. 144.
[235] These were the old wooden steps prior to the 1860 installation of the iron stairway.
[236] Miller, *An East Hampton Childhood*, p. 29.
[237] The Long Islander. March 3, 1849.
[238] Superintendent of Lighthouses for District of Sag Harbor to Stephen Pleasonton. January 16, 1850. Entry 17C: Letters Received from Superintendents of Lights 1803-1852. NARG 26.
[239] Stephen Pleasonton to Edwin Rose, Superintendent of Lights, June 24, 1850. Correspondence of the Light-House Establishment, 1785-1852. Volume 29, p. 265. NARG 26.
[240] Geus, *From Sea to Sea*, p. 60.
[241] *Journal of the Trustees of the Freeholders and Commonalty of East Hampton Town 1845-1870*. p. 90.
[242] Light-House Board to Sag Harbor Superintendent, April 8, 1857. Letters Sent to Superintendents of Lights, 1853-1894. NARG 26.

[243] "Lights and Shadows of Montauk 1832-1857". Montauk Point Lighthouse Museum.
[244] Journal of the Light-House Board, 1851-1908. October 11, 1858. Volume 1854-1862, p. 498. NARG 26.
[245] Journal of the Light-House Board, 1851-1908. October 11, 1859. Volume 1854-1862, p. 537. NARG 26.
[246] Light-House Board to Sag Harbor Superintendent, December 4, 1857. Letters Sent to Superintendents of Lights, 1853-1894. NARG 26.
[247] *Long Islander*. October 1, 1858.
[248] "Found After Thirty Years," *Brooklyn Daily Eagle*, September 9, 1888.
[249] Geus, *From Sea to Sea*, p. 69.
[250] Chairman of Treasury Department, Light-House Board to Capt. L.M. Powell, Inspector. December 30, 1862. Field Records of the Light House Board and Bureau, Third District. Letters from the Light-House Board to the Inspector, 1853-1872. Volume 1862. NARG 26.
[251] Jeannette Edwards Rattray, "Montauk Light Built in 1796 Long In Service," *East Hampton Star*. April 28, 1938.
[252] Letter dated October 31, 1872. Correspondence Received by the Light-House Board, 1853-1900. Volume 312, p. 213. NARG 26.
[253] Rattray, *East Hampton History Including Genealogies of Early Families*, p. 468.
[254] James Devine. "The Montauk Indians and the Montauk Light-house," *Beacon*, 1996, Montauk Historical Society.
[255] Rattray, *East Hampton History Including Genealogies of Early Families*, p. 28.
[256] Journal of Light-house Station at Montauk Point, September, 1875. Entry 80 (NC-31): Lighthouse Station Logs, 1897-1947. NARG 26.
[257] Letter from Jonathan A. Miller to Commodore S L Trenchard, Inspector. August 26, 1875. Correspondence Received by the Light-House Board 1853-1900. Letter Book 379. p. 92. NARG 26.
[258] Letter from Jonathan A. Miller to Commodore S. L. Trenchard, Inspector. August 26, 1875. Correspondence Received by the Light-House Board 1853-1900. Letter Book 379. p. 93. NARG 26.
[259] Letter from S. L. Trenchard to Joseph Henry, Light-House Board. August 30, 1875. Correspondence Received by the Light-House Board 1853-1900. Letter Book 379. p. 92. NARG 26.

[260] Letter from H. S. Havens to Light-House Board. September 27, 1875. Correspondence Received by the Light-House Board 1853-1900. Letter Book 379. p. 181-182. NARG 26.
[261] Letter from S. L. Trenchard to Light-House Board. September 30, 1875. Correspondence Received by the Light-House Board 1853-1900. Letter Book 379. p 157. NARG 26.
[262] Letter from Jonathan A. Miller to Light-House Board. October 19, 1875. Correspondence Received by the Light-House Board 1853-1900. Letter Book 379. p. 281-283. NARG 26.
[263] Ibid. p. 283.
[264] Letter from A. C. Rhind to Joseph Henry, Light-House Board. February 25, 1876. Correspondence Received by the Light-House Board 1853-1900. Letter Book 379. p. 499. NARG 26.
[265] Letter from A. C. Rhind to Joseph Henry, Light-House Board. November 12, 1875. Correspondence Received by the Light-House Board 1853-1900. Letter Book 379. p. 279-280. NARG 26.
[266] "Civil War Letters and Journal of Elbert Parker Edwards," ed. Averill Dayton Geus. 1978.
[267] Ibid.
[268] Rattray, *East Hampton History Including Genealogies of Early Families*, p. 317.
[269] "Civil War Letters and Journals of Elbert Parker Edwards," ed. Averill Dayton Geus, 1978.
[270] Journal of Light-house Station at Montauk Point, August 1875. Entry 80(NC-31): Lighthouse Station Logs, 1897-1947. NARG 26.
[271] Robert Muller, *Long Island Lighthouses Past and Present* (Interlaken: Heart of the Lakes Publishing, 2004), pp. 247-249.
[272] "Long Island Sketches; A New Englander's View of Montauk Point," *Brooklyn Daily Eagle*, October 10, 1872.
[273] Letter from Thomas P. Ripley to Light-House Board. January 13, 1870. Correspondence Received by the Light-House Board 1853-1900. Letter Book 239. p. 535. NARG 26.
[274] Journal of Light-house Station at Montauk Point, November 1875. Entry 80 (NC-31): Lighthouse Station Logs, 1897-1947. NARG 26.
[275] Journal of Light-house Station at Montauk Point, February, 1876. Entry 80 (NC-31): Lighthouse Station Logs, 1897-1947. NARG 26.
[276] "Long Island Sketches; A New Englanders View of Montauk Point," *Brooklyn Daily Eagle*, October 10, 1872.

[277] Journal of Light-house Station at Montauk Point, December, 1876. Entry 80 (NC-31): Lighthouse Station Logs 1897-1947. NARG 26.
[278] Journal of Light-house Station at Montauk Point, March 1876. Entry 80 (NC-31): Lighthouse Station Logs, 1897-1947. NARG 26.
[279] "Lighthouse Drew Visitors Long Ago," *East Hampton Star*, March 7, 1963.
[280] Journal of Light-house Station at Montauk Point. December 1876. Entry 80 (NC-31): Lighthouse Station Logs, 1897-1947. NARG 26.
[281] Letter dated January 29, 1881. Field Records of the Light-House Board and Bureau, Third District. Letters to the Light-House Board from the Inspector. NARG 26.
[282] Journal of Light-house Station at Montauk Point. October 1885. Entry 80 (NC-31): Lighthouse Station Logs, 1897-1947. NARG 26.
[283] "Lighthouse Drew Visitors Long Ago," *East Hampton Star*, March 7, 1963.
[284] Letter from Sandra Clunies to Ann Shengold, Montauk Point Lighthouse Museum, November 1, 2004.
[285] "Lighthouse Log Tells of Blizzard of '88- Which Hit Just 75 Years Ago March 12," *East Hampton Star*, February 28, 1963.
[286] "Journal of Light Station at Montauk Point, October 1, 1874 to June 30, 1890". Lighthouse Station Logs, 1897-1946, Box 107. NARG 26.
[287] "Lighthouse Log Tells of Blizzard of '88- Which Hit Just 75 Years Ago March 12," *East Hampton Star*, February 28, 1963.
[288] Thomas Morrison, Bureau of Accounts, Dept. of State to Frederick Rodgers, US Navy, Thompkinsville, NY. August 29, 1889. "Letters to the Light-House Board from the Engineer 1860-1893". Volume 51, p. 123. NARG 26.
[289] Ibid.
[290] Barbara Borsack, "The Compound," *East Hampton Star*, April 16, 1998.
[291] Jack Otter, "Lighthouse Shines as Altar," *Newsday*, April 19, 1994.
[292] Barbara Borsack, "Tales of the Montauk Light," *East Hampton Star*, May 28, 1998.
[293] Ibid.
[294] Rattray, *Ship Ashore!* pp. 131-132.
[295] Barbara Borsack, "Tales of the Lighthouse," *East Hampton Star*, June 11, 1998.

[296] Jeannette Edwards Rattray, "Lighthouse Log Reveals Old Days at Montauk Pt," *East Hampton Star*, May 5, 1938.
[297] "Lighthouse Nuptials Not the First," *East Hampton Star*, August 4, 1966.
[298] Jeannette Edwards Rattray, "Lighthouse Log Reveals Old Days at Montauk Pt, *East Hampton Star*, May 5, 1938.
[299] John Jacobus to Light-House Board. June 30, 1892. Correspondence Received by the Light-House Board, 1853-1900. Volume 947, p. 1164. NARG 26.
[300] Rattray, *East Hampton History Including Genealogies of Early Families*, p. 217.
[301] "Light Lures Birds to Die," *New York Times*, April 26, 1906.
[302] Muller, *Long Island Lighthouses, Past and Present*, p. 235
[303] Ibid.
[304] Rattray, *Montauk: Three Centuries of Romance, Sport and Adventure*, p. 37.
[305] Jeannette Edwards Rattray, "Lighthouse Log Reveals Old Days at Montauk Pt," *East Hampton Star*, May 5,1938.
[306] Rattray, *Montauk: Three Centuries of Romance, Sport and Adventure*, p. 37.
[307] Ibid. p. 37.
[308] Ibid. p. 37.
[309] Ibid. p. 89.
[310] Jeannette Edwards Rattray, "Lighthouse Log Reveals Old Days at Montauk Pt," *East Hampton Star*, May 5, 1938.
[311] Letter from James G. Scott to Samuel H. Miller, April 5, 1886. Montauk Point Lighthouse Museum.
[312] Inspector Captain C. Thomas to James G. Scott. December 17, 1909. Field Records of the Light-House Board and Bureau, Third District. Correspondence Files, 1901-1939. 626 Aids to Navigation and 601 Operations, Box 10. NARG 26.
[313] James G. Scott to Inspector Captain C Thomas. December 20, 1909. Field Records of the Light-House Board and Bureau, Third District. Correspondence Files, 1901-1939. 626 Aids to Navigation and 601 Operations, Box 10. NARG 26.
[314] Inspector, US Navy to James G. Scott. February 26, 1910. Field Records of the Light-House Board and Bureau, Third District. Correspon-

dence Files 1901-1939. 626 Aids to Navigation and 601 Operations, Box 27. NARG 26.

[315] Robert G. Bachand, *Northeast Lights* (Norwalk, Ct: Sea Sports Publications, 1989), p. 238.

[316] Muller, *Long Island Lighthouses Past and Present*, p. 237.

[317] Letter from Lighthouse Bureau to Department of Agriculture, August 22, 1911. Correspondence of the Bureau of Light-Houses 1911-1939. Box 1004, E50, File 1546E. NARG 26.

[318] Ibid. p. 237.

[319] Rattray, *East Hampton History Including Genealogies of Early Families*, p. 471.

[320] Journal of Light-house Station at Montauk Point, October 1, 1916 to September 30, 1924. Lighthouse Station Logs 1897-1946, Box 107. NARG 26.

[321] Charles Hanson Towne, *Loafing Down Long Island* (New York: Century Co., 1921), p. 122-123.

[322] Letter from Phillips Channell to Arthur Channell, November 16, 1920. Montauk Point Lighthouse Museum.

[323] Journal of Light-Station at Montauk Point, 1917,1921,1923,1928. Entry 80 (NC-31): Lighthouse Station Logs 1897-1947. NARG 26.

[324] Journal of Light-Station at Montauk Point, 1916. Entry 80 (NC-31): Lighthouse Station Logs 1897-1947. NARG 26.

[325] Journal of Light-Station at Montauk Point, 1914. Entry 80 (NC-31): Lighthouse Station Logs 1897-1947. NARG 26.

[326] Journal of Light-Station at Montauk Point, 1919. Entry 80 (NC-31): Lighthouse Station Logs 1897-1947. NARG 26.

[327] Journal of Light-Station at Montauk Point, 1917. Entry 80 (NC-31): Lighthouse Station Logs 1897-1947. NARG 26.

[328] Journal of Light-Station at Montauk Point, 1918. Entry 80 (NC-31): Lighthouse Station Logs 1897-1947. NARG 26.

[329] Journal of Light-Station at Montauk Point, 1928. Entry 80 (NC-31): Lighthouse Station Logs 1897-1947. NARG 26.

[330] Letter from Lighthouse Bureau to Superintendent of Lighthouses, Third District. January 19, 1925. Correspondence of the Bureau of Light-Houses 1911-1939. Box 1004, E50, File 1546E. NARG 26.

[331] Journal of Light-Station at Montauk Point, 1926. Entry 80 (NC-31): Lighthouse Station Logs 1897-1947. NARG 26.

[332] Letter from District Superintendent to the Lighthouse Service, January 22, 1925. Correspondence of the Bureau of Lighthouses 1911-1939. Box 1004 E 50, File 1546. NARG 26.
[333] Interview with Keeper John E. Miller by W. F. Ockenfels. February 10, 1925. Correspondence of the Bureau of Lighthouses 1911-1939. Box 1004. E 50. File 1546E. NARG 26.
[334] Ibid.
[335] Letter from Lighthouse Service to the District Superintendent, February 14, 1925. Correspondence of the Bureau of Lighthouses 1911-1939. Box 1004 E 50, File 1546E. NARG 26.
[336] Letter from Lighthouse Service to the Commissioner, February 19, 1925. Correspondence of the Bureau of Lighthouses 1911-1939. Box 1004 E 50, File 1546E. NARG 26.
[337] Letter from George R. Putnam to the Commandant, US Coast Guard, March 3, 1925. Correspondence of the Bureau of Lighthouses 1911-1939. Box 1004. E 50. File 1546E. NARG 26.
[338] Letter from Robert Moses to George R. Putnam, June 14, 1926. Correspondence of the Bureau of Lighthouses 1911-1939. Box 1004, E50, File 1546E. NARG 26.
[339] Letter from John E. Miller to Superintendent of Lighthouses, Third District. June 24, 1926. Correspondence of the Bureau of Lighthouses 1911-1939. Box 1004, E50, File 1546E. NARG 26.
[340] Letter from Lighthouse Bureau to Robert Moses. July 6, 1926. Correspondence of the Bureau of Lighthouses 1911-1939. Box 1004, E50, File 1546E. NARG 26.
[341] "Montauk Lighthouse at Eastern Tip of Island, Oldest in Service," *East Hampton Star*, April 8, 1927.
[342] "Century-Old Lighthouse Montauk Sight; Popular Mecca For Armies of Tourists," *County Review*, August 17, 1933.
[343] Report of Inspection of Montauk Point Light Station, June 12, 1931. Margaret Buckridge Bock Scrapbook 1930-1943. Montauk Point Lighthouse Museum.
[344] Ibid.
[345] David Behrens, "Keepers of the Lights," *Newsday*, August 6, 1990.
[346] Patrick Fenton, "The Keepers of the Light," *Newsday*, June 2, 1996.
[347] Margaret Buckridge Bock, "Memories of a Light-Keeper's Daughter," *Beacon*, 1987. Montauk Historical Society.

[348] Keatts and Farr, *The Bell Tolls: Shipwrecks and Lighthouses of Eastern Long Island*, p. 121.
[349] Thomas A Buckridge to Superintendent of Lighthouses, July 14, 1935. Correspondence of the Bureau of Lighthouses 1911-1939. Box 1004, E 50, File 1546E. NARG 26.
[350] Keatts and Farr. *The Bell Tolls: Shipwrecks and Lighthouses of Eastern Long Island*, p. 233.
[351] Ibid.
[352] Pelletreau, *A History of Long Island From its Earliest Settlement to the Present Time*, p. 28.
* Thanks to Greg Donohue for his assistance in the preparation of this chapter and providing selected photographs.
[353] Ezra L'Hommedieu to New York Chamber of Commerce, November 19, 1792 in *Journal of the Trustees of the Freeholders and Commonalty of East Hampton Town, 1772-1807* East Hampton, 1927. p. 335.
[354] William Cullen Bryant ed. "Picturesque America", in *Exploring the Past: Writings from 1798 to 1896 Relating to the History of the Town of East Hampton*, ed.Tom Twomey (New York: Newmarket Press, 2000), pp. 305-306.
[355] David Gardiner "Chronicles of the Town of Easthampton", in *Exploring the Past: Writings From 1798 to 1896 Relating to the History of the Town of East Hampton*, ed. Tom Twomey (New York: Newmarket Press. 2000), p. 175.
[356] "Montauk Point, Long Island". *Harper's New Monthly Magazine*. September 1871. p.493.
[357] Richard M. Bayles, *Historical and Descriptive Sketches of Suffolk County* (Port Jefferson: Richard M Bayles, 1874), p. 419.
[358] Charles Lanman, *Recollections of Curious Characters and Pleasant Places* (Edinburgh: David Douglas, 1881), p. 142.
[359] "To Montauk: Brooklynites Take a Long Tramp on the Island," *Brooklyn Daily Eagle*, November 16, 1889.
[360] Martha Bockee Flint, *Early Long Island: A Colonial Study* (New York: G. P. Putnam's Sons. 1896), p.26
[361] Letter from Gilbert H. Edwards to Robert L. Bacon, January 30, 1928. Correspondence of the Bureau of Lighthouses, 1911-1939. Box 1004, E50, File 1546. NARG 26.

[362] O. C. Luther to Bureau of Lighthouses, March 5, 1928. Correspondence of the Bureau of Lighthouses, 1911-1939. Box 1004, E50, File 1546. NARG 26.
[363] Correspondence of the Bureau of Light-Houses 1911-1939. Box 1004, E50, File 1546E. NARG 26.
[364] "Pertinent Facts About Montauk Will Be of Interest to Visitors," *East Hampton Star*, June 21, 1929.
[365] "Kerosene Still Lights Montauk Pt. Beacon," *East Hampton Star*, May 1933.
[366] Jeannette Edwards Rattray, "Montauk Light Built in 1796 Long in Service," *East Hampton Star*, April 28, 1938.
[367] John C. Devlin, "Erosion Imperils Light at Montauk," *New York Times*, January 24, 1958.
[368] "Old Guard to Pass the Torch," *Newsday*, October 2, 1967.
[369] Record of Inspection, January 20, 1967. Montauk Point Lighthouse Museum.
[370] Knut Royce, "Coast Guard to Keep Old Montauk Light," *Newsday*. August 27, 1970.
[371] Record of Inspection. November 15, 1968. Montauk Point Lighthouse Museum.
[372] Letter to Giorgina Reid from Captain G. H. Weller, October 7, 1969. Courtesy of Robert Muller, LI Chapter, US Lighthouse Society.
[373] A corrosion resistant wire container filled with stone fastened together and used for retaining walls, revetments, slope protection, and other structures.
[374] Jeanne Toomey Gray, "Holding Up a Bank," *Suffolk Life*, March 26, 1973.
[375] Record of Inspection. November 23, 1970. Montauk Point Lighthouse Museum.
[376] Record of Inspection. September 24, 1971. Montauk Point Lighthouse Museum.
[377] Record of Inspection. July 24, 1972. Montauk Point Lighthouse Museum.
[378] Marilyn Goldstein, "She Holds the Patent on Tenacity," *Newsday*, October 10, 1984.
[379] Ibid.
[380] Diane Ketcham, "Montauk's Lighthouse: On the Edge of Disaster?" *New York Times*, September 22, 1985.

[381] Ibid.
[382] Ibid.
[383] Ibid.
[384] Bruce Poli, "Montauk Light Dimming?" *New York Times*, October 9, 1983.
[385] Greg Donohue, "Against All Odds; a Lighthouse Looks to the Future". 1996.
[386] Steve Wick, "Lighthouse vs. Erosion; Montauk Historical Society Seeks to Stabilize Bluffs," *Newsday*, February 21, 1989.
[387] Ibid.
[388] Ibid.
[389] Alex Martin, "Dark Days for a Lighthouse. Study to Assess Need for Funds to Bolster It," *Newsday*, December 7, 1990.
[390] Ibid.
[391] "The Daymark." Montauk Lighthouse Museum. Vol. 2 No. 1. March 1992.
[392] "The Storm That Saved the Lighthouse," *Beacon*, 1992. Montauk Historical Society.
[393] Bill Bleyer, "$10 Million Plan for Montauk Light," *Newsday*, March 25, 1993.
[394] Ibid.
[395] Ibid.
[396] Bill Bleyer, "$10 Million Plan for Montauk Light," *Newsday*, March 25, 1993.
[397] George DeWan, "Turning the Tide of Erosion," *Newsday*, June 2, 1996.
[398] Greg Donohue, "The Lighthouse Shines Brighter Than Ever," *Beacon*, 1993. Montauk Historical Society.
[399] Greg Donohue, "Against All Odds: A Lighthouse Looks to the Future." 1996.
[400] "Governor Calls For Action to Protect Historic Lighthouse." NYS Press Release. June 2, 1996.
[401] Ibid.
[402] Ibid.
[403] Ibid.
[404] Bill Bleyer, "Shoring Up Montauk Lighthouse/ Army Corps of Engineers Granted $900G for Study on Erosion Threat," *Newsday*, October 31, 2000.

[405] Debbie Tuma, "Montauk Re-Point," *New York Daily News* ,September 18, 2006.
[406] Ibid.
[407] Bill Bleyer, "Eroding Support," *Newsday.* November 15, 2006.
[408] Ibid.
[409] Corey Kilgannon, "For Montauk, It's Lighthouse vs. Surf's Up!" *New York Times,* November 14, 2006.
[410] Lois Raimondo, "Erosion Project for Lighthouse Nears Completion", *New York Times*, March 8, 1998.
[411] George H. Peters, "The Flora of Long Island," in *Long Island: A History of Two Great Counties, Nassau and Suffolk,* ed. Paul Bailey (New York: Lewis Historical Publishing, 1949),2: 146.
[412] Henry Dering to Tench Coxe, April 5, 1799. Letters to the Bureau of Light Houses 1789-1804. Book C. p. 413. NARG 26.
[413] Henry P. Dering to Samuel Smith, Commissioner of Revenue, September 29, 1815. Correspondence of the Light-House Establishment 1785-1852. Superintendent's Correspondence. NARG 26.
[414] Henry P. Dering to William H. Crawford, Secretary of the Treasury, May 15, 1820. Correspondence of the Light-House Establishment, 1785-1852. Superintendent's Correspondence. NARG 26.
[415] Joseph Lederle to ____, March 19, 1866. Field Records of the Light-House Board and Bureau, Third District. Letters to the Light-House Board from the Engineer, 1860-1893. Volume May 30, 1863 to April 26, 1866. p. 670. NARG 26.
[416] Ibid.
[417] Joseph Lederle to ____, September 23, 1869. Field Records of the Light-House Board and Bureau, Third District. Letters to the Light-House Board from the Engineer 1860-1893. Volume June 1868 to June 1870, p. 411. NARG 26.
[418] Jeannette Edwards Rattray, "Montauk Light Built in 1796 Long in Service," *East Hampton Star*, April 28, 1938.
[419] "Rough Weather on Long Island," *New York Times*, February 13, 1894.
[420] John E. Miller, Keeper to Third District Inspector, December 9, 1917. Field Records of the Light-House Board and Bureau, Third District. Correspondence Files 1901-1939. NARG 26.

[421] Journal of Light Station at Montauk Point, November 1, 1924 to May 31, 1931. Lighthouse Station Logs, 1897-1946. Box 107. NARG 26.
[422] *Beacon*. Montauk Historical Society. 1988.
[423] Ibid.
[424] Peg Winski, *Montauk: An Anecdotal History* (Montauk Historical Society, 1997), p. 34.
[425] Ibid. pp. 45, 47.
[426] Ibid. p. 68.
[427] Ibid. p. 105.
[428] Ibid. p. 124.
[429] Everett S. Allen, *A Wind to Shake the World: The Story of the 1938 Hurricane* (Boston: Little, Brown & Co., 1976), p. 78.
[430] Ibid. p. 79.
[431] Ibid. p. 80.
[432] "Nine More Bodies Found at Beaches," *New York Times*, September 25, 1938.
[433] Journal of Light Station at Montauk Point, March 1, 1936 to August 31, 1940. Lighthouse Station Logs, 1897-1946, box 107. NARG 26.
[434] Recommendation as to Aid to Navigation, October 25, 1938. Correspondence of the Bureau of Lighthouses 1911-1939. Box 1004. File 1546. NARG 26.
[435] Neal Patterson, "Hurricane Swipes City, Batters LI," *New York Daily News*, September 1, 1954.
[436] Robert Parker, "Montauk Staggered, Calls it 'Sneak Punch,'" *New York Daily News*, September 1, 1954.
[437] "Hurricane Rips Eastern Seaboard; No Lives Lost Here," *East Hampton Star*, September 2, 1954.
[438] Ibid.
[439] "South Fork Battered: East Suffolk Hard Hit By Hurricane's Force," *Patchogue Advance*, September 15, 1960.
[440] "Hurricane Donna Roars Across East End," *East Hampton Star*, September 15, 1960.
[441] "Hurricane Esther Finally Dies of Old Age," *East Hampton Star*, September 28, 1961.
[442] "Northeaster Strikes,' *East Hampton Star*, March 8, 1962.
[443] "Freak Gale Pushes Tides Up," *East Hampton Star*, December 5, 1963.

[444] "Winter Gale Endangers Homes," *East Hampton Star*, January 16, 1964.
[445] "Fast Moving Belle Blasts Through LI," *Newsday*, August 10, 1976.
[446] "Hurricane Hits Town But Pulls Its Punches," *East Hampton Star*, October 3, 1985.
[447] "Glancing Blow from Bob Hits Area Hard," *Southampton Press*, August 22, 1991.
[448] "Bob Hits Eastern LI at Low Tide," *East Hampton Star*, August 22, 1991.
[449] "No-Name Storm Slams Coast," *East Hampton Star*, November 7, 1991.
[450] "Storm's Fury Lashes Montauk," *East Hampton Star*, November 7, 1991.
[451] Ibid.
[452] Susan Rosenbaum, "Rain, But Little Harm," *East Hampton Star*, September 23, 1999.
[453] "Storm Warning," *Beacon*, 1993. Montauk Historical Society.
[454] Ibid.
[455] Ibid.
[456] Timothy Dwight, "Journey to Long Island, 1804," in *Journeys on Old Long Island,* ed. Natalie Naylor (Interlaken, NY: Hofstra University/Empire State Books, 2002), pp. 88-89.
[457] David Behrens, "Keepers of the Light," *Newsday*, August 6, 1990.
[458] Joseph P Osborne to Stephen Pleasonton. August 26, 1839. Correspondence of the Light-House Establishment, 1785-1852. Superintendent's Correspondence, Sag Harbor, Volume 1812-1849, p. 194. NARG 26.
[459] David Gardiner, "Chronicles of the Town of Easthampton," in *Exploring the Past: Writings From 1798 to 1896 Relating to the History of the Town of East Hampton,* ed. Tom Twomey (New York: Newmarket Press, 2000) p. 174.
[460] Ibid. p. 175.
[461] Rattray, *Montauk: Three Centuries of Romance, Sport and Adventure*, p. 36.
[462] John W. Barber, "Historical Collections of the State of New York" in *Exploring the Past*, ed. Tom Twomey, p. 230.
[463] Nathaniel S. Prime, *History of Long Island: From its First Settlement to the Year 1845* (New York: Robert Carter, 1845), p. 173.

[464] Lydia Howard Sigourney, *Scenes in My Native Land* (Boston: James Munroe & Co., 1845), p. 49.
[465] Ibid. p. 46.
[466] Winski, *Montauk: An Anecdotal History*, p. 7.
[467] Woodward, *East Hampton: A Town and its People 1648-1994*, p. 147.
[468] Benjamin F. Thompson, *History of Long Island: From its Discovery and Settlement to the Present Time*, ed. Charles J. Warner, 3 vols. 3rd ed. (New York: Robert H Dodd. 1918), 2: 198.
[469] Jared Augustus Ayres. "The Legends of Montauk." Hartford: Edwin Hunt. 1849. p. 117.
[470] Ibid. p. 118.
[471] Ibid. p. 124.
[472] Ibid. p. 125.
[473] "Pedestrian Trip around Long Island," *Brooklyn Daily Eagle*, July 12, 1859.
[474] Ibid.
[475] Ibid.
[476] Walt Whitman, *From Manhattan to Montauk*, ed. Henry M. Christman (New York: MacMillan & Co., 1963), pp. 179, 180, 181.
[477] Ibid. p. 185.
[478] "Montauk and Plover Shooting," *Sag Harbor Corrector*, September 19, 1868.
[479] Woodward, *East Hampton: A Town and its People*, pp. 165-166.
[480] "Montauk Point, Long Island". *Harper's New Monthly Magazine*. September 1871. pp. 481, 483, 487-493.
[481] Ibid.
[482] William Cullen Bryant, "Picturesque America," in *Exploring the Past*, ed. Twomey, pp. 304-305.
[483] Ibid. p. 305.
[484] Bayles, *Historical and Descriptive Sketches of Suffolk County*, p. 415.
[485] Ibid. p. 419.
[486] Ibid. p. 420.
[487] Ibid. p. 421.
[488] Rattray, *Montauk: Three Centuries of Romance, Sport and Adventure*, p. 37.

[489] Lanman, *Recollections of Curious Characters and Pleasant Places*, p. 122.
[490] Ibid. p. 123.
[491] Ibid. p. 141.
[492] William S. Pelletreau, "History of Suffolk County," in *Exploring the Past*, ed. Twomey, p. 326.
[493] "Resorts on Long Island: Montauk Point and Its New Colony," *Brooklyn Daily Eagle,* August 8, 1886.
[494] Ibid.
[495] "A Trip to Montauk: What One Sees at the Eastern End of Long Island," *Brooklyn Daily Eagle*, July 24, 1887.
[496] Ibid.
[497] Ibid.
[498] Ibid.
[499] Ibid.
[500] "To Montauk on a Wheel," *Brooklyn Daily Eagle*, August 6, 1890.
[501] "Observations of the Tourist," *Brooklyn Daily Eagle*, June 3, 1900.
[502] "A Trip to Montauk Lighthouse," *The Tarrytown Argus*, October 15, 1892.
[503] Rattray, *Montauk: Three Centuries of Romance, Sport and Adventure*, p. 8.
[504] Ibid. p. 8.
[505] Marion A. Rowley, "Versatile Reverend," *Long Island Forum*, September 1975.
[506] Eleanor F. Ferguson, *My Long Island*; ed. Anne Nauman (Las Vegas, NV: Scrub Oak Press, 1993), p. 99.
[507] Eugene Armbruster, *Montauk* (New York, 1923), pp. 6-7.
[508] Ibid. p. 8.
[509] Newspaper article. September 1933. Unidentified publication, clipping in Southold Free Library.
[510] Guy Duval, "Early Trip to Montauk as a Boy Recalled," *East Hampton Star*, October 24, 1935.
[511] Letter from Commander of 3rd Coast Guard District to the Commandant, October 11, 1948. Treasury Department.
[512] Bill Bleyer, "The Lighthouse Finds a Keeper," *Newsday*, April 5, 1986.
[513] Thomas Clavin, "Montauk Lighthouse to Be a Museum," *New York Times*, July 6, 1986.

[514] Record of Inspection September 12, 1986. Montauk Point Lighthouse Museum.
[515] "Light Will Still Shine, But Without a Keeper," *Newsday*, September 13, 1986.
[516] Bill Bleyer, "Coast Guard Signing Off at Montauk Point," *Newsday*, April 1, 1987.
[517] Debbie Tuma. "Light Shed on Precious Document," *Newsday*, September 8, 1990.
[518] Anne C. Fullam, "Renovations Upgrade The Keeper's Dwelling In Montauk Lighthouse," *New York Times*, July 5, 1992.
[519] "Gift Shop Restoration," *Beacon*, 1993. Montauk Historical Society.
[520] "Restoring Lighthouse in Montauk," *New York Times*, November 19, 1995.
[521] Alan J. Wax, "Getting the Point Across at Montauk Lighthouse /Brochures Now in 5 Languages to Aid Tourists," *Newsday*, August 10, 1998.
[522] Joe Haberstroh. "Montauk Memorial Honors 110 Lost Fishermen," *Newsday*, October 6, 1999.
[523] Robert J. Hefner, "Montauk Point Light Station, Tower, Oil House and Passage: A Historic Structures Report." Montauk Historical Society. 1989. p. 116.
[524] Betsy White, "The Cistern," *Beacon* 2001. Montauk Historical Society.
[525] "Montauk Point's Brighter Presence," *Newsday*, July 17, 2002.
[526] Janis Hewitt. "Relay," *East Hampton Star*, October 11, 2001.
[527] Russell Drumm, "Home is Where the Light Is," *East Hampton Star*, August 10, 2000.
[528] John S. Saladyga, "A Beacon in Her Life," *Newsday*, September 1, 1988.